DEVELOPMENTS IN WORK AND ORGANIZATION PSYCHOLOGY: IMPLICATIONS FOR INTERNATIONAL BUSINESS

INTERNATIONAL BUSINESS AND MANAGEMENT SERIES

Series Editor: **Pervez N. Ghauri**

Published:

Corporation and Institutional Transparency for Economic Growth in Europe
Oxelheim

Managing Customer Relationships on the Internet
Lindstrand, Johanson & Sharma

The Common Glue
Morosini

Non-Business Actors in a Business Network
Hadjikhani & Thilenius

Managing Networks in Transition Economics
Johanson

European Union and the Race for Foreign Direct Investment in Europe
Oxelheim & Ghauri

International Business Negotiations
Ghauri & Usunier

Intellectual Property and Doing Business in China
Yang

Strategic Alliances in Eastern and Central Europe
Hyder & Abraha

Co-operative Strategies and Alliances
Contractor & Lorange

Critical Perspectives on Internationalisation
Havila, Forsgren & Håkansson

Managing International Business Ventures in China
Li

Business Network Learning
Hakansson & Johanson

The Global Challenge for Multinational Enterprises
Buckley & Ghauri

Network Dynamics in International Marketing
Naude & Turnbull

Other titles of interest:

International Trade in the 21st Century
Fatemi

Globalization, Trade and Foreign Direct Investment
Dunning

International Trade and the New Economic Order
Moncarz

Contemporary Issues in Commercial Policy
Kreinin

Related journals — sample copies available on request

European Management Journal
International Business Review
International Journal of Research in Marketing
Long Range Planning
Scandinavian Journal of Management

For full details of all IBM titles published under the Elsevier imprint please go to:
http://www.elsevier.com/locate/series/ibm

INTERNATIONAL BUSINESS AND MANAGEMENT   VOLUME 20

DEVELOPMENTS IN WORK AND ORGANIZATION PSYCHOLOGY:
IMPLICATIONS FOR INTERNATIONAL BUSINESS

EDITED BY

MANFUSA SHAMS
Open University, England, UK

PAUL JACKSON
Manchester Business School, University of Manchester, UK

Series Editor: Pervez N. Ghauri

ELSEVIER Amsterdam • Boston • Heidelberg • London • New York • Oxford
Paris • San Diego • San Francisco • Singapore • Sydney • Tokyo

Elsevier
The Boulevard, Langford Lane, Kidlington, Oxford OX5 1GB, UK
Radarweg 29, PO Box 211, 1000 AE Amsterdam, The Netherlands

First edition 2006

British Library Cataloguing in Publication Data
A catalogue record for this book is available from the British Library

Library of Congress Cataloging-in-Publication Data
A catalog record for this book is available from the Library of Congress

ISBN-13: 978-0-08-044467-3
ISBN-10: 0-08-044467-9

For information on all Elsevier publications
visit our website at books.elsevier.com

Printed and bound in The Netherlands

06 07 08 09 10 10 9 8 7 6 5 4 3 2 1

Dedication

"For my wife Sallie who made me who I am today, and put up with everything in order to make this book possible".

— *Paul*
December 2005
England, UK

"For my parents, especially for my loving father who throughout his life as a well known judge wrote numerous books in law, jurisprudence, legal matters, legal practice and constitutional issues. His voluminous scholarly writing inspired me to complete this book".

— *Manfusa*
December 2005
England, UK

Contents

List of Figures

List of Tables

Contributors

Asa Björnberg   Department of Organizational Behaviour, London Business School, London, UK

Rob Briner   Organizational Psychology Department, Birkbeck College, London, UK

Ingrid Dackert   Project Management and Organization, Teknik och samhälle/School of Technology and Society, Malmö högskola/Malmö University, Malmö, Sweden

Paul Jackson   Head of Division of Marketing, International Business and Strategy, Manchester Business School, University of Manchester, UK

Tina Kiefer   Organizational Psychology Department, Birkbeck College, London, UK

Judi McLean Parks   John M. Olin School of Business, Washington University, Missouri, USA

Sharon Parker   Australian Graduate School of Management, The University of New South Wales, Sydney, Australia

Manfusa Shams   Department of Science, Open University, England, UK

faye smith   Emporia State University, School of Business, Emporia, Kansas

Paul Sparrow   Manchester Business School, Manchester, UK

Nick Turner   Queen's School of Business, Queen's University,
                         Ontario, Canada

Helen Williams   Leeds University Business School, University of
                         Leeds, Leeds, UK

Pamela Yeow   Lecturer in Human Resource Management and
                        Work Psychology, Kent Business School, University
                        of Kent, Parkwood Road, Canterbury Kent CT2 7PE

Preface

Rapid developments in technology-based work environment, global interdependence in business transactions, tensions in changing organizational culture, and a new dimension in work practice are all parts of the recent development in work and organizational psychology, and International business. With this fast development, an increasingly difficult task is to provide an integrated discussion covering theoretical developments, theory-driven research, new research trends, and dynamics between organizational change and personal development within an enhanced technologically advanced working environment.

A comprehensive work for an edited book in work and organizational psychology is impossible (Dam & Berg, 2004), unless one is selective due to the vast areas covered by Work and Organizational Psychology. Similarly, relational framework to capture changing nature of international business and global interdependence cannot be presented in one edited book due to the sheer volume of work needed to address the ongoing emerging issues as a result of changes in international business spheres across the world.

What would be the best practice for an edited book to showcase selected and representative areas of Work, Organizational Psychology and International Business?

We have made an attempt to answer this question with the use of a phenomenological approach. Taking a reflective practitioner's perspective, our approach has guided us to select experienced authors with longstanding research experiences and deeper insights in both theoretical and practical developments. Our authors have selected topics from their expertise areas where they can make a leading scholarly contribution both at an organizational and an individual level drawing on their personalized academic insights on the relationship between these developmental issues with international business.

Drawing on our personal experiences of being active researchers and academic practitioners in work and organizational psychology, and our exclusive work with international experts in this field, we have also contributed chapters in selected areas. We are aware of potential pitfalls associated with being selective and focusing on certain issues, therefore, we have tried to justify such 'focused' direction to the benefits of the global academic and practitioners community by making an invitation to leading scholars in respective areas from around the world. We believe such a representation of scholars in our edited book will not only show a global interdependence in scholarly work to changes in work and organizational psychology and its relevance to international business, but also to provide diversity and flexibility in presentation for a range of topics which have both local and international relevance. Thoughtful academic insights are therefore grounded in international context, with special attention being given to specific areas of work and organizational psychology.

Students and practitioners of international business are often unaware of developments within psychology, and the purpose of this edited volume is to give authoritative accounts of such developments, applied to key areas of international business, in a form, which is accessible to both students and professional practitioners.

The aims of the book are:

1. to provide authoritative reviews of current psychological knowledge in areas of work and organizational psychology related to international business;
2. to apply psychological knowledge to current issues in international business;
3. to illustrate the applicability of recent research in work and organizational psychology, using case studies, empirical research, and reflective account of research experiences, to international business;
4. to offer a global perspective for work and organizational psychology in international business and management; and
5. to provide a representative collection of work to capture the recent developments in work and organizational psychology within the domain of International business.

Advances in information and communications technology are so rapid that their full implications for the conduct of international business are difficult to discern. Globalization and the recognition of both opportunities and challenges offered by cultural diversity are particular issues, which face organizations, both large and small. In particular, the Internet makes distance irrelevant when communicating with others. Psychology has much to offer to the understanding of these changes. There have been rapid developments in Work and Organizational Psychology in areas such as social identity and work, work and the social context, and the changing nature of work. These are deeply relevant to the area of International Business. However, there is always a delay before research in one discipline begins to inform research and practice in another. A major aim of this edited book is to signpost areas of concerns where interdisciplinary research work can make a significant contribution to bridge the gap in the literature.

Editing a book with a limited time span is not an easy task, especially when we are engaged in other academic work and employment related activities; however, we believe that we have accomplished it competently with the help of our excellent authors and publishers. Over the months, we have developed an excellent academic partnership with our authors, and publishers who are ever so encouraging and patient, and ready to provide practical suggestions with an extended help for editorial work.

Nonetheless, we feel that there may be areas which may have been improved should we get more time and space to invest, and also if we have been allowed to run several meetings with international scholars, national and local businesses to pinpoint areas of recent developments that need academic attention and intervention. We are aware of shortcomings in presentation when we take a particular approach, and also any conflicting views that may be the result of reflexive exercise. However, we are proud of taking such an exceptional step in editing a book on work and organizational psychological issues in international business. The quality of work has never been compromised with the length expected for each chapter; each chapter is unique in content and presentation styles.

In our long journey towards completion we have been encouraged by various people; however most of all, we are grateful to our authors and publishers from Elsevier. Also colleagues from our work place, and our family.

This book aims to take a place in the International Business and academic world.

Dr. M. Shams and Prof. P. Jackson
Editors

Reference

Dam, V. K., & Berg, V. T. P. (2004). Challenges for research in work and organizational psychology: Introduction to the special issue. *Applied Psychology: An International Review*, *53*(4), 481–486.

Acknowledgement

We are grateful to many people for supporting our endeavour to write this book. However, most importantly our authors — Nick Turner, Sharon Parker, Helen Williams, Judy M. Parks, Faye Smith, Asa Bjornberg, Paul Sparrow, Ingrid Dackert, Tina Keifer, Rob Briner, Pamela Yeow, and international experts — Toby Wall, Nigel Nicholson, Peter Warr. Special thanks to Hannah Collett and all other members on the editorial board from Elsevier for providing unlimited support.

Prof. P. Jackson and Dr. M. Shams
(*Editors*)

Introduction
Developments in Work and Organizational Psychology: Implications for International Business

Manfusa Shams and Paul Jackson

Drawing on knowledge from Work and Organizational Psychology, Management and International Business (IB), experts are emphasizing the importance of cross-disciplinary approach to address work and organizational behaviour. Work and organizational psychology share an increasing number of overlapping and complementary issues, thereby giving us an opportunity to get a broad perspective in both these disciplines. The interconnected issues in these disciplines are inseparable; hence, any discussion for one discipline has to be made in relation to another. This book illuminates this interdependency with the presentation of a selection of chapters, and asserts the benefits deriving from such interdependency in the global business and organizational management.

The increasing global interdependency shows the importance of documenting the most recent developments in global business and organizational behaviour, which is strongly influenced by the advancement of information technologies, virtual business transactions, multicultural business partnerships, and expanded virtual businesses across cultures.

Our book aims to present thoughtful analyses of some major developments in work and organizational psychology, with a focus on international business and management. The book is expected to benefit students, researchers, practitioners and employers. We hope our efforts to compile leading authors' work will bring fresh ideas and thought-provoking issues on both theoretical and practical applications of emerging psychological knowledge in work and organizational psychology.

An eclectic approach is taken to showcase the chapters in this book. The authors of each chapter were asked to invest his/her's valuable insights to write a selected chapter with examples from relevant research, utilizing scholarly and reflective arguments to cover the essence of a particular chapter.

Each chapter has adopted an easy-going style to inform readers about the developments in a major area. The discussion in each chapter is assembled with author/s own research and management experiences, thus providing a 'real-life' perspective, highlighting the importance of applying recent developmental issues to the future academic work in the International Business and Management field.

The book has two parts: theoretical discussions and overview of relevant research (family business: an international and cross-cultural perspective; ghost workers: implications of new workforce realities for organizations and their workers; emotions at work: overview of research and implications for practice; mergers, acquisitions and joint ventures: issues of identity and identification; complexity theory: relevance to work psychology and recent developments; and working in glass houses: managing the complex organization), and practical applications and advancement in global market (global human resource management, team working in organizations: implications for workplace safety; approaches in business coaching: exploring context-specific and cultural issues; and future of international business and management: an overview).

Each chapter focuses on a micro- and a macro-approach within an interpersonal framework in business functions and organizational management. The micro approach refers to authors' insights and arguments for, and critical thoughtful analysis of, selected issues; and the macro approach implies the engagement of micro-analysis to the broad contextual and theoretical issues, such as global, local and interdisciplinary contexts, with a strong focus on understanding of the meeting points for and International Business Work Psychology.

The first chapter (Shams and Bjornberg) presents an overview of critical discussion in one of the major developments in International Business — family business and cross-cultural organizational developments. The discussion justifies the unique position of family business in the global market as being 'a stand alone globally connected business and management', where discussion leads to practice, and practice feeds into further knowledge construction for work and organizational behaviour, creating a loop for augmenting critical issues for international business and management within the framework of family and business functions.

The second chapter discusses about 'Team working in organizations with particular emphasis on work place safety' (Turner, Parker and Williams). This chapter has argued that significantly less attention is given to team working contributions to workplace safety than to the positive impact of team working on business performance and employee well being.

The critical and pointed theoretical discussion on 'Changing nature of workforce in organization and implications for organizational identity and working relationship's (Parker and smith)' in Chapter 3 has persistently confirmed the fundamental changes in organizational identity and working relationships made through the systematic influence of new workforce realities (named as 'ghost workers' in the chapter). The presentation deserves credits for advocating controversial and debated issues in the changing nature of workforce in economic sectors across the world.

The 'Knowledge of global human resources management and its applicability to organizations (Sparrow)' in Chapter 4 has drawn a professional account to place human resource management at the core of marketing, corporate communications and information systems, especially, its relevance to cross-cultural practice in organizational management and resource utilizations across cultures.

Chapter 5 offers a critical discussion on 'Organizational merger and business acquisitions (Jackson and Dackert). This chapter aims to showcase the implications of change and integration to economic growth, sustainability and social identification for multicultural teams globally and within a culture.

A solid theoretical groundwork is propounded in Chapter 6 (Yeow and Jackson), 'Complexity theory and the management of change' emphasising knowledge production by workers in business ventures and cross-cultural collaborative managerial enterprises. The authors' have provided an extended theoretical overview of the application of complexity assumptions to work behaviour and management issues at both local and global levels.

In Chapter 7, the authors (Kiefer and Briner) have offered a critical overview of both theoretical and practical implications for 'Emotions at work'. This chapter shows the paramount influence of emotions at work on organizational behaviour and performance, and the way it can impact upon global business transactions, including conceptualizing emotions either to show its pervasive influence to facilitate organizational performance or to hinder inter and intra group's progress within an organization.

Chapter 8 presents (Shams) an introductory note on approaches in business coaching with an example of a research on family business conducted by the author recently. It contains thought provoking issues regarding the appropriateness of coaching approaches to businesses which are built on specific cultural context, hence business function is facilitated by family values and cultural practices.

Chapter 9 by Jackson provides an innovative critical analysis of complexities associated with organizational boundaries, especially the rapid changes in organizations made by uncontrollable external and internal factors, such as corporate communication, organizational identity and strategic alliances.

Chapter 10 summarizes the concerns presented in each chapter for future developments in work and organizational psychology within international business, the complex nature of theoretical developments, and new trends in research to address the interface between work, organizational psychology and international business. Further insights on the contribution of work and organizational psychology to the development of International Business as a discipline within management, and the potential for collaboration between work and organizational psychology and International Business are critically appraised in this chapter.

Concluding the Introduction

The contribution made in this book is only a small part of the major developments made both in Work and Organization Psychology, and in International Business. However, the discussion made in this book is authoritative to the respective field, especially to highlight the 'interdependency' yet to unveil, and the mass upsurge of developments in these two areas, both at a global and a local context.

We hope our readers will be benefited by the critical dialogues presented here to show a new direction of research and academic enterprise, where interdependency than separation is encouraged, closeness than distancing arguments from each discipline is sought, and an assertion for a combined operation to apply relevant knowledge to address major developmental issues in business and organizational behaviour is justified.

Chapter 1

Issues in Family Business: An International Perspective

Manfusa Shams and Åsa Björnberg

Introduction

This chapter aims to provide a critical review of existing literature in family business with particular emphasis on operational definitions, levels of analysis, psychological analysis of family functioning in family business, diversity in family business, and an overview of methodological issues with future directions for family business research.

The chapter focuses on recent developments in international business, managerial psychology and family psychology. The first part of the chapter, which adopts a macro approach, begins with an analysis of definitional difficulties in family firms. This is followed by an overview of the history of family firms, their types, structure and diversity. Following a closer look at a selection of theoretical models used in family business research, attention is given to the specific topic of entry strategies as applied in family firms. The second part of this chapter assumes a more micro approach and addresses the role of the family in family firms, outlining central dimensions of family functioning highlighted by examples from Asia, Africa and Europe. The importance of family for business success is then discussed, as is the lack of a psychological perspective in family business research and related methodological issues encountered by managerial and family business researchers.

With increasing competition in the global economy market, business set up within a family context appears to be the most desirable option for getting the

Developments in Work Organizational Psychology
Copyright © 2006 by Elsevier Ltd.
ISBN: 0-08-044467-9

optimum level of achievements in the economic sector for many developing countries. This is evident from the latest statistics which claims about 65–80% of all businesses in the world family businesses (Nation, 2004), with a sole 80% family business from USA and Europe (Flintoff, 2002). Within this global family business arena, 40% of business originates from the US top level 500 companies, compared to only 5.9% reported to belong to family business within a sample of around 600 in the Labour Force Survey, December 2003–February 2004 in the UK. In Australia around half of all business is family business (Getz & Carlson, 2000). Recent figures from a global sample with varying developmental levels show that families own an average of 75% of businesses, ranging from 85% in Brazil to 51% in Sweden (Astrachan, Zahra, & Sharma, 2003). As such, the academic interest for family business has grown tremendously — and this trend is set to continue.

Recent, fast-paced changes in how people live, work and interact with each other on both global and local levels are reflected in the process and structure of family lives. The family is now a rapidly changing social institution. In the Western world, it has become increasingly heterogeneous, featuring constellations of family members and living arrangements that were uncommon until recent decades. Examples from Northern Europe, which by many is regarded as a forerunner in terms of societal family development, describe delays in marriage or lower marriage rates, increased divorce and separation rates, and more people living single lives (González-López, 2002). To a very large extent, the change in these conditions has resulted from changed relationships between the genders (Castells, 1997).

Worldwide demographic trends show a clear tendency for a global decline in birth rates. Fertility rates have decreased by 50% since 1972, from an average of 6 children per woman to 2.9, a figure which is continuing to decrease rapidly. In fact, almost half of the world's populations currently live in nations of sub-replacement (in order to reproduce a population, a woman must give birth to an average of 2.1 children in her lifespan) (Meyer, 2004). This trend is not limited to Europe, but is also happening in Asia — notable examples include China, Japan and Taiwan. Elsewhere, examples include Uruguay, Mexico and many Caribbean countries (*ibid.*). Simultaneously, life expectancies are prolonged, creating a 'beanstalk syndrome' of thin but tall family trees (Markson, 2003). Contrastingly, areas in the Middle East and Africa are witnessing a rapid population growth. In the long term, this will have a huge impact on labour markets, with labour shortages creating an influx in movement of labour force across the globe on the one hand, and a decrease in social wealth, economic growth and availability of highly educated workers on the other.

As migration across the globe continues to grow, a plethora of sub-cultures featuring unique family types and functioning continues to be created, particularly in the north-western hemisphere. Yet, in a world of expanding communities, global enterprising and emerging virtual arenas, the concept of 'family' still remains a fundamentally important social entity, both economically and emotionally (Becker, 1993), and as a source of both tangible and intangible social capital for immigrant entrepreneurs (Sanders & Nee, 1996). In many developing countries, small and micro family firms constitute the foundation and prerequisite for economic development.

PART I

Defining Family Business

On a simplistic level, family business is defined as an economic organisation originating from a family, controlled and managed by family members (Table 1.1). The anthropological approach defines family business as a generational transmission of delivering economic power to family members with a typical family

Table 1.1: Operational definition of family business.

- *Psychological:* emphasis on the psychological processes such as leadership, communication and relationship, management hierarchy, business behaviour, family values and family functioning

- *Sociological*: emphasis on family business as a social unit, equity in legitimate share of a business and execution of decisions and management

- *Anthropological*: emphasis on generational transmission of economic activity transfer with a typical family prototype for execution of family business

- *Biological*: emphasis on evolutionary aspects of family business in which genetic factors predominately influence the transmission process of family business

- *Complimentary*: emphasis on firm ownership and management, and intention of family members to achieve intra-organisational family-based relatedness practice, and values to sustain external pressures to the maintenance of family business. Sociological definition offers family business as a social unit in which equity in legitimate share of a property is ensured through execution of decisions and management for business owned from old generation within a family setting (for a full discussion, see Ferraro (2002)). Litz (1995) has proposed two complementary approaches to define family business: a structure-based approach (intra-organisational family-based relatedness) indicating firm ownership and management, and an intention-based approach showing the intention of family members to achieve and/or maintain intra-organisational family-based relatedness. The difference between these two approaches is on the degree of intra-organisational family-based relatedness used to define family business.

The psychological definition refers to the functional aspects and the execution patterns of these functions with a defined objective and goal towards family business. Family business is a business organisation for and by the family engaging in economic activities. However, the empirical definition stresses the functions or involvements of family members in a business set up by family members. In other words, family ownership and management define the family firm. In the field of family-firm research, operational definitions sometimes also include the family firm's *perception per se* as a family firm, and/or its *intention* to transfer ownership/management to a succeeding generation, thus narrowing the scope for inclusion. Both theoretical and empirical definitions are interlinked in such a way as to suggest that the absence of one cannot be compensated for by the inclusion of the other in the definitional query. Thus, a business set up by and for family members requires members' involvement for its functioning to such an extent as to regulate its functioning. A critique of family business definitions shows conceptual challenges in defining family business and as such, ambiguity in the definition persists (Chua, Chrisman, & Sharma, 1999). An alternative paradigm for definition is suggested, viz., 'cross-generational sustainability in visions for family business'. Here family members' sustained interests are more important than power transfer strategy between generations.

The most widely accepted definition of family business is that of a business owned, managed and governed by one or more generations of family and/or family members, and in which values, visions and missions laid down by their founders are strictly maintained (McCrea, 1997).

Historical Context in Family Business

The history of family business can be presented in terms of clusters representing the economic status of a particular time period, cultural/family tradition, impact of immigration on the economy sector, economic trends for ethnic minority groups, alternatives to formal employment, diasporas and social identity and global interdependence.

Each of these areas are characterised by the dominant influence of one major socio-cultural trajectory, for example, economic recession at a particular time leading to self-employment involving family members, large influx of immigrants necessitating the emergence of family business in the absence of employment elsewhere, and family succession issues in business leading to a continuity in family business.

Pre-Industrial

Before the industrial revolution, during the agricultural era, family firms were the backbone of all economic activities in all societies (De Roover, 1963). Although the industrial revolution has resulted in an upsurge of family businesses across the world, the stability of family business was subjected to a turbulent environment, with absence of a legal system to secure and enforce property rights (Colli, 2002). The recent historical perspective shows a less hostile and more stable family business due to increasing legal and socio-political protection and attention to such types of establishments (Cassis, 1997; Casson, 2000).

Industrial

The early phase of family business growth was occupied by small and medium sized family firms. These were characterised by flat organisational structure and internal succession patterns, relying upon self-financing or an local and informal credit sources and local of stock-market finances. Consequently, they were less modernised in production technology and labour relations — and less profitable (Colli, 2003) occupied the early phase of family business growth. This was followed by more technologically advanced family businesses, although resistance to bring any changes in the family dynasty was prevalent, leading to sustained growth and innovation in capital and technology-intensive industries (Sargant, 1961). This 'short-sightedness' in family firms (Payne, 1984; Sargant, 1961) affecting the endurance and continuity, as such the 'three-generation paradigm' (start-up and early growth, consolidation and decline), is reported in the literature (Dyer, 1986; Jones & Rose, 1993). During the post-industrial revolution, global interdependence, technological advancement, merging and decline of non-family-owned enterprises show an enduring legacy for family business (Pollak, 1985).

The history of family business needs to incorporate ethnic minority groups (Heck, 2004) and as such diverse streams of historical perspectives can be drawn within the main root of family history literature. For an extensive family-history for ethnic minority groups see Barratt, Jones, and Mcevoy (1996) and Small bone, Ram, Deakins, and Baldock (2003).

The historical context of family business is difficult to analyse due to their heterogeneity and diverse functionality associated with ascension and/or descent of family firms in the pre- and post-industrialised periods.

Types of Family Business and Family Business Structure

The nature and types of family businesses are predominantly determined by the managerial structure, ownership patterns, sizes, production types and performance (Holland & Boulton, 1984). Holland and Boulton (1984) in an early attempt to sketch the penetration of family into family business showed four types of structures for the family–business relationship — pre-family (founding of business, centralised power and focus on survival and succession), family (entry of family members, de-centralised power and dispersed amongst family members, focus on expansion and stability), adaptive family (developing business partnership with non-family members, centralised power for management and stock ownership, focus on improving performance) and post-family (merger and acquisition of new organisations, power-transfer to new organisation and focus on new developments).

Dyer (1988) has proposed four types of family business — paternalistic, laissez-fare, participative and professional, and the classification is based on three distinctive dimensions of founder centrality: between-ness, closeness and connectivity. Recently, Zahra, Hayton, and Salvato (2003) described family business in relation to non-family business; this may be a more pragmatic approach identifying the essential features of family business that are in sharp contrast to non-family business. The 1997/2000 national family business survey in the USA has used a household sampling frame, such as ownership, management control, family involvement and multiple generations to define family business (Heck & Stafford, 2001; Winter, Fitzgerald, Heck, Haynes, & Danes, 1998). As such, family business types can be categorised according to how a family business is operationalised/defined (Heck, 2004).

The critical review of family business types and structure shows an overlap in the discussion for seeking definitional certainty and types of business structure, suggesting that underlying theoretical models and theories are more important to explore if family business is a homogeneous concept. However, the literature shows a frequent use of several major concepts in articulating family business: ownership, governance, succession, management, leadership and performance; and less frequent use of business characteristics such as gross income, expenditure and profits, business size, the influence of family culture and ethnicity on business, motivation, commitments and values underpinning family business behaviour (Muske & Fitzerald, 2002; Masuo, Grace, & John, 2002; Harris, 2003). Based on the above discussion, the following two diagrams (Figures 1.1 and 1.2) are presented to illustrate the definitional constraints for family business types.

A change in family business was noted from the early 1980s until the 1990s due to the decline in many industrial organisations, crisis in the survival of many

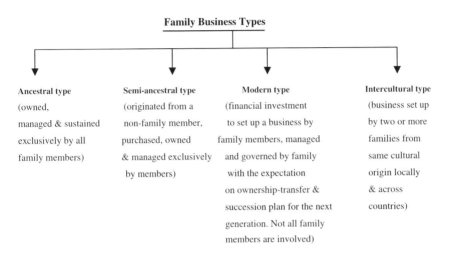

Figure 1.1: Family business types.

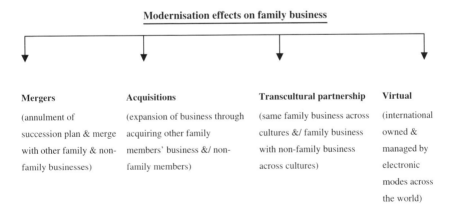

Figure 1.2: Modernisation effects on family business.

state-owned organisations and financial pressure of private businesses (Colli, 2002, 2003). The uncertainty and business failures were accountable for the changing structure of family businesses. Figure1.2 shows the transformation in family businesses due to the economic decline, industrial revolution and modernisation.

Diversity within Family Businesses

Family business is diversified by size, nature of business, ethnic origin of the founders, the way business is performed, namely, use of technology and staff, multinational and localised context. As yet, no single published paper has been identified that has addressed diversity in family business, although each of the areas within diversity has been widely researched in the management literature (e.g., Wang, Watkins, Harris, & Spicer, 2004; Einhorn, 2000; Westhead, 2003; Bell, Crick, & Young, 2004; Birley, 2001).

Small Family Businesses

A critique of the literature suggests an imbalance in researching diversity issues within family business, with a tendency to research more on small-firm business, multinational businesses and ethnic minority businesses in the management literature. Several reasons can be offered to explicate this tendency, for example, small family businesses are easy to access, manageable and less time-consuming to research. A second reason is that large profit-making organisations usually represent multinational companies across the world, and are difficult to recruit for research purposes. Cross-validation is also difficult to achieve for multisite-based businesses, and lastly family business is largely represented by ethnic minorities in the UK and the USA (Barrett et al., 1996). The discussion in this section therefore will be made in three major areas: ethnic minority family business, small family business and multinational family business.

Family Business and Ethnic Minority Groups

It is estimated that ethnic minorities are making a large contribution to the national family business outputs both in Britain and the USA. For example, in Britain an estimate by the National Westminster Bank (Bank of England, 1999) shows that approximately 50% of all new businesses are from ethnic minorities (Office for National Statistics (ONS), 1999). The ethnic minority businesses are dominated by South-East Asian, Chinese and Afro-Caribbean immigrant communities.

Typical ethnic minority businesses are small-sized, predominantly corner-shop-style firms in inner-city areas, groceries, clothing retail and restaurants. They feature family tradition and typical within-group (co-ethnic) social networking, leadership styles and a patriarchal business environment. The intersection of culture and business behaviour needs to be extrapolated in order to establish the relations. Ethnic minority business entry is not dictated by a single motivational factor such as family tradition to embrace economic activities in adult life. Instead, a mixture of cultural, economic, societal structural, political and migrational factors contributes towards the entry processes. The blending factor in ethnic minority business entry is called 'embeddedness' by Kloosterman, Leun, and Rath (2000). The inseparable bond between small business and ethnic minority groups has suggested the increasing rate of success (Ram & Jones, 1998; Sanders & Nee, 1996) in small business activities, although no homogeneous relations have been noted for ethnic minority groups influencing small business success trends. Rather, the diversity in ethnic minority business is observed which is accountable to cultural attributes, such as family tradition, migration motives, religion, family links, business experience and educational attainment. However, two powerful social factors — gender and power relations — are common in all ethnic minority families when impacting upon small business activities (Ram, Abbas, Sanghera, Barlow, & Jones, 2001).

Generational Family Business

Interestingly, in contrast to the influence of generational trends in family business, recent research critically has critically put forward the explanation of the alternative employment paradigm for the second generation due to the increasing evidence that many family business owners prefer to have an alternative employment for their children (Metcalf, Moodod, & Virdee, 1996). However, such alternative employment provision is conditional upon educational and labour market success elsewhere (Goldthorpe, Llewellyn, & Payne, 1980). Some studies insist on acknowledgement of the involvement of the second-generation family members as predominantly an outcome of limited labour market choices, lack of social networking and exertion of power relations and gendered labour within the household (Lee, 2002). The possibility of exerting transferable skills from a family setting to a small business setting cannot be ruled out and recent research is now arguing for an inclusive 'insiders' perspective in family business, namely, a shift in attitude towards family business from a second-generation perspective. The changing dynamics in the cross-generational aspects of ethnic family businesses will be further discussed in the second part of this chapter.

Using a critical and interpretative approach, Ainsworth and Cox (2003) argued for the examination of issues of identity, power, control and resistance to ascertain organisational culture in small family business. In contrast to small family business, large family business groups are hardly researched (Morck & Yeung, 2003).

Virtual Family Businesses

The multinational family business and global enterprises are providing significant insights into the growth of economy, transformation of business strategies, management and market focus in conjunction with cultural patterning of 'doing business' across the world. The ability and interest of family business to make it international is restrictive due to resource issues at its disposal, hence much of the transfer of business strategy and management is done virtually (Bell et al., 2004). For example, focus is now on new technologies (information technology and biotechnology) to make knowledge-intensive family business a global enterprise.

A number of associations have taken the forefront in delivering information on international family business, for example, the International Family Business Programme Association (http://nmq.com/ifbpa), the Family Firm Institute (http://ffi.org) and the Family Business Network (http://www.fbn-i.org/). However, more research initiatives are required to address functional processes in multinational family business and global family business (the former refers to a collection of family business enterprises from families of diverse cultural backgrounds and the latter refers to one single family business with a worldwide network of businesses governed by the family only).

Models of Family Business

Family business has been characterised as a unique economic organisation for the pattern of ownership, governance, management, and succession influencing the organisation's goals, strategies, structure and the functional strategies to transfer succession power to the next generation (Figure 1.3) (Chua et al., 1999). Unlike any other organisational issues proposed by psychologists, the discussion of family business organisations is problematic due to its volatile nature.

Family Business Models Based on Theories of Family

The voluminous literature of family business has offered a number of theoretical explanations for the way family business functions and the strong influence of family functioning *per se* on family business. The widely used theoretical models

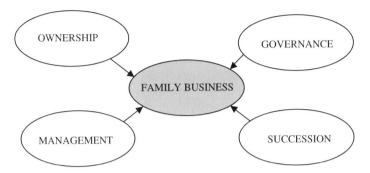

Figure 1.3: Widely used component of the family firm definition.

of family functioning are family ecology theory (focuses on families as they inter-act with the environment (Bubolz & Sontag, 1993)), family development theory (focuses on changes in family life cycles (Rodgers & White, 1993)), family systems theory (emphasis on intervention in family business (Whitechurch & Constantine, 1993)) and family resource management theory (discusses personal and managerial resources to underpin a strategy for economic growth in the family (Deacon & Firebaugh, 1988)). The reciprocal influence of family on business and business on family has been documented (Olson, McCubbin, Barnes, Larsen, Muxen, & Wilson, 2003).

A detailed critical analysis of one major theory, viz., family systems theory, gives emphasis to the sustainability of both the family and business and seeks further research to verify the inseparable bond between family and business in family business with the examination of key variables, such as size, structure, composition, type, functionality, management activities, styles and outcomes (Heck, 2004). In line with this theory, 'the sustainable family business model' (Stafford, Duncan, Danes, & Winter, 1999) emphasises the sustainability of the family business system and treats family and business systems equally in the discussion.

Current Models of Family Business

Current models of family business lack depth with regards to the key functions of family business ownership, governance and execution of business activities within a family context (Nicholson, 2004). To bridge this gap, agency theory (Fama & Jensen, 1983) is used in the behavioural economic and family business literature (Schulze, Lubatkin, & Dino, 2003). The basic tenet of agency theory is that management decisions are strongly influenced by the ownership status of each decision maker who serves on a corporation's board of directors. Agency theory addresses the problems in divergent relations between stakeholders and agents, and their disproportionate risk tolerance. It furthermore suggests the ownership pattern in a family business and problems associated with fractional ownership among family members, for example, self-governing interests can overtake the firm's unitary general interests. Agency theory complements as well as contradicts many issues proposed by the corporate governance theory, which focuses primarily on public firms and overlooks family business and within-group/ingroup economic activities.

Other models of family business rely on the functional interface between family and business and as such these models are developed to explain family business as a dual system rather than a single unit. For example, Davis and Taguiri's (1989) model features membership in overlapping family, ownership and management groups. Davis and Stern (1988) modified Davis and Taguiri's model with additional elements in the analysis of family business, adaptation, growth and survival, intergenerational as well interpersonal process of families and demand on market and technological influences.

In contrast to this dual system model, 'Fundamental Interpersonal Relations Orientation' (FIRO) proposed by Danes, Zuiker, Arbuthnor, Kean, and Scannell (1998) offers a single system explanation for family business. The model thrusts on three major components to sustain external pressure for survival and success — inclusion, control and integration.

Family Business Models in International Context

None of the early models of family business take into account international perspective, that is, to what extent these models are generalisable across countries, and what would be the variables that should be incorporated into these models. If family business is the tradition and the only sanctioned means for economic activities, then involvement in the family business becomes mandatory for all family members. Birley (2001) cautioned about the misleading attempt to generalise family business as a homogeneous groups indicating distinctive differences in terms of attitudes towards family business amongst various countries, for example, Japanese and American participants considered their business as a family business, participants from Poland and Italy did not do so implying three possible explanations for such differential attitudes towards family business — 'the family in', 'the family out' and 'the family-business jugglers' attitudes. The 'family in' attitude asserts the definite entry of family members into the business and taking the succession while the 'family out' and family-business jugglers' attitudes are indecisive in terms of entry into the family business.

The theoretical models in the literature are clearly inadequate to explicate culturally mediated factors in family business and a holistic approach encompassing all cross-cultural variables in family business and entry to family business, with specific reference to the changing nature of family business across cultures/societies. Theoretical development must be attested by international cross-collaboration in family business research.

Entry Strategies in Family Business

Family business is now regarded as one of the strong engines of the post-industrial growth process with powerful holdings of economy activities by generations' entrepreneurial talent, loyal commitment to sustain all external pressures to keep the business running exclusively by the family and corporate independence (Wang et al., 2004). Entry to the family business depends on succession stages, such as pre-arrival and post-arrival stages (Figure 1.4) (Sharma, Chrisman, & Chua, 2003; Dyck, Mauws, Starke, & Mischke, 2002; Gordon & Rosen, 1981). Succession is thus considered as the single most powerful entry route and a process to internalise a successor into the operation of family business, ensuring effective transmission of values and objectives (Garcia-Alverez, Lopez-Sintas, & Gonsalvo, 2002).

Various models are proposed to characterise succession process, and among them is the three-level model proposed by Stavrou and Swiercz (1998). The first level is characterised by family members (usually offspring) in the pre-entry stage in which learning about business operations from the incumbent takes place, followed by the second stage which is primarily an entry stage into the business and necessary integration into the business environment and finally, the final stage of succession in the form of taking over managerial/executive position. Gersick, Lansberg, Desjardins, and Dunn (1999) have stressed 'two stage models' of

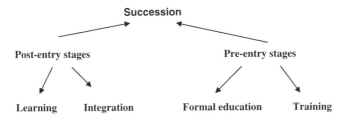

Figure 1.4: Single most powerful entry strategy: succession.

succession. The first stage is pre-entry where socialisation in the family business takes place and the second stage is 'late entry' where rather than entry after the first pre-entry period, a brief period of outside education and employment/training precedes entry to the business.

Creativity and Novelty in Entry Strategies

Fletcher's (2004) critique of family business provides significant insights into the intersections between family process and business activities. The three-dimensional developmental model (family/business/ownership) proposed by Gersick, Davis, McCollom, and Lansberg (1997) was critically reviewed to suggest the addition of a fourth dimension, intergenerational transition/intergenerational emergence and creativity in entrepreneurship, for example, drawing on past events, experiences and practices, seeking new opportunities in the market, networking, new ideas and concepts, reproduction of modern technological input into business practices etc. The emphasis here is to enter the family business on a creative path where family members are not possibly accepting the business environment, rather originating, developing and implementing their own ideas, experiences, training and aspirations.

Social Psychological Processes in Business Entry

The social psychological explanations for entry to family business are overshadowed by the powerful interpretations from sociological and anthropological viewpoints. Although there is no systematic research trend or literature to suggest that important social psychological variables, such as family values, needs for achievement and aspiration, social identity, self-esteem etc. can explicate family business entry, few researchers have suggested the plausible effects of these variables on the decision making, acceptance of family values and traditions towards entrepreneurship (Chua et al., 1999; Westhead & Cowling, 1998). One of the important variables overlooked in the literature is the influence of educational achievements to generate business initiatives within the community, usually when educational attainment is so low as to persuade someone to end up with developing a business strategy for the family to sustain economic pressure. This applies particularly to immigrant groups in a country (Shams & Jackson, 1994).

Strong paternalistic attitudes towards business succession often create tensions and conflicts among family members leading to uncertainty about the continuity of the business, and family members' unwillingness to carry over the management of family business. This is called 'Buddenbrooks effect', schematising the inadequacy of successors to obtain the same achievements as the founder (Colli, 2002, 2003). However, this effect is not evident in all cultures, especially in a collectivist culture where strong family commitment and holdings of family ideologies and values along with the altruistic attitudes towards family members serve as a grounding force for a firm family business (Dutta, 1996). Similarly, Japanese '*zaibatsu*' refers to written constitutions for family members to which all members of the family must adhere (Neubauer & Lank, 1998). Although commitment and involvement are prerequisites to both continuity and success of a family business, Chua et al. (1999) showed that family involvement is a weaker predictor of business succession compared to goals, intentions and behaviour of family members.

Despite a large literature pool on succession issues in family firms, the literature for business entry is inconclusive and lacks empirical support. In addition, the modernisation effect on family business is hardly discussed in the literature, including international and global family business enterprises. International collaboration in examining organisational issues, including entry path towards family business across cultures/countries and the technological advancement to speed up the entry route, such as virtual entry and cyberspace connections in family business can enlighten our understandings of social psychological processes in family business. Inclusion of the ecology of community in the discussion of family business can add further insights on the sustainable progress of family business, particularly for culturally diverse and ethnic minority groups (Shams, 2005).

PART II

The Role of Family Functioning in Family Firms

Family is an inseparable term in family business, implying that the essential family functions determine family business functions and vice versa (Heck, 1998; Rogoff & Heck, 2003). Despite this, family functioning has received remarkably little attention in the field of family business (Katila, 2002; Nicholson, 2004). As mentioned previously in this chapter, much attention has been devoted in defining 'family business', yet no efforts have been made to define the concept of 'family' — the entity that differentiates these firms from others. 'Family' is a difficult concept to capture and define — perhaps the only thing that can be agreed upon is that it refers to a group of people (Katila, 2002), most of whom are genetically related. This argument puts forward that the family is a not only a biological unit, but also a social creation, a product of our cultural communities.

When considering the inextricable link between family business and family functioning, the cultural differences that apply play a central part — not only variances between regionally and politically defined cultures, but also within the firm and the family itself. Restrictions and freedoms apply according to the societal parameters and cultural frame of reference that operate. These dictate the roles of and dynamics between women, men and children (toddlers through to teenagers) in the family, and create the attitudes that perpetuate these practices. Different expectations and different values — shaped by such influences as exerted by religion or fiscal and social policy — affect family functioning and family enterprises on many levels. For example, matrimony and inheritance laws are a direct function of the values that operate in a given culture. Institutional arrangements for balancing work and family also have a vital role to play in terms of practical family functioning, labour market participation and family demographic trends (Castells, 1997). This creates the scene in which the three overlapping circles of family, business and ownership are set to interact.

In family business, three basic influencing factors shape the organisational culture: first, the family culture and functioning as determinants for family leadership; secondly, the national culture/ethnicity (including economy); and thirdly, the sectoral influences (such as the use of technology and operational differences). The section below will focus on the first two of these factors, starting with a theoretical overview of family functioning from a psychological perspective, followed by a brief summary of cross-cultural organisational research. A synthesis of these approaches is then presented, with relevant examples.

A Psychological Perspective on Family Functioning in Family Business

It is challenging if not impossible to express a coherent, international view of family functioning. From the outset, studies of the family were restricted to the fields of sociology and anthropology. The field has now developed to spawn theories in an array of disciplines, including psychology, psychiatry, linguistics, communications, home economics, nursing, social work (Grotevant & Carlson, 1989) and economics (Becker, 1993). Family psychologists in the Western world have attempted to distil vital aspects of family functioning based on the universal roles, tasks, processes and emotions that all families experience. These are expected to vary in accordance with the different stages in the family life cycle (Carter & McGoldrick, 1980). For example, the newly formed, nuclear family with young children is more likely to be close-knit compared to a family with children in their late teens and that has gone through divorce. Reference to the life cycle brings two important dimensions to the understanding of the family: a normative dimension and a time dimension. The normative dimension ensures that the family is viewed in accordance with what is normal for a family in a given historical and cultural perspective. The time dimension ascertains that the family must be understood as a continuously changing and developing system with a past, present and future (Schødt & Egeland, 1994). Even under the assumption that the dimensions of family functioning are universal, the interpretation and outcomes for families may be radically different in one part of the world compared to the other. An illustration of this is Baumrind's (1972) report that authoritarian parenting is associated with assertiveness in African-American girls, whereas their white European counterparts associate it with fearful, timid behaviour.

The majority of psychological theories that focus on the more specific aspect of family functioning stem from practices in family therapy, and are thus founded on a clinical basis. Forefathers of family therapy such as Minuchin (1974) and Bowen (1976) both built their respective approaches on general systems theory. Systems theory describes the family as a social system that interacts with its environment through a varying degree of open or closed boundaries, utilising negative and positive feedback for regulating states of morphogenesis (change promoting) and homeostasis (equilibrium maintaining) (Falicov, 1988; Schødt, & Egeland, 1994). Recently, more attention has been brought to the notion of family normality (Walsh, 1993). Also, Bray (1995) points out that the field has shifted from viewing the family as a coherent whole to being discussed in terms of critical aspects of functioning as specific processes and interaction between family members. This makes for a more flexible scope, particularly when considering the dynamics of transgenerational family teams that often operate in family businesses.

There are numerous family theories that all take a similar yet slightly different view of family functioning. Provided below is a selected overview of models in psychology that aim to describe family functioning in more detail, most of which have attempted to create a systematic deconstruction of whole family functioning by ordering them into psychometric measures.

Among the most widely used model is the Circumplex Model of Marital and Family Systems (Olson, 1998; Olson & Defrain, 1994; Olson et al., 1992), and deriving from family systems and family developmental theory. Its main postulation lies in the balance between the two strong dimensions of adaptability and cohesion. Adaptability is here seen as the extent to which the family system is flexible and able to change. Cohesion describes the degree to which an individual is separate from or connected to the family system (Olson, 1988). Other theorists, while applying a general systems perspective, place more emphasis on family dynamics and the interaction between the individual and family process (Skinner, Steinhauer, & Santa-Barbara, 1983) or the social ecological climate

(Moos & Moos, 2002). Williamson pioneered a synthesis of the multigenerational approaches to family functioning, building a focus of many generations to explain family development and change (described in Williamson & Bray, 1988). Other vital contributions to family theory are concerned with parenting styles (such as Baumrind, 1968; Darling & Steinberg, 1993; George & Bloom, 1997), family emotional functioning (e.g., Lowman, 1981) and family stress and coping (see, for example, Hobfoll & Spielberger, 1992).

Conceptual overviews of the above and many more models of whole family functioning provide a delineation of the most frequently occurring dimensions that are utilised in this field of research (Fisher, 1976; Grotevant & Carlson, 1989; Bray, 1995; Touliatos, Perlmutter, & Strauss, 1990). The most recent review is Grotevant and Carlson's meta-analysis of 17 self-report family measures (1989). Conceptual groupings feature firstly **Structure**, referring to constellations of intrafamilial relationships, including roles and distances, coalitions and triangulations. Secondly, **Process** refers to conflict solving, adaptability, communication and control. Thirdly, **Affect** describes affective expression, responsiveness, involvement and intimacy. Fourthly, **Orientation** includes values and norms, cultural/intellectual/religious orientation and extrafamilial factors, such as support groups outside the family circle. The final and fifth conceptual grouping refers to **Other** aspects that are more specific to the theoretical approach, and feature, for example, family health, intergenerational intimidation and financial problems.

Although it has been argued otherwise (Bray, 1995) most family measures have been developed in a clinical context. They thus feature sensitive items that would not be acceptable to the larger part of the family business population, whose members are notoriously private. Secondly, and related to the first point, many of them are oriented towards pathology, touching upon issues such as alcohol or physical abuse. Thirdly, the vast majority of the reviewed models is circumscribed to smaller (nuclear) family units, and do not take the extended family or multiple generations into account, with the exception of Bray, Williamson and Malone (1984) and Lowman (1981). The ongoing development of the Family Climate Scales by Björnberg and Nicholson (2004) addresses these issues, and includes those dimensions believed to explain a significant portion of the activity of the family as a unit (Forman & Hagan, 1983) and are applicable in a *family business context*. These are presented in Figure 1.5.

Building on a comprehensive review of the literature described above, the model includes the following dimensions, along the conceptual groupings of Family Process, Family Intergenerational Style and Family Cohesion: **Open Communication** is defined as family members' ability to openly express themselves and be receptive to the expressions of others in the family system; **Adaptability** refers to the family system's inherent flexibility, self-belief and

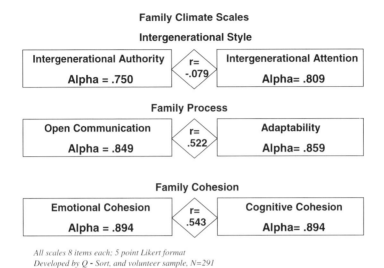

Figure 1.5: Reliability of the family climate scales: cronbach alphas and main factor intercorrelations.

cooperativeness in its ability to face challenges or solve problems; **Intergenerational attention** is defined as responsiveness of older generations, as expressed in their recognition and initiative to safeguard and promote the needs of individuals of younger generations; **Intergenerational authority** is defined as demandingness of older generations as expressed in their decision making, behaviour control and boundary creation for individuals of younger generations; **Emotional Cohesion** (family feelings) is seen as the degree of closeness experienced in the family system expressed in terms of positive or negative emotion; and finally, **Cognitive Cohesion** (shared norms and values) represents the degree to which family members share the same world view, or rather, degree of closeness or distance between family members in terms of how much their norms and values are shared. These dimensions (represented in Figure 1.6) will be referred to in the discussion below on family functioning in family firms across cultures.

Cross-Culture Organisational Research

The most commonly used description of cultural comparisons is that of Hofstede (2001). He speaks of four dimensions, deep-seated mental formulae that run like

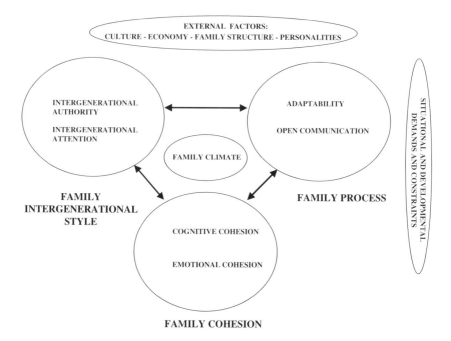

Figure 1.6: Dimension of family functioning.

programmes through any society, resulting from the universal need for order. They show contrasting attributes of the extreme poles, but since they represent continuous scales, cultures and nations, they paint a picture in grey tones rather than black and white in terms of these dimensions. The first among these is Power Distance. This dimension describes a society's sense of hierarchy, indicating the degree of inequality of power in a given dyad. In cultures that have large power distance, such as the Philippines, Malaysia and Indonesia, subordinates expect to be told what to do, and the ideal boss is seen as a benevolent autocrat or good father. The second dimension, Individualism–Collectivism, represents the sense a person has of being psychologically separate from and independent of others, or alternatively inextricably linked via bonds of obligations, and incorporated into a network of others. Examples of collectivist societies are Venezuela and India, and individualist societies are, for example, the USA and the UK.

The other two dimensions are Uncertainty–Avoidance, and Masculinity–Femininity. The former reveals the extent to which members of a culture feel threatened by unknown or uncertain situations and tend to behave in ways, which reduce anxiety. Societies noted as having strong uncertainty–avoidance are, for example,

Greece and Japan, whereas societies with low uncertainty–avoidance are, for example, Denmark and Hong Kong. The latter dimension separates 'masculine' societies, in which gender roles are distinct (e.g., Austria and Japan) from 'feminine' societies, where gender roles overlap — as in Sweden and the Netherlands. The most recent addition to these four dimensions is the long-term versus the short-term orientation. The poles of this dimension are reminiscent of Confucian thinking, with persistence and thrift on one end, and personal stability and respect for tradition on the other. Eastern cultures score high on a long-term orientation, Western countries score rather low and developing countries the lowest.

An alternative description of a cross-cultural approach to the study of organisational behaviour is the work of Trompenaars (1993). He describes cultures as varying along five basic orientations: universalism vs. particularism, individualism vs. collectivism, neutral vs. emotional orientation, specific vs. diffuse orientation and achievement vs. ascription orientation. These overlap with the dimensions put forward by Hofstede to a certain extent. In the analysis below, the main focus will be given to the work of Hofstede.

Family Functioning in Family Firms Across Cultures

So what do these dimensions mean for family businesses? What effects do different types of family functioning have for the family business — and how much does this depend on a given culture?

When studying the impact of culture on organisational behaviour and family functioning, there is a tendency to look for differences. However, three factors need to be taken into consideration. First, despite the differences, significant similarities also exist, in the shape of universal roles (e.g., parent or sibling roles), emotions and approaches that operate in these arenas. Secondly, there are probably more differences within than between cultures. No doubt all families are unique. Individual personality configurations also exert a great influence (Nicholson, 2003), particularly in positions of leadership. Thirdly, one also needs to take into account not only the above-mentioned effect of family functioning on the business, but also the effect of the business on family functioning — the 'backwash' of the business into the family culture — creating residuals, cohesion or even splits in the family.

An inherent duality has been noted in family firms, where key cultural strengths are simultaneously key weaknesses (sometimes referred to as bivalent attributes) (Nicholson & Björnberg, 2004; Allio, 2004; Tagiuri & Davis, 1996) owing to the complexity of having two systems operating in one context. This is a balancing act with which many business-owning families are familiar. For example, the flexibility and quick decision making of informal and personal networks may also be related to an absence of planning and gaps in communication. Similarly, the stability, continuity and long-term perspectives applied by many family firms may lead to conservatism, rigidity and a tendency to be ingrown (Nicholson, 2003).

In order to illustrate the dimensions of family functioning mentioned previously in this section against particular cultural backgrounds, examples from South Asian firms in the UK, Asian firms in Kenya and firms in Finland are discussed below. These examples feature succession, a vulnerable and critical stage in the evolution of a family firm, as a highlighting issue.

Intergenerational Authority and Attention

Power distance is closely related to the concepts of parenting styles, and thus intergenerational authority. In this context, it includes relationships between family members that are separated by more than one generation. Within organisations, power distance is commonly examined in the relationship between the superior and subordinate (Hofstede, 2001). Consultative processes taking place between superior and subordinate are less common in decision making in societies that feature large power distance. This can have a strong effect on fundamental family business matters, such as succession planning and intergenerational cooperation.

In the case of succession, intergenerational authority and attention both play significant roles. The latter is significant in terms of socialisation of the potential successors in a family business context, including formal preparation such as education and training, work experience and informal preparation, for example, development of relationships (Morris, Williams, & Nell, 1996). The former plays a significant role not only in the process of succession but has also moulded the structure that the successor will be entering into. To a certain degree, intergenerational authority defines what kind of leader the successor is replacing and will perhaps even continue to work with over a period of time.

As mentioned previously in the chapter, certain background factors play a specific role in the particular succession situation of ethnic minority family firms. Bachkaniwala, Wright, and Ram's (2001) qualitative study of South Asian family firms in the UK sheds some light on what influences the entry of family members into ethnic family firms.

(1) They are subject to the dynamic push and pull of second generation potential successors — the push into the family business exerted by a blocked upward mobility for ethnic minorities and prevailing discrimination on the labour

market, and the pull of higher levels of education and less corporate discrimination of the second generation towards more desirable positions in large organisations (Bachkaniwala, Wright, & Ram, 2001).

(2) The second generation has less knowledge of their native culture and language (Wong, McReynolds, & Wong, 1992) due to assimilation in the host country's culture — thus a lesser degree of cultural attachment (*ibid.*). This may also imply a lesser extent of shared norms and values in the generational divide (lower cognitive cohesion).

A high level of power distance is featured in many countries in the South Asian region (Hofstede, 2001). Veneration of older members of the family is an important aspect of family life (Janjuha-Jivraj & Woods, 2002), thereby suggesting a higher level of intergenerational authority, a factor that comes into play in the ramifications of succession. In their study, Bachkaniwala, Wright, and Ram (2001) found that the offspring's educational qualifications and external employment opportunities, growth and development prospects in the family firm play a specific role in the succession processes. Additional, distinctive factors negatively influencing the interest of the second generation were long and unsociable working hours due to tight market niches and the extreme focus and dependence on a co-ethnic clientele. However, the authors concluded that the differences in approach to succession in the cases studied were influenced by the founder's background and sector.

Findings from the Asian family business community in Kenya is unlike the sample mentioned above, inasmuch as many of these businesses have already gone through a first succession. Experiences of unplanned successions that caused devastating splits, both in terms of the family and the business, have prompted a determined effort to increase transgenerational communication in the attempt to create a long-term strategy. Findings also identify non-active family members as having considerable influence during succession, in particular the mothers, who act as 'silent buffers' between generations. Culture and experiences are seen as strong factors influencing attitudes towards succession, yet there is a shift in the younger generation, whereby less emphasis is placed on the religious-ethnic community for support. Also, lesser emphasis on filial obligation was found in the Kenyan cases, and thereby a stronger tendency towards separation of ownership and management (Janjuha-Jivraj & Woods, 2002).

These examples highlight something very fundamental in terms of the context within which the family system operates. In the case of Kenya, the religious-ethnic community has played a very central role, not only for the perpetuation of a cultural identity but also in terms of social welfare (featuring community-based schools, hospitals and financial institutions) (*ibid.*). In Britain, these groups have less tangible characteristics to rely upon. Therefore, with each generation's increasing desire to integrate in the community, the emphasis on the religious-ethnic community diminishes (*ibid.*). Asian firms in the UK thus face a double challenge — not only are they caught between generations, they are also caught between a more collectivist versus a more individualist culture, in Hofstede's terminology (2001). In addition, Asian family firms run a greater risk of discord between family members, since the likelihood of extended family involvement is more common (Janjuha-Jivraj & Woods, 2002). This places extra weight and pressure on virtually all aspects of family functioning, but perhaps particularly on communication, adaptability and intergenerational style. Preliminary results from a multicultural sample of the Family Climate Scales indicate that intergenerational authority is unrelated to the other dimensions of family climate, with the exception of communication and adaptability (Björnberg & Nicholson, 2004). As we shall see below, communication and adaptability are both key factors in the succession process, not least for the establishment of trust and continuity in the relationships between family members.

Adaptability

Adaptability is of fundamental importance to the family and business systems, particularly in the light of an increasingly versatile and demanding market. For example, it influences strategic formulation, determining consolidation or diversification, and determines the ability to manage change. Adaptability also denotes the openness of a system. A family system with rigid boundaries is more likely to keep its environment at a greater distance, thus being less likely to take in outside advice or involve non-family. The type of leadership emanating from enmeshed family situations will have direct effects on the type of family governance system applied — or indeed, the presence of one in the first place.

In societies that display strong uncertainty avoidance, there is an emotional need for rules, regardless of them being effective or not. There is more resistance to innovation, and motivation comes by security and esteem or belongingness (Hofstede, 2001). For example, Yokozawa and Goto (2004) show that long-lived family firms in Japan apply cautious innovation and financial conservatism. These practices can be traced back to the writing of family constitutions in Japan, outlining risk management structures that reflect periods of economic and political turmoil, such as the Genroku period (1688–1704) and World War II (*ibid.*) Hofstede's fifth dimension of long-term versus short-term orientation is inevitably a factor that applies in this case, on the basis of a historical need to prepare for a more distant future. Family firms in some cultures may also favour a very traditional route in terms of succession, again exemplified by the Japanese tradition of business heritage being given to the eldest male son (Hambata, 1991).

Although evidence from the United States shows that there is a linear relationship between adaptability and family health (Cluff, Hicks, & Madsen, 1994) (the more adaptable the family, the more healthy it is likely to be), an overly flexible approach in a *family business context* can result in a lack of planning and unclear boundaries. This may, in turn, impede the level of preparation for the generational shift. Murray (2002) describes the role of anxiety as one of either catalyst or inhibitor in the transition stages of the family firm (sample derived from the UK). Her description features anxiety as the central challenge facing the key individuals in the generational transition process, and the skill with which an enterprising family system manages this anxiety can be determining for the survival of the firm. Problem solving, a sub-feature of adaptability, is therefore also crucial for this and similar processes in the family firm.

Emotional and Cognitive Cohesion

The marriage of the rational and the emotional, as described by Murray (2002), is yet another example of the bivalent attributes of the family firm, as mentioned above. Emotional cohesion is very important, for example, in relationship building, not only within the firm but also with community stakeholders (Nicholson & Björnberg, 2004). For such activities, the emotional fulfils a rational function. Cognitive cohesion is vital for creating a strong and unified leadership based on norms and values that are shared and understood by family, and easily communicated to non-family. A lack of both cognitive and emotional cohesion may be a breeding ground for unwanted and destructive relationship conflicts, and can cause rifts that negatively influence both the family and the business. Kellermanns and Eddleston (2004) suggest that relationship conflicts in family firms are moderated by the degree of altruism among family members. In collectivist cultures, strong family commitment, family ideologies and values and altruistic attitudes towards family members serve as a grounding force for the family business (Dutta, 1996). However, just as the absence of cohesion may cause states of fragmentation, dysfunctionally high levels of cohesion may in some cases also lead to the system becoming closed and enmeshed (Nicholson, 2003).

An illustration of emotional and cognitive cohesion in the overlap of family and business functioning is provided by Katila (2002) in her description of Finnish farm businesses. What makes these businesses special is the fact that the farm is simultaneously a workplace and a home, sharply at odds with the dominating form of social organisation that segregates the two (*ibid.*). One of the norms of the yeoman moral order in Finland is that of unpaid family labour. The virtue of industriousness is still highly valued among the rural population in

Finland, including the youth. Combined with the norm of unpaid family labour, this virtue serves the core value of the moral order: the continuity of the family farm. Monetary incentives play an irrelevant role in terms of family labour on these farms. Instead, the social obligations to kin and the promise of future position as an owner-manager are the primary motives for work (Katila, 2002). The collectivism referred to by both Hofstede (2001) and Trompenaars (1993) thus features strongly in this subculture of family firms.

Succession processes in these firms is highly gendered. Only boys are expected and trained specifically to continue the family farm into the next generation. Girls are trained in this respect only when they are the only children in the family (Katila, 2002). Family roles are clearly defined in this case, and reflect what Hofstede (2001) refers to as a 'masculine' society. Family values incorporated into the running of the business are perpetuated in a very traditional manner, most likely due to the nature of the sector rather than due to the national Finnish culture at large, which Hofstede found to be on the feminine side (*ibid.*).

The fundamental significance of emotional and cognitive cohesion for the perpetuation of the family firm is illustrated by this case. In addition, it shows how these dimensions of cohesion encompass not only the family, but also the larger community. Love for the land and the work, as a part of your body and soul, featured strongly in these relationships. Equally, guilt and shame were core emotions and motivational drivers in the chain of continuation. Discontinuation or loss of the farm was seen as forbidden and thus shameful, since it would waste all of the work of all previous generations (Katila, 2002). The authority in the family system conveying these feelings and norms was embodied by the parents in the socialisation process, and internalised as the voice of conscience, is the moral order.

Open Communication

The role of communication is so vital and fundamental that it encompasses all of the above dimensions. One specific aspect of communication that was touched upon is that of transgenerational family teams, which begs the question 'How is culture transmitted across generations?'

According to Bennett, Wolin, and McAvity (1988), symbolic communication in the shape of rituals enacts the family identity, and is a systematic way of perpetuating it. As condensed versions of family life as a whole, rituals clarify roles, delineate boundaries and define rules. In addition to more subtle components of the family's gestalt, family-level beliefs encompass concepts such as ethnicity, religiosity and work ethic. The authors see rituals as categorised into three general groupings: celebrations, traditions and patterned routines. For family businesses, having family constitutions or councils as part of the family governance system is one way in which the family identity is ritualised and expressed in the business. These, if used correctly, constitute a pathway of communication between the family and the business, and often contain directions on how to manage succession. Other ritualistic behaviour is manifested in the numerous ways that culture finds expression in the everyday life of the organisation, for example, in the shape of myths, stories, artefacts and habits (Schein, 2004). The merged cultural identity of the organisation and the family is maintained in the subtle and sometimes outspoken exchange between the structure and processes that have evolved and continue to evolve in their joint, yet separate life cycles. In effect, basic assumptions of family identity translate into values upon which the organisation remembers, operates and prepares for the future. Simply put, its identity is the way in which the family views reality — and reacts accordingly (Bennett, Wolin, & McAvity, 1988).

As was mentioned previously, Bachkaniwala, Wright and Ram (2001) argue that in order to run ethnic minority businesses, culture-specific knowledge and language is needed. Therefore, succession options may be typically generated within not only the kinship group, but also in the co-ethnic network. The challenge faced by these firms in particular, and other family firms in general, is the maintenance and continuation of the cultural framework, although the succession does not necessarily take place within the kinship group. However, continuity of family identity is not advantageous in all families (*ibid.*). Indeed, dysfunctional patterns and rituals can be very destructive and hard to alter.

Culture management is becoming an increasingly pertinent issue, in particular as family businesses are widening their scope, not only in terms of size, but also when they straddle more than one culture in a global arena.

The Importance of Family for Business Success

As can be seen, the stability of family business depends to a great extent on intergenerational relationships and communication patterns (Wang & Poutziouris, 2003). Cohesion within the family also ensures optimal performance in family business. Although a tendency to keep family business within the family is predominant among the old family firms, relatively new and multiple business holders show interest in quality of work, financial security, innovation, personal and social advancement, corporate citizenship and job security (Tagiuri & Davis, 1992). Gersick et al.'s (1999) model emphasizes the third generation's encounter in a competitive business market with skilled entrepreneurship and business expertise, usually through training and external networking (Figure 1.7).

Despite initiatives towards the modernisation of family business, participation from family business organisations is alarmingly low (Matley, 2000). This has serious implications for those failed family businesses because a direct association has been reported between business success rate and undertakings of training initiatives (Westhead & Storey, 1997). Kelly, Athanassiou, and Crittenden (2000) proposed a founder centrality model to elucidate the powerful role of the founder in family business from a social network perspective. To cite from Hollander and Elman (1988), 'the culture of the business becomes, at least in part, an embodiment of the founding personality'; this culture then influences operational style that in turn affects both the development of the business and its ability to respond to change.

Recent literature suggests that three dimensions in family communication and decision-making characterise family business relations and success (Dyer & Handler, 1994). The first one is between representing power (Krackhardt, 1990) distribution in the form of decentralised decision-making and equity in distributing information however not at the expense of divorcing managerial control from the founder. The second dimension, 'closeness centrality', refers to independent

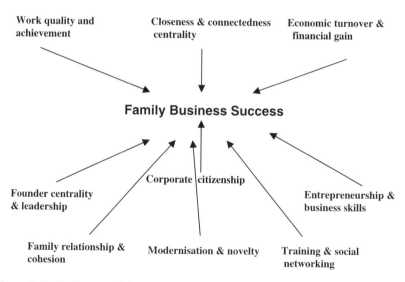

Figure 1.7: Indicators of family business success.

or divisive communication and networking (Freeman, 1979) by the founder with other management group members without the help of intermediaries, as such an independent decision as to whom to approach first is determined by the central management only. The third dimension, 'connectivity centrality', refers to the top management's abilities to connect with selected top management group members (Watts & Strogatz, 1998).

A growing interest is observed to interconnect family businesses around the world to promote commerce and industry, and for economic growth in a family. Carney and Gedajiovic (2002) proposed a co-evolutionary model to present notions of interdependence, path dependence and system openness in the development of family business groups. They have made specific reference to agency theory in which human motivation and interests can have a paramount influence on the relational infrastructure of family businesses around the world. Family relations are critical for business flourish, and to personalise it in terms of family norms, values and practices (Wang & Poutziouris, 2003; Wang et al., 2004). Healthy family relations can enhance the succession process as well as bring effective continuity of the business within the sanctioned family framework. Recent data from a sample of UK family firms demonstrates that the 'family' is not only viewed as a cultural strength, but is also predictive of family firm performance (controlling for firm size) (Nicholson & Björnberg, unpublished data). Although 'family' was also described as a cultural weakness, it was not negatively associated with firm performance in this case. However, it provided another example of the 'bivalent' attributes of the family firm, as mentioned above. Marshall (2002) in a national data set analysis in the USA has confirmed the latent importance of family relations manifesting successful business outcomes; the latent factors identified are conflict resolution styles (flexible vs. rigidity) and leadership styles (cooperative vs. autocratic). These two dimensions differ according to the size of the business (Dierickx & Cool, 1989), and the founder member's personality, values and practising styles are also taken into consideration (Kets de Vries, 1996).

The management literature is still underrepresented in providing systematic evaluation of the important aspects of family relations in enhancing business performance and effective execution of business plans by the family members, for example, communications patterns (face-to-face meetings as well as electronic devices) as driving force to shape up family business and successful succession over generations. In addition, psychological theorising and explanations are inadequate to examine the intersection between family relations and business performance. Recent developments in the psychology of family business, as described in the section above, are aimed at bridging that gap.

Methodological and Ethical Issues

Methodological issues are less discussed and prioritised in the family business, although recent changes in technology, and global interconnections in family business field demand a critical analysis for the development of innovative methods and professional intervention strategies. However, methodological concerns in family business are consistently showing the predominant use of some methods, thereby questioning the validity and generalisable power of measurements for all types of family business research. The constraints inherent in conducting family business research are first of all problems in identifying family business as they are not listed separately within the self-employed category (see, for example, Labour Force Survey, LFS listing), and family businesses are reluctant to be identified even for research purposes and to disclose information regarding their business history, and activities (Handler, 1989; Schulze et al., 2003; Wang, 2004). This could well be the main reason for the lack of longitudinal studies in family business (Brockhaus, 1994). Other possible reasons are problems in mapping out research issues within the family business domain, and lack of resources to underpin professional and ethical issues in family business research that can most often lead to a more formal indirect research approach, such as telephone interviewing (Small bone et al., 2003) and secondary data sources that Garcia-Alvarez and Lopez-Sintas (2002) followed by the grounded theory approach (Glasser & Strauss, 1967) called 'theoretical sampling'. Additionally, the use of differing operational definitions of family firms also poses a methodological hazard, particularly when comparisons between quantitative studies are attempted. This also substantially reduces the scope for conducting meta-analyses of such studies.

Methods in Family Business Research

There is a growing trend in family business research to undertake qualitative methods in all types of family business including business with international focus (Axelsson & Johanson, 1992; Bell, 2004). This is due to the fact that family businesses usually do not agree to invest time and energy for research purposes, especially when the benefits are not clearly stated, there is also a fear for invading their privacy. As a result of these apprehensions, qualitative method is believed to be the only reliable method (Carson, Cromie, McGowan, & Hill, 1995) to collect information on family business as it allows the effective use of a phenomenological approach (Pires & Stanton, 2003) to understand the interface between working and family lives. Several methods, such as case study (Eisenhardt, 1989), multiple case studies (Larsson, 1993; Yin, 1994), ethnography (Ram, 1999), interpretive, critical incidence (Chell & Rhodes, 1999), discourse analysis (Fairclough, 1995), focus groups (Blackburn & Stokes, 1998) and observational study (Lee & Marshall, 1998), are usually applied. Case study is the most widely used method among qualitative methods in family business as it allows a rich understanding of family processes in business. It can also be applied to a multiple-business site simultaneously or independently, and using pattern matching for case data (McCucheon & Meredith, 1993), the information gives refined spatial, familial and ownership functions in various case sites (Ainsworth & Cox, 2003). Parker (2000) calls this approach a 'generalisable grammar, flexible to establish a fundamental unity or normative consensus in organisational aspects of family business' (Casey, 1999; Gabriel, 1999; Young, 2004). However, Zimmerman and Szenberg (2000) warned about the use of qualitative techniques such as case study in international business research since cultural problems such as understanding family business in various cultures, interpreting data and understanding of culture may contaminate international research strategy in family business

Alvarez and Ercilia (2002) have successfully used both qualitative and quantitative methods in family business. The triangulated approach is suitable for researching small family firms (Swartz & Boaden, 1997). Other approaches in family business research are action research, participatory observation and internet survey (Westbrook, 1995; Rao & Perry, 2003). Action research is particularly helpful when family business is seeking expert advice on any aspects of their business management, and functional capability, output target and market strategies. Researchers in this case can implement their findings in the research in conjunction with the family business protocol/strategy using action-research technique.

Ethical and Professional Practice

The ethical and professional issues in family business are hardly discussed in the literature as an independent area for enquiry. Although business ethics is one of the most popular subject areas in business and management psychology, however, the recent publications on business ethics is showing growing concerns for inappropriate use of ethical queries in business organisations, and failing professional accountability to address business ethics in courses and study programmes (Bruce, 2004; Merritt, 2004; Young, 2004). Trevino and Weaver (2003) report on ongoing challenging and conflicting issues for business ethics with the changes in technology, culture, politics, workforce diversity, business activities and internationalisation. However, none of the recent publications have discussed ethical issues for undertaking research in business, professional accountability to ensure the maintenance of code of conduct while accessing confidentiality and any concerns relating to the breach of business confidentiality, with particular reference to family business.

Methodological Concerns

Despite the growing concerns for accessing family business for research purposes (Ram, Abbas, Sanghera, Barlow, & Jones, 2001), fear of breach of confidentiality as a prime factor for low participation and response returns, debriefing issues after the interview, and family business participants' involvement in the research process are hardly discussed, although these are the strong factors interfering with research participation and articulating research processes. Shams et al. (2004–2005) have addressed these important issues in their research with Asian family businesses in which a website is created to provide the potential participants access to information about the rationale, aims and objectives of the research with implications for minority businesses. The debriefing issue in this research has been addressed through a proposal for a social networking event for all participants with a major focus on disseminating information on research outcomes during the event.

The discussion of methodology is definitely giving some indications of future research prospects in family business where innovative methodologies and action research may overtake the traditional normative use of mainly qualitative methods and questionnaires, to underpin research outcomes leading to conceptual and theoretical developments of emerging issues in family business.

Conclusion: Future of Family Business

Family business is regarded as one of the most dominant forms of economic enterprise throughout the world (La Porta, Lopez-de-Silanes, & Shlieifer, 1999), and a popular means to achieve economic independence in conjunction with family values and support. Yet research in this prospective economic behaviour is not extensive, partly because it is shared by a number of social-science disciplines, such as management and business studies, economics and politics, psychology, applied social sciences. An integrated literature with diverse research paradigms to address key research issues in relation to an 'insider's perspective' in family business is needed. The insider's perspective here calls for a re-examination of operational issues on family businesses, viz., identity, power, control, communication, values, aspirations and resistance (Ainsworth & Cox, 2003). An international perspective on family businesses needs to find a common theoretical ground on which effective discussion about psychological issues in family business can be made at the expense of divorcing cultural differences in family business functioning. The problematic issue of finding a common theoretical platform of psychological importance has been debated in Shams and Jackson (2005).

The analysis in this chapter reflects some of the concerns from the existing literature and expressed legitimately when it says family business is excluded in the mainstream organisational research (Hoy, 2003). Most of the educational materials such as recommended textbooks and course content do not support the delivery of family business and as such hardly any discussion about family firms has been held in the educational literature for further and higher studies.

The discussion in this chapter has highlighted several underdeveloped areas in family business research:

- Definitional differences in categorising family businesses.
- Conceptual difficulties of placing family in family business.
- Lack of psychological explanations for family business behaviours.
- Absence of research on organisational issues in family business, particularly from family as an employee perspective.
- Inadequate theorising about family business functions and generational succession.
- Neglect of diversity in family business research.
- Less research on methodological development and advancement leading to inconclusive findings and validity issues for sample representations (in most of the cases, the sample is a convenient sample, readily available and willing to participate rather than following on pre-determined criteria).
- Ethical issues and professional practice in family business research are hardly discussed.
- The essence of international business and virtual family business requires research attention.
- Issues for funding family research, international and interdisciplinary research projects have not been given appropriate attention.

In spite of these shortcomings, recent work focusing on the psychology of family business and family functioning is beginning to show encouraging developments in conceptualising family business from a psychological perspective. Increasing technological advancement and cultural dependency are calling for a disciplinary approach to capture international family business in order to include new areas into the theoretical explanation. Future research should pay attention to cross-cultural issues in family business, family business strategies in cross-national collaboration, and applications of family functioning models to family business research.

As mentioned previously in this chapter, the field of family business research is in need of further theoretical development. With more developed, empirically testable theories, cross-disciplinary collaboration will be made easier, empirical data will be improved and the understanding of the nature of the subject matter will be enhanced.

Contemporary overarching trends on the level of social change that are of particular interest for the analysis of family are: individualisation, democratisation and globalisation (Crow, 2002). The international perspective on family business applied in this chapter has highlighted both global and interpersonal trends, taking into account the characteristics of different cultural backgrounds.

Demographic and socio-political changes that have taken place over recent decades pose a particular challenge for family businesses on several levels, and are expected to continue doing so. For instance, the effect of declining birth rates in some parts of the world and increased birth rates in other parts will continue to encourage the growth of a globally mobile workforce. Also, the thinning of family trees — with an increasingly aged population — will inevitably provide a smaller gene pool for succession within families. Thus, we are likely to witness an increased tendency or preference for professionalisation of family firm leadership groups as a result. As such, more family businesses will be family-owned rather than family-managed.

The notion of the family being subject to a process of 'democratisation' is also central in this respect. Giddens (1998) posits that if a contemporary family is to be durable, it must provide scope for individual choice and input into the decision making for its members. Arising from this is not only higher levels of flexibility, but also an increased tension between autonomy and togetherness in family life, leading to different styles of negotiation over family resources such as time, household labour and money (Björnberg & Kollind, 2003). As we have shown in this chapter, this tension takes shape when individuals in family businesses find themselves in not only the generational gap, but also in the grey zone of cultural overlap. Despite this growing need for autonomy and individual freedom, it is clear that obligations, structural constraints and social solidarity continue to prevail in the family system — perhaps more so in the non-Western world. These opposing forces are further confounded by the complexity involving task, process and relationship conflict in family business, which remains one of most serious challenges in creating sustainable family business success. This is especially the case for the next generation, who will enter an informal contract of employment within a family setting (Kellermanns & Eddleston, 2004).

It is not our task to make value-laden statements about the best type of family or firm functioning but rather, continue to ask ourselves: How does the process of adjustment between national, organisational and family cultures take place, and what can be done to facilitate family firms to find their own way towards success and sustainability? Increasing partnerships between researchers and family business organisations can help us to document recent developments in family business organisations and thus foresee future prospects in international business within and between entrepreneurial families in the world economy.

Acknowledgement

We are grateful to Prof. Nigel Nicholson who provide constructive and critical comments on an earlier version of this chapter. Åsa Björnberg's contribution was supported by the ESRC grant no. RES-000-22-0302.

References

Ainsworth, S., & Cox, W. J. (2003). Families divided: Culture and control in small family business. *Organization Studies, 24*(9), 1463–1485.

Allio, M. K. (2004). Family businesses: Their virtues, vices and strategic path. *Strategy & Leadership, 32*(4), 24–33.

Alvarez, G., & Ercilia, U. (2002). Contingency table: A two-way bridge between qualitative and quantitative methods. *Field Methods, 14*(3), 270–287.

Astrachan, J. H., Zahra, S. A., & Sharma, P. (2003). *Family-sponsored ventures.* The entrepreneurial advantage of nations: First annual global entrepreneurship symposium. New York: United Nations Headquarters.

Axelsson, B., & Johanson, J. (1992). Foreign market entry: The textbook vs the network view. In: B. Axelssson, & G. Easton (Eds), *Industrial networks: A new view of reality* (pp. 218–234). London: Routledge.

Bachkaniwala, D., Wright, M., & Ram, M. (2001). Succession in South Asian family businesses in the UK. *International Small Business Journal, 19*(4), 15–27.

Bank of England. (1999). *The financing of ethnic minority firms in the UK: A special report.* London: Bank of England.

Barratt, G. A., Jones, T. P., & Mcevoy, D. (1996). Ethnic minority business: Theoretical discourse in Britain and North America. *Urban Studies, 33*(4), 783–810.

Baumrind, D. (1968). Authoritarian v. authoritative parental control. *Adolescence, 3*, 255–272.

Baumrind, D. (1972). An exploratory study of socialization effects on black children: Some black-white comparisons. *Child Development, 43*, 261–267.

Becker, G. (1993). *A treatise on the family.* Cambridge: Harvard University Press.

Bell, J., Crick, D., & Young, S. (2004). Small firm internationalization and business strategy. *International Small Business Journal, 22*(10), 23–56.

Bennett, L. A., Wolin, S. J., & McAvity, K. J. (1988). Family identity, ritual and myth: A cultural perspective on life cycle transitions. In: C. Falicov (Ed.) *Family transitions: Continuity and change over the life cycle.* New York: The Guilford Press.

Birley, S. (2001). Owner-manager attitudes to family and business issues: A 16 country study. *Entrepreneurship: Theory and Practice*, 63–76.

Björnberg, U., & Kollind, A.-K. (2003). Att leva själv tillsammans. Jämställdhet, autonomi och gemenskap i parrelationer. *(Living together on individual principles. Equality, autonomy and togetherness in couple relationships)* Malmö: Liber.

Björnberg, Å., & Nicholson, N. (2004). *Family climate: The development of new measures for use in family business research.* London Business School working paper.

Blackburn, R., & Stokes, D. (1998). Dialogues with business owners: Focus groups in SME research. Paper presented at ISBA 21st national small firms and research conference, Durham University, 18–20 November.

Bowen, M. (1976). Theory in the practice of psychotherapy. In: P. Guerin (Ed.), *Family therapy: Theory and practice.* New York: Gardner Press.

Bray, J. H. (1995). Family assessment – Current issues in evaluating families. *Family Relations, 44*(4), 469–477.

Bray, J. H., Williamson, D. S., & Malone, P. E. (1984). Personal authority in the family system – development of a questionnaire to measure personal authority in intergenerational family processes. *Journal of Marital and Family Therapy, 10*(2), 167–178.

Brockhaus, R. H. (1994). Entrepreneurship and family business research: Comparisons, critique, and lessons. *Entrepreneurship: Theory and Practice, 19*(1), 25–38.

Bruce, H. D. (2004). Managing ethics in business organizations: Social scientific perspectives. *Personnel Psychology, 57*(2), 556–558.

Bubolz, M. M., & Sontag, M. S. (1993). Human ecology theory. In: P. G. Boss, W. J. Doherty, R. LaRossa, W. R. Schumman, & S. K. Steinmets (Eds), *Sourcebook of family theories and methods: A contextual approach.* New York: Plenum.

Carson, D., Cromie, S., McGowan, P., & Hill, J. (1995). *Marketing and entrepreneurship in SME's: An innovation approach.* Hemel Hempstead: Prentice-Hill.

Carter, B., & McGoldrick, M. (Eds) (1980). *The changing family life cycle: A framework for family therapy* (2nd ed.). New York: Gardner Press.

Casey, C. (1999). Come, join our family: Discipline and integration in corporate organizational culture. *Human Relations, 52*(2), 155–178.

Cassis, Y. (1997). Big business. *The European experience in the twentieth century.* Oxford: Oxford University Press.

Casson, M. (2000). *Enterprise and leadership, studies on firms, markets and networks.* Chletenham: Elgar.

Castells, M. (1997). The power of identity. *The information age: Economy, society and culture* (Vol. II). Oxford, MA: Blackwell.

Chell, E., & Rhodes, H. (1999). The development of a methodology for researching vertical relations in SMEs. Paper presented at the British Academy of Management Annual conference, Manchester Metropolitan University, 1–3 September.

Chua, J. H., Chrisman, J. J., & Sharma, P. (1999). Defining the family business by behaviour. *Entrepreneurship: Theory and Practice, 23*(4), 19–39.

Cluff, R. B., Hicks, M. W., & Madsen, C. H. (1994). Beyond the circumplex model: A moratorium on curvilinearity. *Family process, 33*(4), 455–470.

Colli, A. (2002). Family firms in comparative perspective. In: F. Amatori, & G. Jones (Eds), *Business history around the world at the turn of the century.* Cambridge: Cambridge University Press.

Colli, A. (2003). *The history of family business, 1850–2000.* Cambridge: Cambridge University Press.

Crow, G. (2002). Families, moralities, rationalities and social change. In: A. Carling, S. Duncan, & R. Edwards (Eds). *Analysing families. Morality and rationality in policy and practice.* London: Routledge.

Danes, S. M., Zuiker, V., Arbuthnor, J., Kean, R., & Scannell, E., (1998). Business and family goals and tensions. *Fifth annual international family business program association proceedings.* San Antonio, TX, July 23–25.

Darling, N., & Steinberg, L. (1993). Parenting style as context: An integrative model. *Psychological Bulletin, 113*(3), 487–496.

Davis, J. A., & Taguiri, R. (1989). *Bivalent attributes of the family firm.* Santa Barbara, CA: Owner managed Business Institute.

Davis, P., & Stern, D. (1988). Adaptation, survival, and growth of the family business; an integrated systems perspective. *Family Business Review, 1*(1), 69–85.

Deacon, R. E., & Firebaugh, F. M. (1988). *Family resource management: Principles and applications.* Boston: Allyn and Bacon.

De Roover, R. (1963). *The rise and decline of the Medici Bank, 1397–1494,* Cambridge, MA: Harvard University Press.

Dierickx, I., & Cool, K. (1989). Asset stock accumulation and sustainability of competitive advantage. *Management Science, 35,* 1504–1511.

Dutta, S. (1996). *Family business in India.* New Delhi: Sage Publications.

Dyer, W. G. (1986). *Cultural change in family firms: Anticipating and managing businesses and family transition.* San Francisoc and London: Jossey-Bass Publishers.

Dyer, W. G. (1988). Culture and continuity in family firms. *Family Business Review, 1,* 37–50.

Dyer, W. G., & Handler, W. (1994). Entrepreneurship and family business: Exploring the connections. *Entrepreneurship: Theory and Practice, 19,* 71–84.

Dyck, B., Mauws, M., Starke, F. A., & Mischke, G. A. (2002). Passing the baton: The importance of sequence, timing, technique, and communication in executive succession. *Journal of Business Venturing, 17,* 143–162.

Einhorn, B. (2000). Look who's taking Asian digital. *Business Week, 36*(69), 102–107.

Eisenhardt, K. M. (1989). Building theory from case study research. *Academy of Management Review, 14*(4), 532–550.

Fairclough, N. (1995). *Critical discourse analysis: The critical study of language.* London: Longman.

Falicov, C. (1988). Family sociology and family therapy contributions to the family development framework: A comparative analysis and thoughts on future trends. In: C. Falicov (Ed.), *Family transitions: Continuity and change over the life cycle.* New York: The Guilford Press.

Fama, E., & Jensen, M. C. (1983). Separation of ownership and control. *Journal of Law and Economics, 26,* 301–325.

Fletcher, D. (2001). Experiencing "professional management" in the small, family firm. Paper presented to 17th European group on organization studies colloquium, Lyon, France, 5–7 July.

Fletcher, D. (2004). Interpreneuralship organizational (re)emergence and entrepreneurial development in a second generation family firm. *International Journal of Entrepreneurial Study, 10,* 34–48.

Flintoff, J. P. (2002). Managing to keep the family happy. Financial Times, 21 August. *Behaviour and Research, 10* (1/2), 34–48.

Fisher, L. (1976). Dimensions of family assessment: A critical review. *Journal of Marriage and Family, 2,* 367–382.

Forman, B. D., & Hagan, B. J. (1983). A comparative review of total family functioning measures. *American Journal of Family Therapy, 11*(4), 25–40.

Freeman, L. C. (1979). Centrality in social networks. *Social Networks, 1,* 215–239.

Gabriel, Y. (1999). Beyond happy families: A critical reevaluation of the control–resistance–identity traingle. *Human Relations, 52*(2), 179–203.

Garcia-Alverez, E., Lopez-Sintas, J., & Gonsalvo, P. (2002). Socialization patterns of successors in first-to second generation family businesses. *Family Business Review, XV*(3), 189–203.

George, E. L., & Bloom, B. L. (1997). A brief scale for assessing parental child-rearing practice: Psychometric properties and psychosocial correlates. *Family Process, 36*(1), 63–80.

Gersick, K., Lansberg, I., Desjardins, M., & Dunn, B. (1999). Stages and transitions: Managing changes in the family business. *Family Business Review, XII*(4), 287–297.

Gersick, K. E., Davis, J. A., McCollom, H. M., & Lansberg, I. (1997). *Generation to generation: Lifecycles of family business.* Boston, MA: Harvard Business School Press.

Getz, D., & Carlson, J. (2000). Characteristics and goals of family- and owner-operated businesses in the rural tourism and hospitality sectors. *Toursim Management, 21,* 547–560.

Giddens, A. (1998). *The third way: The renewal of social democracy.* Cambridge: Polity Press.

Glasser, B. G., & Strauss, A. L. (1967). *The discovery of grounded theory: Strategies for qualitative research.* New York: Aldine de Gruyter.

Goldthorpe, J., Llewellyn, C., & Payne, C. (1980). *Social mobility and class structure in modern Britain.* Oxford: Clarendon Press.

González-López, M. (2002). A portrait of Western families: New models of intimate relationships and the timing of life events. In: A. Carling, S. Duncan, & R. Edwards (Eds), *Analysing families. Morality and rationality in policy and practice.* London & New York: Routledge.

Gordon, G. E., & Rosen, N. (1981). Critical factors in leadership succession. *Organisational Behaviour and Human Performance, 27,* 227–254.

Grotevant, H. D., & Carlson, C. I. (1989). *Family assessment: A guide to methods and measures.* New York: Guilford Press.

Hambata, M. (1991). *Crested kimono: Power and love in the Japanese business family.* New York: Cornell University Press.

Handler, W. C. (1989). Methodological issues and consideration in studying family business. *Family business Review, 1*(4), 257–276.

Harris, J. (2003). Widening the radius of trust; Ethnographic explorations of trust and Indian business. *Journal of the Royal Anthropological Institute, 9*(40), 755–764.

Heck, R. K. Z. (Ed.) (1998). The entrepreneurship family: Refocusing on the family in business. In: *The entrepreneurial family* (pp. 1–7). Needham, MA: Family Business Resources Publishing.

Heck, R. K. Z. (2004). A commentary on "entrepreneurship in family vs non-family firms: A resources-based analysis of the effect of organizational culture". *Entrepreneurship Theory and Practice*, 383–389.

Heck, R. K. Z., & Stafford, K. (2001). The vital institution of family business: Economic benefits hidden in plain sight. In: G. K. McCann, & N. Upton (Eds), *Destroying myths and creating value in family business* (pp. 9–17). Deland, FL: Stetson University.

Hobfoll, S. E., & Spielberger, C. D. (1992). Family stress: Integrating theory and measurement. *Journal of Family Psychology*, 6(2), pp. 99–112.

Hofstede, G. (2001). *Culture's consequences* (2nd ed.). Thousand Oaks, CA: Sage.

Holland, G. P., & Boulton, R. W. (1984). Balancing the family and the business in family business. *Business Horizons*, (March–April), 16–21.

Hollander, B. S., & Elman, N. S. (1988). Family owned business: An emerging field of inquiry. *Family Business Review*, 1, 145–164.

Hoy, F. (2003). Legitimizing family business scholarship in organizational research and education. *Entrepreneurship: Theory and Practice*, 417–422.

Janjuha-Jivraj, S., & Woods, A. (2002). Successional issues within Asian family firms. Learning from the Kenyan experience. *International Small Business Journal*, 20(1), 77–94.

Jones, G., & Rose, M. B. (1993). *Family capitalism*, London: Frank Cass (special issue of Business History: 35).

Katila, S. (2002). Emotions and the moral order of farm business families in Finland. In: D. Fletcher (Ed.), *Understanding the small family business*. London: Routledge.

Kellermanns, F. W., & Eddleston, K. A. (2004). Feuding families: When conflict foes a family firm good. *Entrepreneurship: Theory and Practice*, 28(3), 209–228.

Kelly, L. M., Athanassiou, N., & Crittenden, W. F. (2000). Founder centrality and strategic behavior in the family-owned firm. *Entrepreneurship: Theory and Practice*, 25(2), 27–43.

Kets de Vries, M. F. R. (1996). *Family business: Human dilemmas in the family firm.* Boston: International Thomson Business Press.

Kloosterman, R., Leun, J., & Rath, J. (2000). Mixed embeddedness: (In)formal economic activities and immigrant business in the Netherlands. *International Journal of Uervan and Regional Research*, 23(2), 253–267.

Krackhardt, D. (1990). Assessing the political landscape: Structure, cognition, and power in organizations. *Administrative Science Quarterly*, 35, 342–369.

Larsson, R. (1993). Case survey methodology: Qualitative analysis of patterns across case studies. *Academy of Management Journal*, 36(6), 1515–1546.

La Porta, R., Lopez-de-Silanes, F., & Shlieifer, A. (1999). Corporate ownership around the world. *Journal of Finance*, 54, 471–517.

Lee, Y. (2002). Gender differences in business success among business managers of family business: Evidence from the 1997 and 2000 national family business studies. *Consumer Interests Annual*, 48.

Lee, K. C., & Marshall, R. (1998). Measuring influence in the family decision making process using an observational method. *Qualitative Market Research: An International Journal*, 1(2), 88–98.

Litz, A. R. (1995). The family business; toward definitional clarity. *Academy of Management Proceedings*, 99–104.

Lowman, J. (1981). Love, hate and the family: Measures of emotion. In: Filsinger, E., & Lewis, R. (Eds), *Assessing marriage: New behavioural approaches* (pp. 55–73). Los Angeles: Sage.

Maccoby, E. E., & Martin, J. A. (1983). Socialization in the context of the family: Parent–child interaction. In: P. H. Mussein (Series Ed.), & E. M. Hetherington (Vol. Ed.), *Handbook of child psychology: Vol. 4. Socialization, personality and social development* (4th ed., pp. 1–101). New York: Wiley.

Markson, E. W. (2003). *Social gerontology today: An introduction.* Los Angeles: Roxbury.

Marshall, J. P. (2002). The impact of business owner's conflict management and leadership styles on succession planning in family-owned businesses. Dissertation Abstracts International Section a: Humanities & Social Sciences, *62*(10-A), 3470.

Masuo, D., Grace, F., & John, Y. (2002). A comparison of single manager family business households in 1997 and 2000. *Consumer Interests Annual, 48*, 1.

Matley, H., (2000). Training and the small firm. In: S. Carter, & D. E. Jones. (Ed.), *Enterprise and small business: Principles, practice and policy* (pp. 323–336). London: Prentice-Hall.

McCrea, B. (1997). Growing a family business, one step at a time. *Industrial Distribution, 86*, FA7–FA10.

McCucheon, D. M., & Meredith, R. J. (1993). Conducting case study research in operation management. *Journal of Operations Management, 11*(3), 239–256.

Merritt, J. (2004). Welcome to ethics 101. *Business Week*, (3904), 90.

Metcalf, H., Moodod, T., & Virdee, S. (1996). *Asian self-employment: The interaction of culture and economics in England.* London: Loci Studies Institute.

Meyer, M. (2004). Birth dearth. *Newsweek*, September 27.

Minuchin, S. (1974). *Families and family therapy.* Cambridge, MA: Harvard University Press.

Moos, R. S., & Moos, B. S. (2002). *Family environment scale manual* (3rd ed.). Palo Alto, CA: Mind Garden.

Morck, R., & Yeung, B. (2003). Agency problems in large family business groups. *Entrepreneurship: Theory and Practice*, 367–382.

Morris, M. H., Williams, R. W., & Nell, D. (1996). Factors influencing family business succession. *International Journal of Entrepreneurial Behaviour and Research, 2*(3), 68–81.

Murray, B. (2002). Understanding the emotional dynamics of family enterprises. In: D. Fletcher (Ed.), *Understanding the small family business.* London: Routledge.

Muske, G., & Fitzerald, A. M. (2002). Copreneurs – who continues and why? Evidence from the 1997–2000 national family business studies. *Consumer Interest Annual, 48*, 1.

Nation. (2004). Baker&McKenzie: unique needs of family firms. *Nation*, (The Thailand), July, 26.

Neubauer, F., & Iank, A. G. (1998). *The family business: Its governance for sustainability.* New York: Routledge.

Nicholson, N. (2004). *Gene politics: A new view of family business.* London Business School Working Paper.

Nicholson, N., & Björnberg, Å. (2004). Evolutionary psychology and the family firm: Structure, culture and performance. In: S. Tomaselli, & L. Melin (Eds), *Family firms in the wind of change.* Research Forum Proceedings, Lausanne: IFERA.

Office for National Statistics (ONS). (1999). *The ethnic minority populations of Great Britain: Latest estimates.* London: Office for National Statistics.

Olson, D. H. (1988). Family types, family stress and family satisfaction: A family developmental perspective. In: C. Falicov (Ed.), *Family transitions: Continuity and change over the life cycle.* New York: The Guilford Press.

Olson, D. H., & Defrain, J. (1994). *Family assessment (United States).* Mayfield, CA: Mountain View.

Olson, D. H., McCubbin, H. I., Barnes, H., Larsen, A., Muxen, M., & Wilson, M. (1992). *Family inventories.* Minneapolis: Life Innovations Inc.

Olson, P. D., Zuiker, V. S., Danes, S. M., Stafford, K., Heck, R. K. Z., & Duncan, K. A. (2003). Impact of family and business on family business sustainability. *Journal of Business Venturing, 18*(5), 639–666.

Parker, M. (2000). *Organizational culture and identity: Unity and division at work.* London: Sage.

Pollak, R. A. (1985). A transaction cost approach to families and households. *Journal of Economic Literature, 33,* 581–608.

Pires, G., & Stanton, J. (2003). Identifying and reaching an ethnic market: Methodological issues. *Qualitative Market Research: An International Journal, 6*(4), 224–235.

Ram, M. (1999). Managing autonomy: Employment relations in small professional service firms. *International Small Business Journal, 17*(2), 13–30.

Ram, M., & Jones, T. (1998). *Ethnic minorities in business.* Milton Keynes: Small Business Research Trust.

Ram, M., Abbas, T., Sanghera, B., Barlow, G., & Jones, T. (2001). Making the link: Households and small business activity in a multicultural context. *Community, Work and family, 4*(3), 327–347.

Rodgers, R. H., & White, J. M. (1993). Family development theory. In: P. G. Boss, W. J. Doherty, R. laRossa, W. R. Schumm, & S. K. Steinmetz (Eds), *Sourcebook of family theories and methods: A contextual approach.* New York: Plenum.

Rogoff, E. G., & Heck, R. K. Z. (2003). Evolving research in entrepreneurship and family business: Recognizing family as the oxygen that feeds the fire of entrepreneurship (introductory editorial note for special issue). *Journal of Business Venturing, 18*(5), 559–566.

Sanders, J., & Nee, V. (1996). The family as social capital and the value of human capital. *American Sociological Review, 61,* 231–249.

Sargant, F. (1961). *Ownership, control and success of large companies.* London: Sweet and Maxwell.

Schein, E. H. (2004). *Organisational culture and leadership* (3rd ed.). San Francisco, CA: Jossey-Bass.

Schødt, B., & Egeland, T. A. (1994). Från systemteori till familjeterapi. *(From systems theory to family therapy).* Lund: Studentlitteratur.

Schulze, W. S., Lubatkin, M. H., & Dino, R. N. (2003). Exploring the agency consequences of ownership dispersion among the directors of private family firms. *Academy of Management Journal, 46*(2), 179–195.

Shams, M. (2005). Developmental issues in indigenous psychologies: Sustainability and local knowledge. *Asian Journal of Social Psychology, 8*(1), 39–50.

Shams, M., & Jackson, R. P. (1994). The impact of unemployment on the psychological well-being of British Asians. *Psychological Medicine, 24*(2), 347–357.

Shams, M., & Jackson, R. P. (Eds.), (2005). Bringing psychology to all societies. Special issue of *The Psychologist, 18*(2), 77.

Sharma, P., Chrisman, J. J., & Chua, J. H. (2003). Succession planning as planned behaviour: Some empirical results. *Family Business Review, XVI*(1), 1–15.

Skinner, H., Steinhauer, P., & Santa-Barbara, J. (1983). The family assessment device. *Canadian Journal of Community Mental Health, 2*(2), 190–210.

Small bone, D., Ram, M., Deakins, D., & Baldock, R. (2003). Access to finance by ethnic minority business in the UK. *International Small Business Journal, 21*(30), 291–314.

Stafford, K., Duncan, A. K., Dane, S., & Winter, M. (1999). A research model of sustainable family businesses. *Family Business Review, XII*(3), 197–208.

Stavrou, E. T., & Swiercz, P. M. (1998). Securing in family businesses: Exploring the effects of demographic factors on offspring intentions to join and take over the business. *Journal of Small Business Management, 37*(3), 43–61.

Swartz, E., & Boaden, R. (1997). A methodology for researching the process of information management in small firms. *International Journal of Entrepreneurial Behaviour and Research, 3*(1), 53–65.

Tagiuri, R., & Davis, J. A. (1992). On the goals of successful family companies. *Family Business Review, V*(1), 43–62.

Tagiuri, R., & Davis, J. A. (1996). Bivalent attributes of the family firm. *Family Business Review, 9*, 199–208.

Touliatos, J., Perlmutter, B. F., & Strauss, M. (1990). *Handbook of family measurement techniques.* Newbury Park: Sage.

Trevino, K. L., & Weaver, R. G. (2003). *Managing ethics in business organizations: Social scientific perspectives.* Palo Alto, CA: Stanford.

Trompenaars, F. (1993). *Riding the waves of culture.* London: Brealey.

Walsh, F. (1993). Conceptualization of normal family process. In: F. Walsh (Ed.), *Normal Family Process.* New York: Guilford Press.

Wang, U., & Poutziouris. P. (2003). Micheal Stone Ltd: Balancing family business tradition with entrepreneurial growth. In: A. Jolly (Ed.), *The growing business handbook* (6th ed., pp. 137–145), London: Kogan Page.

Wang, Y., Watkins, D., Harris, N., & Spicer, K. (2004). The relationship between succession issues and business performance: Evidence from UK family SMEs. *International Journal of Entrepreneurial Behaviour and Research, 10*(1), 59–84.

Watts, D. J., & Strogatz, S. H. (1998). Collective dynamics of small-world networks. *Nature, 393*, 440–442.

Westhead, P. (2003). Company performance and objectives reported by first and multi-generation family companies: A research note. *Journal of Small Business and Enterprise Development, 10*(1), 93–105.

Westhead, P., & Cowling, M. (1997). Performance contrasts between family and non-family unquoted companies in the UK. *International Journal of Entrepreneurial Behaviour and Research, 3*(2), 30–52.

Westhead, P., & Storey, D. (1997). *Training provision and development of small and medium-sized enterprises.* Research Report No. 26. London: HMSO.

Whitechurch, G. G., & Constantine, L. L. (1993). Systems theory. In: P. G. Boss, W. J. Doherty, R. laRossa, W. R. Schumm, & S. K. Steinmetz (Eds), *Sourcebook of Family Theories and Methods: A contextual approach.* New York: Lenum.

Williamson, D. S., & Bray, J. H. (1988). Family development and change across generations: An intergenerational perspective. In: C. Falicov (Ed.), *Family transitions: Continuity and change over the life cycle.* New York: The Guilford Press.

Winter, M., Fitzgerald, M. A., Heck, R. K. Z. Haynes, G. W., & Danes, S. M. (1998). Revisiting the study of family businesses: Methodological challenges, dilemmas, and alternative approaches. *Family Business Review, 11*(3), 239–252.

Wong, B., McReynolds, B. S., & Wong, W. (1992). Chinese family firms in the San Francisco Bay Area. *Family Business Review, 5*(4), 355–372.

Yokozawa, T., & Goto, T. (2004). Some characteristics of Japanese long-lived firms and their financial performance. *Fifteenth FBN Annual World Conference Research Forum Proceedings.* Copenhagen, Denmark, September.

Young, E. (1989). *On the naming of the rose: interests and multiple meaning as elements.*

Young, S. (2004). Ethics: The key to understanding business and society. *European Business Forum,* (18), 78–80.

Yin, R. K. (1992). *Case Study Research: Design and methods,* (2nd ed.) Thousand oaks, CA: Sage.

Zahra, S. A., Hayton, J. C., & Salvato, C. (2003). Organizational culture and entrepreneurship in family firms: A resource-based analysis. Paper presented at the Theories of the family enterprise conference. University of Pennsylvania, Philadelphia.

Zimmerman, S. A., & Szenberg, M. (2000). Implementing international qualitative research: Techniques and obstacles. *Qualitative Market research; An International Journal, 3*(30), 158–164.

Chapter 2

Teamworking in Organizations: Implications for Workplace Safety[1]

Nick Turner, Sharon K. Parker and Helen M. Williams

Introduction

Teamworking in organizations is increasingly popular (Waterson et al., 1999; West, Borrill, & Unsworth, 1998). Given this growth in popularity, it is important to understand the consequences of teams for outcomes such as business perform-ance and employee well-being. Considerable literature has investigated these out-comes (Parker & Wall, 1998). However, an outcome of teamworking that has received significantly less attention is that of occupational safety. To date, occu-pational safety has not been seen widely as an indicator of team effectiveness.

When it works well, teamworking brings with it tremendous benefits, with teams achieving much more than the individuals working alone. For example, a story in *The Times* (2000) highlighted how a cockpit crew on a jetliner responded quickly and effectively to a deranged passenger bursting into the cockpit. Yet, teamworking can also go wrong, sometimes with terrible human consequences. The following two stories illustrate the potential dark side of work teams for

[1]This chapter is based, in part, on Chapter 3 (The effect of teamwork on safety processes and out-comes) by N. Turner and S. K. Parker in J. Barling and M. R. Frone's (Eds), The psychology of work-place safety. Copyright © 2004 American Psychological Association. Adapted with permission. All three of the current authors contributed equally to this adapted version. Financial support from the Social Sciences and Humanities Research Council of Canada and the Offshore Division of the UK Health and Safety Executive helped to make collaboration on this chapter possible.

safety. Top management teams in the UK faced "corporate manslaughter" charges for negligence over managing workplace safety (Mathiason, 2001), while gangs of UK trackside maintenance workers reported being unclear about procedures for working on broken rails which put occupational and public safety in jeopardy (McVeigh, 2000).

In this chapter, we explore how working in teams might help or hinder occupational safety. We use workplace safety as an exemplar by which to explore issues surrounding teamworking in organizations more generally. In particular, we review the rather limited set of existing studies that look at teamworking and safety, and we develop ideas about how to further research on this topic. First, however, we need to define what we mean by "team."

Teams and Team Effectiveness

Guzzo and Dickson (1996) defined a team, or work team, as "made up of individuals who see themselves and who are seen by others as a social entity, who are interdependent because of the tasks they perform as members of a team, who are embedded in one or more larger social systems (e.g., community, organization), and who perform tasks that affect others (such as customers or coworkers)." (pp. 308–309) This definition highlights that teams are more than a set of co-located or geographically distributed individuals; team members are interdependent and need to coordinate their activities to achieve their goals.

There is a vast literature investigating the antecedents of effective teamworking, and over the decades many different models and frameworks of team effectiveness have been proposed (e.g., Salas, Stagl, & Burke, 2004; Sundstrom, McIntyre, Halfhill, & Richards, 2000). In this chapter, we do not provide a thorough review of the teamworking literature because many comprehensive reviews exist already (e.g., Cohen & Bailey, 1997; Guzzo & Dickson, 1996; Salas et al., 2004; Sundstrom et al., 2000). Rather, our focus here is more specific and is concerned with what the teamworking literature can tell us about safe working within organizations. At this point, however, it is useful to draw broad conclusions from the literature on team effectiveness.

A clear goal in teamworking research is to understand what factors influence the effectiveness of teams. In a thorough review of the teamworking literature, Sundstrom et al. (2000) concluded that models of teamworking cover five broad categories of factors, which relate to team effectiveness: *organizational context* (e.g., rewards, training, and leadership); *team composition and size* (e.g., knowledge, skills and abilities of team members, demographic diversity, and team size); *teamwork design* (e.g., autonomy, performance feedback, and interdependence);

intra-team processes (e.g., cohesion, communication, conflict, and coordination among members of the team); and *external team processes* (e.g., communication, coordination, and integration with people/teams outside the team). Both the labels of these categories (Sundstrom et al., 2000) and the propositions regarding how the categories relate together differ across frameworks. For example, models that are broadly referred to as "input-process-output" models of team effectiveness propose that certain team characteristics (e.g., teamwork design) have their effect via intra-team processes (e.g., team cohesion).

An important question in this area of research concerns exactly what is meant by an "effective" team. Unfortunately, there is little consistency in the criteria of effectiveness used within both empirical research and theoretical frameworks (e.g., Sundstrom et al., 2000). As with antecedents of effectiveness described above, many different categorizations exist, and definitions vary widely. Particularly useful, however, is Cohen and Bailey's (1997) distinction between three types of effectiveness criteria: performance-related (e.g., quality and quantity of outcome), attitudinal (e.g., job satisfaction, organizational commitment), and behavioral (e.g., turnover, absenteeism). Within this taxonomy, workplace safety is considered to be a set of behavioral criteria (e.g., injuries, safety-related behaviors), although safety has had relatively little attention as an indicator of team effectiveness.

In attempting to understand what factors affect the safety of work teams, it is tempting to assume that many of the same determinants of good work performance will also positively affect workplace safety. Unfortunately, we cannot assume this to be the case, especially since antecedents of team effectiveness are often found to differentially predict different team outcomes (Sundstrom et al., 2000). For example, while it is possible that a high workload is associated with higher team productivity, a high workload might result in more injuries yet more proactive behaviors (e.g., anticipating hazards, taking initiative to prevent accidents) with respect to safety. It is therefore important that academics, students, and practitioners alike give greater consideration to the issue of safety in work teams and not automatically assume that safety is restricted to the numbers of workplace injuries. However, before discussing the research literature relating teams and safety, in the next section we define what we mean by "safety."

Safety

A traditional approach to conceptualizing and operationalizing safety is to assess statistics such as days away from work and injury frequencies (or near-misses). These measures are convenient for researchers because collaborating organizations often record such data for regulatory purposes. However, they also suffer from reporting biases (e.g., individuals often do not want to report injuries for fear of repercussions), and injury numbers tend to capture extraordinary events (since fortunately, injuries are usually rare), making these "objective" outcomes potentially both unreliable and invalid.

A different approach is to assess employees' safety-related behaviors. For example, Simard and Marchand (1995) asked supervisors to rate their teams' propensity to engage in safety-related initiatives; that is, how attuned the workforce was in preventing injuries by recognizing potential hazards in advance of injuries that may occur. Minor injury indexes (e.g., Frone, 1998; Hemingway & Smith, 1999; Zohar, 2000) are also reliable indicators of more frequently occurring injuries. They are less prone to socially desirable response sets than open-ended questions about severe injuries, and indeed often predicate more severe, yet less frequently occurring injuries.

When considering safety in this chapter, we include both traditional measures of negative events (e.g., injuries, near-misses) as well as concepts that assess employees' safety-related behaviors, including those directed toward the maintenance of safety (e.g., complying with safety procedures), coping with hazards (e.g., handling errors once they have occurred), and a proactive approach toward safety (e.g., safety-related initiative or citizenship behaviors).

Existing Research on Teams and Safety

Research on teams with safety as an outcome has mostly concerned one of three types of teams: health and safety committees (HSCs), "self-managing" or "autonomous" teams (sometimes called "self-managing teams") situated in a range of organizational settings (e.g., manufacturing or service sector), and airplane cockpit crews. Although all classify as teams according to Guzzo and Dickson's (1996) criteria, these teams also vary in important ways.

Health and Safety Committees

HSCs tend to be what Cohen and Bailey (1997) refer to as *parallel teams*, which bring "together people from different areas of the organization to carry out tasks alongside the day to day functioning of the organization." (p. 242) That is, members work on core job tasks outside this team and their membership of the HSC is an extra role or task from their regular work. Consequently, members tend to be less homogenous and less interdependent than in the case of autonomous work teams, with individuals in HSCs often representing distinct departments, jobs, and hierarchical levels of the organization. Participation is typically voluntary in HSCs, whereas it tends not to be in autonomous teams and cockpit crews. Further, HSCs tend to only meet on a periodic (e.g., monthly) basis.

Autonomous Teams

In contrast, autonomous work teams usually involve relatively homogenous teams of shopfloor or service employees working closely together to carry out their core daily tasks. Autonomous work teams grew out of the socio-technical systems approach that originated at the Tavistock Institute in London, England, during the 1950s (e.g., Trist & Bamforth, 1951). The core feature of this theory is the distinction between social and technical subsystems in organizations, and the proposal that firms design in parallel both the human or social system and the technical system in an organization. Applying this theory to the design of jobs resulted in development of *autonomous work teams* in which teams of employees are able to decide on their own methods of working, and be responsible for handling as many operational problems as possible they encountered at the source. In practice, although there are variations in the level of self-management, members of autonomous teams typically have discretion over day-to-day operational decisions, as well as input into the running of the team (e.g., selecting new members). The potential benefits of self-managing teams for employee well-being and for organizational performance have been widely documented (see Goodman et al., 1988; Parker & Wall, 1998; Wellins et al., 1991). Because autonomous teams tend to have stable membership, Cohen and Bailey (1997) refer to them as "work teams."

Cockpit Crews

The final type of team that has been investigated in relation to safety is the cockpit crew. Cockpit crews are similar to autonomous work teams in that they are work teams with team members carrying out their core tasks in a relatively autonomous way, yet cockpit crews are made up of highly trained specialists, team membership changes frequently (e.g., captains and first officers on commercial airliners do not always work together), and team sizes are often quite small. Additionally, cockpit crews undertake highly interdependent tasks in an environment that has the potential for a high degree of operational uncertainty and in which the cost of errors is high. The key differences between the three types of teams described above are summarized in Table 2.1.

The value of considering safety issues across these rather distinct types of teams is that we obtain a broad perspective of the ways in which teamworking

Table 2.1: Summary of differences between health and safety committees, autonomous work teams, and cockpit crews.

Criteria	Health and safety committees	Autonomous work teams	Cockpit crews
Type of team	Parallel	Work	Work
Composition	Multi-functional	Multi-functional/specialist	Multi-functional
Interdependence	Low	Moderate to high	High
Basis for selection	Voluntary	Recruited	Recruited
Stability of membership	Stable	Stable	Changeable
Typical size	Moderate to large	Moderate	Small
Frequency of contact	Periodic	Day to day	Often itinerant
Autonomy	Low	High	Moderate

might influence this outcome. We first discuss evidence about HSCs and their impact on safety, followed by a discussion of autonomous work teams and their effect on safety. For cockpit crews, we aim to apply ideas from this much more developed research area to other organizational teams. We then draw together common threads, and make recommendations for future research.

Health and Safety Committees (HSCs)

HSCs are the keystone of official workplace safety programs in many organizations. For example, in the United States, HSCs are the most common form of safety-specific employee participation, existing in 75% of organizations with over 50 employees and in 31% of organizations employing fewer than 50 people (Commission of the Future of Worker–Management Relations, 2001). HSCs usually consist of representatives from the workforce and management, and there is typically one per organization or site. HSCs discuss, make recommendations, and initiate action on workplace health and safety issues with the aim of reducing the numbers of injuries and illnesses in the workplace (Eaton & Nocerino, 2000). We now summarize three of the most recent and rigorous studies in the area.

Key Studies on HSCs

Using data from eight manufacturing plants in a US building-products company, O'Toole (1999) investigated how the presence of HSCs affected organizational safety outcomes, and whether voluntary or mandatory implementation of HSCs in these plants moderated their effectiveness using a quasi-experimental research design. Quasi-experimental studies use experimental designs within field settings so as to minimize threats to the validity of the study findings (Shadish, Cook, & Campbell, 2002). They typically have two teams of participants: those who experience an intervention (in this case the implementation of HSCs), who are referred to as the "experimental" team or condition, and those who do not experience an intervention, who are referred to as the "control" team or condition. The quasi-experiment differs from a pure experiment in this regard because participants are not randomly assigned to teams or conditions. O'Toole's study was also longitudinal, which means that it had both pre- and post-implementation data collection. The idea is that outcomes should change in the experimental team between the pre- and post-implementation time points, whereas there should be no change in the control team outcomes because they did not experience the intervention. The strength of such longitudinal quasi-experimental research designs is that they help control for alternative explanations in the data. If only the experimental team is tested, then how can we be sure that it is the intervention that caused a change in the outcome? By showing that those who experienced the intervention changed, but those who did not experience the intervention did not change (despite having similar experiences in other aspects of their work), it helps us to be more confident in concluding that it is the intervention that caused the change in outcome.

More specifically, within O'Toole's study, six of the plants implemented HSCs either in the last half of 1991 or the first half of 1992 (i.e., experimental condition), and the remaining two plants did not implement HSCs during this period (i.e., control condition), despite equal opportunity to do so. Additionally, three of the six plants that implemented HSCs did so to comply with regulatory requirements; the other three plants implemented HSCs on a voluntary basis (i.e., they were not required by either regulatory or organizational pressures to do so). To assess the effect on safety, two forms of data were collected between 1987 and 1996: the Occupational Safety and Health Administration (OSHA) Recordable Injury Rate (i.e., rate of occupational injuries per 100 employees per year based on the employer's OSHA logs) and OSHA Severity Rate (i.e., rate of either days lost or restricted work activity per 100 employees per year based on OSHA lost time injuries).

The results supported the value of HSCs on safety. The six plants that implemented HSCs experienced less severe injuries overall, and the plants that had established HSCs on a voluntary basis experienced fewer injuries than those plants that had introduced HSCs because they were required by law. The two plants that did not implement HSCs had no changes in either injury frequency or severity over the study period.

Whereas O'Toole's (1999) study examined HSCs in plants from a single organization, Reilly, Paci, and Holl (1995) examined how the internal composition of HSCs across multiple UK manufacturing organizations affected company injury rates. These researchers found significant differences between HSC membership and the injury rates of the associated workplace. Controlling for industry-related background variables, organizations with joint consultative HSCs (i.e., those that had members from both union and management) had between 3.4 and 5.7 fewer injuries per 1000 employees, when compared to those with non-consultative HSCs. In particular, the greater the proportion of union-chosen members on these committees, the fewer the injuries. This study provides some positive evidence for the benefits of labor involvement in safety-improvement activities.

In an effort to probe more deeply what factors make for an effective HSC that will positively affect safety, Eaton and Nocerino (2000) conducted an analysis of a stratified sample of public organizations and departments in New Jersey, USA. Some of the organizations had HSCs ($n = 180$), while others did not ($n = 247$). Injury and illness data were collected from the New Jersey Department of Labor for the years 1988 and 1989 on a joint sub-sample ($n = 251$) of these two categories. Surprisingly, results from the analyses suggested that the presence of HSCs was associated with more lost workdays from injuries. How can this be explained? The fact that this study used single-year change in injuries as its outcome raises a criticism often leveled against cross-sectional studies of this sort. That is, because the data are just collected at one point in time, we cannot differentiate cause and effect. It could be that the presence of HSCs led to more lost workdays due to injuries. Alternatively, it could be that organizations with greater numbers of lost days injuries are more likely to implement HSCs. These two possibilities underlie the two explanations offered by Eaton and Nocerino (2000) in discussing their findings. First, organizations with HSCs may be more likely to report workplace injuries, when compared to organizations less committed to the reporting process and often without HSCs. Second, in the absence of a measure of workplace hazards, it is possible that HSCs are a proxy for more dangerous workplaces.

Despite this counterintuitive result for HSCs presence in relation to injury rates, there was nevertheless evidence that greater worker involvement with HSCs (i.e., higher proportion of non-management members), and greater non-management involvement in agenda setting, was associated with fewer reported injuries among those workplaces that had HSCs. This complements earlier findings (e.g., O'Toole, 1999; Reilly et al., 1995) that suggest that it is important to involve non-managerial employees to improve health and safety at work.

HSC and Safety: Summary of Evidence

One theme that emerges from two of the three studies (i.e., Reilly et al., 1995; Eaton & Nocerino, 2000) is that greater employee involvement in HSCs, as well as in general safety-related initiatives, is related to better safety outcomes. This suggests that team composition, which is highlighted as a key factor in the team effectiveness literature, is also important to safety outcomes. The finding is also consistent with the general participation literature, which shows that employee involvement facilitates the successful implementation of new initiatives (Lawler, 1992). Several processes might explain this finding (Parker & Wall, 1998). For example, greater employee involvement in HSCs could mean that better solutions are generated because employees possess local expertise that managers do not possess. Another possibility is that the involvement of employees could enhance the likelihood that changes are accepted by the workforce (e.g., employees on the HSCs can use their influence to persuade the workforce to change their approach).

Autonomous Work Teams

Autonomous work teams, as their name suggests, have members that autonomously carry out operational tasks. Just like it was important to consider the value of employee involvement in HSCs effectiveness, it is also important to understand whether the degree of autonomy possessed by the teams affects safety outcomes. Does autonomy result in a heightened sense of responsibility and ownership for safety, greater knowledge of workplace risks, and increased opportunity to anticipate and act on hazards (Parker & Turner, 2002)? Or does autonomy, and the lack of direct supervision this entails, encourage team members to go beyond their abilities without having an integrated understanding of the work system (e.g., knowing the knock-on effects of one team's actions on those of another's)?

In relation to these competing hypotheses, the evidence is unclear. The lack of clarity arises from the many definitions of autonomous teamworking, different research designs, variations across contexts, multiple levels of analysis, and the use of a range of safety outcomes. We explore some of the existing studies in more detail.

Key Studies on Autonomous Work Teams and Safety

The first comprehensive investigation of the effect of autonomous teamworking on safety was conducted by Eric Trist and colleagues at the Tavistock Institute in the UK. Trist et al. (1963) studied a UK coal mine that underwent significant changes in work organization and mechanization after World War II. The study examined large teams (in some cases up to 50 people) operating under different mining conditions and with varying types of pit technology. The research team collected qualitative and quantitative data over several years on aspects of these teams and their performance. A key focus of the investigation was differences between two "panels" of teams involved in coal mining.

Over several five-month phases, in response to varying levels of workload, one panel of teams restricted its team members to single tasks (termed "conventionally organized," or Number 1 panel), whereas the other panel of teams rotated its members between functions and tasks (what the researchers called "fully composite," or Number 2 panel). The panels were adjacent to each other in the pit, physical conditions were identical, and both used exactly the same technology. Additionally, the teams consisted of employees with comparable qualifications and experience, membership was self-selected, and neither panel looked to management for guidance on how day-to-day work should be organized. Thus, the panels were very similar to each other on all variables except their work organization.

After 10 months in the conventionally organized panel, the researchers found a significant rise in absence caused by injuries at the coalface. This picture contrasted with the fully composite panel of teams, which rotated its miners systematically through multiple tasks, and who had no change in absence due to injuries over the same period. Trist et al. (1963) explained their findings in terms of the latter workers' higher levels of stimulation, reduced boredom, and a reduced fatigue caused by monotony. It is also possible that members of the fully composite teams acquired greater knowledge and understanding of all tasks, and were therefore able to co-ordinate their actions with other members and operate more safely.

Trist et al. then embarked on another a second large-scale, longitudinal project of work reorganization in the Rushton coal mine (Trist, Susman, & Brown, 1977). Overall, there was some positive evidence that safety improved for the autonomous work teams. Employees involved in the work redesign felt that the experiment with autonomous teamworking had a strong, positive effect on safety. More objective ratings of safety proved to be similarly positive. Both on-site observations of safety behaviors and independent ratings from inspectors showed that there was a marked improvement over the study period in safety behaviors such as compliance with procedures in the experimental teams. However, the number and severity of violations varied across the study period and did not drop significantly for the experimental teams.

However, although some of the safety indicators were positive, the researchers suggested that the "public claims…about the safety improvements at Rushton have been overstated." (Goodman, 1979, p. 229) First, there was a very strong desire among managers and unions to improve mine safety, and, as such, safety was a strong focus in the training and feedback that the experimental teams received

(Goodman, 1979). It is therefore possible that some of the ratings (e.g., observations of safety behavior) might be confounded with the socially desirable goal of the intervention to improve safety. Second, archival data tends to highlight infrequent and specific incidents. Third, it is not clear to what extent any improvements in safety behaviors were attributable to autonomous teamworking rather than safety-specific initiatives (e.g., extensive safety training) that occurred concurrently. Thus, while positive, the results from this study are far from definitive.

In the early 1990s, Pearson (1992) conducted an important investigation over 1 year into the introduction of autonomous work teams in a heavy engineering shop. A particular strength of this study was its Solomon four-team design. This type of research design is similar to the pre- and post-test quasi-experimental design we discussed earlier, but it also assesses whether the pre-test data collection has influenced the participants (Walton Braver & Braver, 1988). This is done by splitting the experimental and control teams into two and having half of each team receiving both a pre- and post-test and the other half only a post-test. In this way, in addition to checking that there are effects within the experimental team but not in the control team, analyses can also be conducted to check that there is no difference in the post-test results of those in the experimental team who had a pre-test and those who did not.

Interestingly, Pearson (1992) found that injuries for the autonomous teams stayed the same over the experimental period. On the surface, this looks as though there was no link between autonomous work teams and safety. However, it should be noted that the team injury rate for the non-autonomous team increased over the same period, which suggests that autonomous work teams in some way prevented or reduced injuries that would have otherwise increased. Pearson observed that the members of autonomous work teams often discussed safety in their meetings, whereas the non-autonomous teams relied solely on safety representatives or a safety officer, both of whom were external to the team, to detect unsafe practices. These findings suggest that factors such as greater communication and increased ownership of safety outcomes among team members helped to keep injuries down.

An issue with Pearson's study is that it is not clear from the descriptions as to what degree the autonomous teamworking initiative also involved coaching team leaders about safety. In other words, was the prevention of injuries caused by the work redesign itself or was it attributable to active coaching of the team leaders? Zohar (2002), for example, has found strong links between how supervisors behave in relation to safety and employee safety outcomes. This study, like that of Trist et al. (1977), highlights the difficulty of isolating the effect of autonomous work teams from other co-occurring initiatives.

Nevertheless, a benefit of Pearson's (1992) study was the explicit recognition of the changes in technology (i.e., the introduction of a production and maintenance system that limited the autonomy that operators had) might have limited the success of the teams. Such plausible yet often unmeasured influences on work organization need to be considered in future research in this area. Additionally, this study high-lights the need to assess the degree to which any autonomous team initiative is indeed successful in changing the nature of the work and actually in increasing employees' job control. Without establishing that the work redesign had its intended effects on jobs (e.g., increasing autonomy), one cannot really make any definite conclusions about its effect on outcomes.

The next study we consider was conducted within the service sector, contrast-ing to the studies reviewed so far that have focused on manufacturing environ-ments. Using a cross-sectional, quasi-experimental design (i.e., a comparison of experimental and control teams but with only a post-test data collection), Cohen and Ledford (1994) examined differences between traditionally managed teams and autonomous teams in a telecommunications firm. The researchers matched the teams across functions, such that pairs of teams consisted of a traditionally managed team (which formed the control team) and an autonomous team (which formed the experimental team).

Some quality of work life variables (i.e., job satisfaction, social satisfaction, and organizational commitment) were negatively linked with the number of days missed due to injury or illnesses, but there were no associations between these same predictor variables and number of injuries sustained. This suggests that the autonomous team initiative might have enhanced individuals' motivation to come back to work faster after injuries, but it does not appear to have led to a reduced occurrence of injuries. A further analysis comparing the matched pairs of teams found no significant differences between the traditionally managed and autonomous teams on either injury frequency or number of days missed.

What might explain these null findings? Cohen and Ledford (1994) suggested that this experiment placed no particular emphasis on workplace safety, in con-trast to previous studies (e.g., Trist, Susman, & Brown, 1977; Pearson, 1992). Thus, it might be that autonomous teams involve employees taking on more responsibility for key team goals (e.g., cost, quality), and, if safety is not one of those team goals, then there is no reason to expect that work redesign should change it. For example, one reason that increased autonomy as beneficial is because it allows employees to deal more effectively with, and prevent, uncer-tainties such as breakdowns (Parker & Wall, 1998). If there are few uncertainties, or if the uncertainties do not involve much safety-related risk, then enhanced autonomy is not likely to positively affect safety, at least via this mechanism.

However, it is important to note weaknesses in Cohen and Ledford's (1994) design that might make such conclusions premature. The study is cross-sectional (i.e., data collected only at one time point) so one does not know what the teams' safety levels were like prior to any work redesign. Also, the assignment of teams to experimental and control teams was not random, hence there might have been differences between those teams that chose to become autonomous compared to those that remained traditionally organized (e.g., because of the types of technology or unsupportive supervision) that confound any straightforward comparison. Finally, we have no clear evidence of how autonomous the autonomous teams really were.

A recent contribution to our understanding of the effect of teamworking on safety is Hechanova-Alampay and Beehr's (2002). These researchers asked a 10-member representative team of trained assessors to reach consensus on 22 attributes (e.g., decision making on team rules, problem-solving, improving work processes, and internal training processes) to assess the level of self-management of each of 24 manufacturing teams. The use of raters to assess self-management is a strength of this study because, as noted above, studies have often not checked to see if the autonomous work teams were indeed autonomous. The ratings were then correlated with safety-related outcomes. The findings suggested that greater team self-management is related to safer working (assessed via unsafe behaviors and aggregated injuries). Unfortunately, the study is limited in its ability to draw causal inferences due to the cross-sectional design (see discussion above for an explanation of this issue), the lack of a control team, and the susceptibility of archival injury data to reporting biases and other threats to validity.

In summary, the quasi-experimental and correlational studies reviewed so far suggest positive links between autonomous teamworking and safety. Nevertheless, these studies do not isolate which features of autonomous work teams are important in promoting safety. For example, is it the expanded autonomy that is important or is it a result of improved team processes? Nor do they determine if it is the concurrent introduction of other safety initiatives that was key. The next set of studies allows a closer examination of what particular work characteristics associated with autonomous teamworking might be important.

Cross-level Studies of Operational Teams and Safety

The previous studies we have discussed in terms of autonomous work teams have taken what is called a pure team-level approach, which involves relating aggregated work team scores (e.g., aggregations of individuals' perceived job autonomy) to aggregated team outcome scores (e.g., aggregated individual injuries). In contrast, cross-level studies take a mixed approach like aggregating work team scores in the team-level approach, but relate them to individual-level outcomes. Recent studies into teamworking and safety have made headway in this area by using multiple levels of analysis.

In two studies, Simard and Marchand (1995, 1997) examined a sample of 1061 work teams across 97 Canadian manufacturing plants. In the first study (Simard & Marchand, 1995), multi-level models were developed to predict teams' safety initiative (e.g., their propensity to take personal initiative for improving safe work conduct and suggest ideas to supervisors about improving safety), whereas in the second study (Simard & Marchand, 1997) the focus was on predicting teams' safety compliance (e.g., their propensity to comply with rules, follow supervisors' advice). The authors distinguished team-level ("micro") antecedents, such as work processes and risk, characteristics of the team, and supervision characteristics, from organizational-level ("macro") antecedents, such as top management commitment to safety and socioeconomic context. All of the outcomes and predictors were assessed using supervisory ratings.

The team-level antecedents emerged as the best predictors. A participatory approach to safety management was the most important predictor of safety compliance (Simard & Marchand, 1995). When supervisors and employees were both involved in safety-related activities on the shopfloor, teams were more likely to anticipate hazards, make suggestions, and put pressure on the organization to make safety improvements. Team cohesion and cooperation between team members and supervisors, as well as elements of task autonomy and uncertainty, were also positively associated with teams taking safety initiatives.

A cooperative team-supervisor relationship was the strongest predictor of team compliance (Simard & Marchand, 1997). To a lesser degree, participatory styles of supervisory management of safety and team cohesion were also important. In contrast to the safety initiative study, no elements of work organization such as task autonomy were significantly related to safety compliance.

Although these studies had several benefits, one limitation was that all of the team variables as well as the outcome variables were derived from supervisors' responses. It is possible that having supervisors rate their teams on positive characteristics (e.g., cohesion) might encourage self-enhancing biases, thus inflating the true relationship between team processes and a socially desirable outcome like safety behaviors. For example, supervisors who get along better with their teams might have a tendency to rate their teams higher on both team processes and safety outcomes (i.e. a "halo" effect). A second limitation is that only firms with more than 70 employees were included in this sample, which restricts the extent to which the models are generalizable to smaller enterprises.

The final study that we report in this section is like the Simard and Marchand (1995, 1997) studies in that it used a cross-level strategy. Hofmann and Stetzer (1996) investigated 21 teams in a chemical processing plant, and assessed how several team-level factors (i.e., team process, safety climate, and intentions to approach other team members engaging in unsafe behaviors) and one individual-level factor (i.e., perceptions of role overload) affected team safety (i.e., unsafe behavior, injuries). There was some support for the hypothesis that the relationship between task-oriented team processes (e.g., planning and coordinating efforts, sharing information about work-related events) and unsafe behaviors would be mediated by the intention to approach team members engaged in unsafe acts, although there was some complexity surrounding the finding (i.e., it was supported when using one statistical technique, but not another). Understanding multilevel mechanisms like this, by which teamworking seems to affect safety, is a severely under-researched topic.

Summary of Findings and Potential Mechanisms

The diversity in the studies we have reviewed, in content and methodology, makes it difficult to clearly assess how safety performance is affected by autonomous teamwork. Nevertheless, themes are identifiable. All major investigations of autonomous work teams and safety (e.g., Trist, Higgin, Murray, & Pollock, 1963; Trist et al., 1977; Pearson, 1992; Hechanova-Alampay & Beehr, 2002), with the exception of the Cohen and Ledford (1994) study, suggest positive safety consequences of this work redesign. Certainly, no study showed negative safety consequences. It appears that autonomous forms of work design promote safer working through mechanisms such as greater felt responsibility and ownership for safety, increasing team member communication, and reducing boredom. Another plausible mechanism is that autonomous work teams increase employees' understanding about each other's tasks and the wider unit, thereby enhancing collective safe working.

In trying to understand the particular aspects of this work design that are most important for safety, the cross-level studies are especially valuable. Employee involvement in safety activities, task autonomy (or "non-routine" work organization), team processes (e.g., cooperation, planning and coordination), and leadership behaviors positively influenced safety outcomes. It is interesting to observe the consistency between these findings and the general team effectiveness literature that highlights the importance of organizational context, teamwork design, and intra-team processes (Sundstrom et al., 2000).

Cockpit Crews

The third category of team that has been considered extensively in the safety domain is cockpit crews. It is typically assumed in this literature that cockpit staff need to work as a team, which contrasts with the research on HSCs and autonomous teams that often focuses on whether team structures are more effective than non-team structures. The focus in the cockpit crew literature is mostly on the effectiveness of the team and how effectiveness is affected, influenced by team processes. Working as a "crew" in cockpits requires very tight coordination to process large amounts of information in short periods of time. Members need to share information, issue and acknowledge commands, and to ask questions about flight operations and conditions. Therefore, it is perhaps not surprising that research in this context has concentrated on team processes, such as the crew's ability to communicate with each other.

A common approach to assessing safety in this context has been to observe crews and their behavior during flights. For example, as part of a large human factors project based at the University of Texas at Austin, researchers have used expert observers on over 3500 domestic and international airline flights to record systematically various threats to safety, how they are managed by the crew (e.g., whether they detect and respond to error), as well as detailed information on the types of the errors (Helmreich, Klinect, & Wilhelm, 1999). Crew error is typically defined as "action or inaction leading to deviation from team or organizational intentions" (Helmreich, 2000, p. 781), and can come in various forms (e.g., intentional non-compliance errors, procedural errors, communication errors, proficiency errors, and operational decision errors; Helmreich & Foushee, 1993). An advantage of this observational approach is that it overcomes some of the problems of using accidents (e.g., airplane crashes) as the only safety outcome. Airplane crashes are rare (fortunately), which means such data typically have limited variance. Crashes are also affected by multiple factors (e.g., weather conditions) in the flight system, some of which cannot be controlled by crew members. Observational data can be more "proximal," direct, and statistically reliable.

There is a very large amount of research on cockpit crews, with the general conclusion that team processes influence safety-related outcomes such as errors (for comprehensive reviews of this and the related area of Crew Resource Management, see Foushee, 1984; Wiener & Nagel, 1988; Wiener, Kanki, & Helmreich, 1996; Helmreich & Merritt, 1998). Rather than repeat these summaries, our goal here is to showcase some innovations used in studying safety in cockpit crews that have implications for teams in other organizational contexts. In particular, we describe an informative analytic technique for understanding team processes and their consequences, and report on the potential role of knowledge-based processes in safety.

Linguistic Analysis of Crew Communication

Crew communication is recognized as vital for safety and performance outcomes, but it is an interesting question to consider exactly how and why communication is important. Sexton and Helmreich (2000) used simulated flights on Boeing 727s to investigate via linguistic analysis *how* crew members used language. The researchers assessed two dimensions: (1) the use of first person plural (i.e., we, our, us) and first person singular (i.e., I, my, me) words, and (2) achievement-oriented language, such as words like "try," "effort," and "goal." The researchers argued that use of first person plural words provided a gauge of how oriented the speaker was to seeing the crew as a team (in essence, asserting a form of team identity), while achievement-oriented words are indicative of the crew working toward a successful outcome (rather like the concept of goal orientation (Locke & Latham, 1990).

Researchers found that the usage of language differs as a function of both crew job position and workload, as well as between members of the same cockpit crew. For example, captains used the first person plural (e.g., "we") more frequently than either first officers or flight engineers, particularly during high-workload segments. There was also a linear increase in the use of first person plural across time suggesting increasing familiarity. However, perhaps most intriguingly, use of first person plural words and words indicative of achievement were positively related to performance and communication, and negatively to error rates. For example, the captain's use of achievement words in an earlier segment was strongly related to fewer errors by the flight engineer in a later flight segment. The important point here is that language use both reflects, and constructs, important team processes such as team identity and familiarity.

Although focusing more specifically on communication, this study shows that, as was the case for autonomous work teams and consistent with the team effectiveness literature, intra-team processes are critical. What is unique about this study is the linguistic approach, which could be highly informative in the studies of other types of organizational teams. For example, Pearson's (1992) study suggested better safety performance among autonomous work teams, and this was attributed to these teams assuming greater responsibility for safety rather than seeing it as just the responsibility of safety personnel. One hypothesis with regards to the other types of teams we have discussed thus far is that members of the autonomous work teams would make more first person plural references (e.g., "we") in relation to safety, whereas members of the conventional teams might talk more about safety in terms of "they"?

Knowledge-Based Processes

The above study highlighted the importance of communication. A further important element for cockpit crews is having a mutual understanding of the nature of events relevant to safety and flight efficiency. Such a "shared mental model" enables individuals to make sense of and engage with their environment (e.g., Cannon-Bowers & Salas, 2001; Mohammed & Dumville, 2001). Team members' mental models shape team processes and performance (e.g., Mathieu, Heffner, Goodwin, Salas, & Cannon-Bowers, 2000).

The importance of shared mental models and mutual understanding gives rise to the question as to how such understanding is developed. Blickensderfer, Cannon-Bowers, and Salas (1998) highlighted the value of cross-training as a way to provide crew members with opportunities to perform each other's roles, thereby providing a basis for a greater common understanding. Evidence supporting the role of cross-training has come from studies using undergraduate student samples on flight simulators. For example, using a computerized flight simulator, Volpe, Cannon-Bowers, Salas, and Spector (1996) randomly assigned 80 undergraduate male students to dyads in one of four conditions in a 2×2 between-subjects design: high workload with cross-training; low workload with cross-training; high workload without cross-training; and low workload without cross-training. Cross-training took the form of verbally presenting team members with information about the other's roles. Results showed that this form of cross-training was associated with better communication and simulator performance. A follow-up study drawn from US Navy recruits (Cannon-Bowers, Salas, Blickensderfer, & Bowers, 1998) used a more cognitively demanding simulator with greater task interdependence. In this case, cross-training involved training the team members in each other's duties. Teams that had cross-training showed more knowledge of other team members' jobs and the wider unit (interpositional knowledge) and more effective team functioning.

These two studies suggest that gaining greater interpositional knowledge can enhance team functioning, and hence lead to safer performance. These conclusions converge with our earlier speculation that one of the ways in which autonomous work teams might enhance safety is through expanding team members' knowledge of other team members' jobs and the wider unit (in essence, interpositional knowledge). The cockpit crew studies thus point to knowledge-based mechanisms as a way of understanding how teams affect safety. From a more general perspective, training is included in the organizational context category in Sundstrom et al.'s (2000) taxonomy. However, training has not always been found to affect measures of effectiveness (e.g., Campion, Medsker, & Higgs, 1993; Eden, 1985). It is therefore important that research identifies the types of training that are beneficial, and the situations in which they are most likely to have an effect. Cross-training might be a particularly important contributor to team effectiveness because of its consequences for developing shared mental models and greater understanding among team members.

Conclusions

Positive Implications of Teamwork

The research we have described in this chapter suggests that team structures within organizations can have positive consequences for workplace safety. Teams can provide a structure for employee involvement in decision-making, as in the case of HSCs. Research suggests that having a HSC is related to a lower organizational injury rates, especially if the HSC is voluntarily introduced and contains representatives of the workforce rather than just managers. Consistent with this literature, studies of autonomous work teams suggest that this work design, which has as a core feature greater collective autonomy, is associated with better safety in day-to-day operations. The studies on autonomous work teams pointed to the importance of employee participation in safety-related activities and task autonomy as determinants of teams' safety behaviors, particularly safety initiatives. Collectively, one could conclude that an important way to enhance workplace safety is to increase employee involvement, either in the form of greater employee participation in safety-related decision-making (e.g., HSCs) or in the form of greater task or team autonomy. We discuss the potential mechanisms by which these effects might occur shortly.

In the literature on autonomous teams, although the direct evidence is rather limited, effective team processes (e.g., team cohesion, cooperation, team planning) are also implicated as determinants of workplace safety. Researchers investigating cockpit crews would not be surprised by this conclusion: they have demonstrated links between team processes, particularly crew communication, and safety-related outcomes such as errors. Indeed, given that the main reason for teams is to coordinate action around interdependent tasks, it would be strange if team processes like coordination did not impinge on safety. The practical implication from this is that one should not only train team members in task-related aspects of the job, but also in the interpersonal and process skills that can make or literally break a team. Providing teamwork training appears to be important, not just for team performance but for safety as well.

Finally, an important contribution to safety is also likely to be of a high-quality interaction between supervisors and employees (i.e., cooperative leadership). This was evident in the studies showing the consequence of joint HSCs, and the type of interaction between supervisors and their teams over safety activities as was evident in the research on autonomous teams. This finding complements studies showing the importance of safety focused leadership (e.g., Zohar, 2002), and suggests the practical value of leadership training and development for safety in the workplace.

In sum, the team characteristics found to be important on safety outcomes coinciding with those described in the broader literature on team effectiveness. To re-visit Sundstrom et al.'s taxonomy that we introduced at the beginning of the chapter, aspects of organizational context (i.e., training and leadership), team composition and size (i.e., proportion of union-representatives, proportion of non-management members), teamwork design (i.e., autonomy, non-routine work organization), and intra-team processes (i.e., communication, cohesion) have all found to be related to safety outcomes. Of course, a relative shortage of rigorous field studies, especially those focusing on HSCs and autonomous work teams, combined with highly diverse methods, measures, and settings, makes it important to qualify such a conclusion.

A Possible Dark Side to Teams?

Thus far we have mostly focused on the potential positive outcomes of teamwork for safety. However, the possibility exists that teamwork could reduce safety under some circumstances. For example, in the case of implementing autonomous teams, role clarity is often reduced as a result of new roles and the possibility of diffused responsibility, thereby resulting in greater likelihood of accidents. Other problems might arise because this form of teamworking is poorly implemented or is implemented at the same time as other changes with negative consequences on safety (e.g., downsizing; see Probst, 2004).

Another way that teamwork could negatively affect safety is through its potential negative effects on team processes. For example, team members might engage in social loafing and reduce their efforts (Karau & Williams, 1993), and "teamthink" might result in poor quality decision-making (Janis, 1982). More generally, the benefits of teamworking usually arise because of the coordination of individual efforts, but these coordination processes can fail. For example, Tjosvold (1990) identified situations in which flight crew teams failed to coordinate effectively, such as crew members not being able to discuss opposing views openly.

Thus, teamwork might have detrimental effects on safety under some circumstances. We need to do more research to understand how likely these negative effects are, whether they outweigh the potential positive benefits and whether it is possible to intervene to limit the negative effects (e.g., via training).

Future Directions

Although promising, the above conclusions about the advantages and disadvantages of teams in terms of workplace safety must be considered provisional due to the relatively small number of robust studies. A straightforward yet recurrent appeal, therefore, is for more rigorous studies, such as longitudinal designs combined with reliable indicators of safety. In the course of discussing the existing literature, we also identified several methodological issues that would need to be considered in future research. Next, we suggest some other important ways forward.

Gaps from the Teamworking Literature

As we discussed above, many of the factors that impact upon safety have also been found to be predictors of other aspects of team effectiveness. Due to the scarcity of research relating teams and safety, it makes sense to draw on the wider team effectiveness literature in identifying other potential antecedents that would be worthy of investigation. We identify some, though by no means all, of the possibilities here.

The predictors of team safety fall into four out of the five categories of factors of team effectiveness identified by Sundstrom et al. (2000). It would therefore seem fruitful to investigate other predictors within the already identified categories. For example, how do the intra-team processes such as conflict affect safety? Are rewards an important aspect of the organizational context when safety is considered as a key outcome? Does team size affect safety-related attitudes and behavior? In addition, to our knowledge no research has investigated how external team processes (the fifth category identified by Sundstrom et al. 2000) affects safety, yet the way in which teams communicate and integrate is likely to be key. For example, the quality and quantity of communication between HSCs and the rest of the organization is likely to affect the degree to which HSCs can effectively influence safety outcomes.

The wider context within which organizations are embedded is another key issue that has been largely overlooked in the literature on teams and safety. Many models of team effectiveness incorporate context (e.g., Sundstrom et al., 1990) and it is likely that a consideration of contextual variables will help further our understanding of team safety. The only study (i.e., Cohen & Ledford, 1994) of autonomous work teams that did not report positive consequences for safety was one that was conducted in a very different context (i.e., an organization in which safety was perhaps less salient) than the other existing studies that were conducted in manufacturing settings. This discrepancy alone alerts us to the need to consider context. Some of the research reviewed above has made a special effort to do this (e.g., Trist et al., 1977; Pearson, 1992; Cohen & Ledford, 1994) and provides examples for future contributions in this area. In addition, growing interest in multilevel studies in teams and safety research (e.g., Hofmann & Stetzer,

1996; Simard & Marchand, 1995, 1997) implicitly moves studies in this area toward the importance of contextual influences.

Attention to Mechanisms

Several researchers have speculated on mechanisms by which teams can affect safety, but these have rarely been investigated. One advantage of understanding significant mechanisms is that it will help to identify when particular interventions are likely to be appropriate. For example, consider the possible ways in which autonomous work teams might impinge on safety. First, autonomous work teams might enhance safe working via motivational mechanisms, such as employees feeling greater responsibility for and ownership of safety. Autonomous work teams might also improve team interaction. For example, by being autonomous, team members might communicate directly with each other rather than communicating via a supervisor. This form of work redesign, as we have already speculated, might enhance knowledge and understanding (e.g., interpositional knowledge), which in turn means employees make fewer errors and work more safely. These are just some of the ways that autonomous work teams might result in a safer workplace. If we have a better understanding of such processes, then we can more easily ensure that work structures and supports are put in place to maximize the likelihood of the work redesign's success.

New Challenges

With work environments constantly changing, new challenges emerge and their impact upon teams and safety need to be considered. Two trends brought about by globalization that are of particular importance are increasing levels of racio-ethnic and cultural diversity within teams and the more frequent need for teams to work in a virtual and distributed way. As yet, no research has investigated the safety implications of either diversity or virtual teamworking. In this section, we therefore hypothesize what these implications might be and call for researchers to explore these issues empirically in the near future.

Team diversity refers to the degree of difference between team members with respect to given characteristic. Particularly salient within international business is diversity in ethnicity and culture. Most research of this type has focused on racio-ethnic diversity and typically it has been found to have negative implications on important outcomes. For example, greater racio-ethnic diversity within teams has been found to be associated with less prosocial organizational behavior (Kizilos, Pelled, & Cummings, 1996, cited in Williams & O'Reilly, 1998), lower performance (Kirkman, Tesluk, & Rosen, 2001; Townsend & Scott, 2001). Furthermore, team members who are dissimilar from other team members in terms of their racio-ethnic background have been found to have less psychological commitment to their organization (Tsui, Egan, & O'Reilly, 1992) and lower perceptions of team performance (Riordan & Weatherly, 1999). Such diversity has also been found to be negatively associated with intra-team processes such as communication (Hoffman, 1985) and social integration (Kirchmeyer, 1995). Given that the research on teams and safety reviewed above suggests that intra-team processes positively affect safety-related outcomes, it is therefore likely that racio-ethnic diversity will have a negative effect upon team safety via its negative effects on team processes.

Despite this rather negative warning, some studies have found national/cultural diversity to have positive effects on performance (e.g., Earley & Mosakowski, 2000; Elron, 1997). It is therefore also possible that diversity might have a positive effect on some aspects of safety. For example, diverse teams have the potential for more creative solutions (Williams & O'Reilly, 1998) and therefore may be better at generating solutions to safety issues within the workplace.

In sum, diversity might have both positive and negative effects on safety outcomes. On the one hand, diversity creates the potential for more creative problem-solving. On the other , it tends to have a negative effect on the social integration of teams. Future research would do well to explore these possibilities, as well as highlight the mechanism by which diversity might have an impact so that any potential negative effects can be mitigated.

Another key issue with emerging internationalization is virtual or distributed teamworking. While most teams these days use communication technologies (e.g., e-mail, telephone), virtual teams have to rely to a greater extent on such technologies because they have limited opportunities to meet face-to-face (Axtell, Fleck, & Turner, 2004). To our knowledge, no research to date has investigated the implications of virtual teamworking on safety outcomes. Research does, however, suggest that virtual teams tend to communicate less frequently (e.g., Sosa, Eppinger, Pich, McKendrick, & Stout, 2002), be less collaborative (e.g., Kraut, Fussell, Brennan, & Siegel, 2002), less cohesive (e.g., McGrath & Hollingshead, 1994), have lower levels of affective trust (e.g., Rocco, Finholt, Hofer, & Herbsleb, 2000, cited in Axtell et al., 2004), and less mutual knowledge and contextual understanding (e.g., Cramton, 2001; Sole, & Edmondson, 2002). In essence, virtual teams have weaker relational ties (Axtell et al., 2004) than traditional co-located teams. Consequently, it would seem reasonable to expect virtual teams to have a negative effect on safety again via the impact on intra-team processes.

On a more positive note, however, it has been suggested that a lack of social cues in virtual teamworking might lead to team members being less inhibited and less likely to conform to norms (Sproull & Kiesler, 1986), which in turn could lead to less focus on the differentiation of status among team members and thus more equal participation (e.g., Sproull & Kiesler, 1986). Laboratory research supports such a suggestion insofar as there is more equal participation among teams using computer-mediated technology than those using face-to-face communication (e.g., Herschel, Cooper, Smith, & Arrington, 1994). It is possible therefore that members of virtual teams might be more likely to raise safety-related issues to other team members and they might be more likely to suggest ways of working safer that go against the team's normal procedures. If this was to be the case, then virtual teams might have a positive impact upon safety, especially safety initiative and participation.

A Final Word

On the one hand, it seems that teams can provide a structure for greater employee involvement in decision-making, greater social support, more information sharing, and more participative styles of leadership — all aspects likely to promote safer working. On the other , introducing teams per se is no automatic guarantee of success, and there is the potential for negative outcomes such as diffused responsibility, miscommunication, and role ambiguity. Although research has made some progress, we still need to know much more about how best to design and structure teams, what sorts of team processes are most important, and how teams should be led if we are to promote important outcomes. Viewing teams through the lens of an important outcome such as workplace safety provides a nuanced perspective on many factors that can make them succeed or fail.

References

Axtell, C. M., Fleck, S. J., & Turner, N. (2004). Virtual teams: Collaborating across distance. In: C. L. Cooper & I. T. Robertson (Eds), *International organizational psychology, review* (Vol. 19, pp. 205–248). Chichester, UK: Wiley.

Barker, J. R. (1993). Tightening the iron cage: Concertive control in self-managing teams. *Administrative Science Quarterly, 38,* 408–437.

Blickensderfer, E., Cannon-Bowers, J. A., & Salas, E. (1998). Cross-training and team performance. In: J. A. Cannon-Bowers & E. Salas (Eds), *Making decisions under stress: Implications for individual and team training* (pp. 299–311). Washington, DC: American Psychological Association.

Campion, M. A., Medsker, G. J., & Higgs, A. C. (1993). Relations between team characteristics and effectiveness: Implications for designing effective work teams. *Personnel Psychology, 46,* 823–850.

Cannon-Bowers, J. A., & Salas, E. (2001). Reflections on shared cognition. *Journal of Organizational Behavior, 22,* 195–202.

Cannon-Bowers, J. A., Salas, E., Blickensderfer, E., & Bowers, C. A. (1998). The impact of cross-training and workload on team functioning: A replication and extension of initial findings. *Human Factors, 40,* 92–101.

Cohen, S. G., & Bailey, D. E. (1997). What makes teams work: Team effectiveness research from the shop floor to the executive suite. *Journal of Management, 23*(3), 239–290.

Cohen, S. G., & Ledford, Jr, G. E. (1994). The effectiveness of self-managing teams: A quasi-experiment. *Human Relations, 47,* 13–43.

Commission of the Future of Worker-Management Relations. (nd.). Safety and Health Programs and Employee Involvement. Retrieved June 22, 2001, from http://www.dol. gov/dol/_sec/public/media/reports/dunlop/section7.html.

Cramton, C. D. (2001). The mutual knowledge problem and its consequences for dispersed collaboration. *Organization Science, 12*(3), 346–371.

Delbridge, R., Turnbull, P., & Wilkinson, B. (1992). Pushing back the frontiers: Management control and work intensification under JIT/TQM factory regimes. *New Technology, Work and Employment, 7,* 97–106.

Earley, P. C., & Mosakowski, E. M. (2000). Creating hybrid team cultures: An empirical test of international team functioning. *Academy of Management Journal, 43,* 26–49.

Eaton, A. E., & Nocerino, T. (2000). The effectiveness of health and safety committees: Results of a survey of public-sector workplaces. *Industrial Relations, 39,* 265–290.

Eden, D. (1985). Team development: A true field experiment at three levels of rigor. *Journal of Applied Psychology, 70,* 94–100.

Edmondson, A. (1996). Learning from mistakes is easier said than done: Team and organization influences on the detection and correction of human error. *Journal of Applied Behavioral Science, 32,* 5–28.

Elron, E. (1997). Top management teams within multinational corporations: Effects of cultural heterogeneity. *Leadership Quarterly, 8,* 393–412.

Flap, H., Bulder, B., & Ölker, B. V. (1998). Intra-organizational networks and performance: A review. *Computational & Mathematical Organization Theory, 4,* 109–147.

Foushee, H. C. (1984). Dyads and triads at 35,000 feet: Factors affecting team process and aircrew performance. *American Psychologist, 39,* 885–893.

Foushee, H. C., & Helmreich, R. L. (1988). Team interaction and flight crew performance. In: E. L. Weiner, & D. C. Nagel (Eds), *Human factors in aviation* (pp. 189–225). San Diego, CA: Academic Press.

Frone, M. R. (1998). Predictors of work injuries among employed adolescents. *Journal of Applied Psychology, 83,* 565–576.

Goodman, P. S. (1979). *Assessing organizational change: The Rushton quality of work experiment.* New York: Wiley.

Goodman, P.S., Devadas, R., & Hughson, T. L. G. (1988). Groups and productivity: Analyzing the effectiveness of self-managing teams. In J. P. Campbell, R. J. Campbell et al. (Eds.), *Productivity in organizations: New perspectives from industrial and organizational psychology* (pp. 295–327). San Francisco: Jossey-Bass.

Guzzo, R. A., & Dickson, M. W. (1996). Teams in organizations: Recent research on performance and effectiveness. *Annual Review of Psychology, 47*, 307–338.

Hechanova-Alampay, R. H., & Beehr, T. A. (2002). Empowerment, span of control and safety performance in work teams after workforce reduction. *Journal of Occupational Health Psychology, 6*, 275–282.

Helmreich, R. L. (2000). On error management: Lessons from aviation. *British Medical Journal, 320*, 781–784.

Helmreich, R. L., & Foushee, H. C. (1993). Why crew resource management? Empirical and theoretical bases of human factors training in aviation. In: E. Wiener, B. Kanki, & R. Helmreich (Eds), *Cockpit resource management* (pp. 3–45). San Diego, CA: Academic Press.

Helmreich, R. L., Klinect, J. R., & Wilhelm, J. A. (1999). Models of threat, error, and CRM in flight operations. *Proceedings of the tenth international symposium on aviation psychology* (pp. 677–682). Columbus, OH: Ohio State University.

Helmreich, R. L., & Merritt, A. C. (1998). *Culture at work in aviation and medicine.* Aldershot, UK: Ashgate.

Hemingway, M. A., & Smith, C. S. (1999). Organizational climate and occupational stressors as predictors of withdrawal behaviours and injuries in nurses. *Journal of Occupational and Organizational Psychology, 72*, 285–299.

Herschel, R. T., Cooper, T. R., Smith, L. F., & Arrington, L. (1994). Exploring numerical proportions in a unique context: The team support systems meeting environment. *Sex Roles, 31*(1/2), 99–123.

Hoffman, E. (1985). The effect of race-ratio composition on the frequency of organizational communication. *Social Psychology Quarterly, 48*, 17–26.

Hofmann, D. A., & Stetzer, A. (1996). A cross-level investigation of factors influencing unsafe behaviors and accidents. *Personnel Psychology, 49*, 307–339.

Jackson, S. E., Joshi, A., & Erhardt, N. L. (2003). Recent research on team and organizational diversity: SWOT analysis and implications. *Journal of Management, 29*(6), 801–830.

Janis, I. L. (1982). *Teamthink*. Boston: Houghton Mifflin.

Johns, G. (2001). In praise of context. *Journal of Organizational Behavior, 22*, 31–42.

Karau, S. J., & Williams, K. D. (1993). Social loafing: A meta-analytic review and theoretical integration. *Journal of Personality and Social Psychology, 65*, 681–786.

Kirchmeyer, C. (1995). Demographic similarity to the work team: A longitudinal study of managers at the early career stage. *Journal of Organizational Behavior, 16*, 67–83.

Kirkman, B. L., Tesluk, P. E., & Rosen, B. (2001). The impact of race heterogeneity and team leader-member demographic fit on team empowerment and effectiveness. Paper presented at the 15th annual meeting of the Society for Industrial and Organizational Psychology, New Orleans.

Kizilos, M., Pelled, L., & Cummings, T. (1996). *Organizational demography and prosocial organizational behavior.* Unpublished manuscript.

Kraut, R. E., Fussell, S. R., Brennan, S. E., & Siegel, J. (2002). Understanding the effects of proximity on collaboration: Implications for technologies to support remote collaborative work. In: P. Hinds, & S. Kiesler (Eds), *Distributed work* (pp. 137–162). Cambridge, MA: MIT Press.

Landsbergis, P. A., Cahill, J., & Schnall, P. (1999). The impact of lean production and related new systems of work organization on worker health. *Journal of Occupational Health Psychology, 4*, 108–130.

Lawler, E. E. (1992). *The ultimate advantage: Creating the high involvement organization.* San Francisco: Jossey-Bass.

Locke, E. A., & Latham, G. P. (1990). *A theory of goal setting and task performance.* Englewood Cliffs, NJ: Prentice-Hall.

Mathiason, T. (2001). Safety crackdown as work deaths rise. *The Observer*, August 12, p. 4.

Mathieu, J. E., Heffner, T. S., Goodwin, G. F., Salas, E., & Cannon-Bowers, J. A. (2000). The influence of shared mental models on team process and performance. *Journal of Applied Psychology, 85*, 273–283.

McGrath, J. E., & Hollingshead, A. B. (1994). *Teams interacting with technology. Ideas, evidence, issues, and an agenda.* Thousand Oaks, CA: Sage Publications.

McVeigh, T. (2000). Repair bungles add to chaos on railways. *The Observer*, November 12, p. 6.

Mohammed, S., & Dumville, B. C. (2001). Team mental models in a team knowledge framework: Expanding theory and measurement across disciplinary boundaries. *Journal of Organizational Behavior, 22*, 89–106.

Neal, A., & Griffin, M. A. (2004). Safety climate. In: J. Barling & M. R. Frone (Eds), *The psychology of workplace safety*. Washington, DC: American Psychological Association.

O'Toole, M. F. (1999). Successful safety committees: Participation not legislation. *Journal of Safety Research, 30*, 39–65.

Occupational Safety and Health Administration (OSHA). (1991). *Hearing report on OSHA reform.* Retrieved from the OSHA Standard Interpretation and Compliance Letters web site: http://www.oshaslc.gov/OshDoc/Interp_data/I19911101.html.

Parker, S. K., & Turner, N. (2002). Work design and individual work performance: Research findings and an agenda for future inquiry. In: S. Sonnentag (Ed.), *The psychological management of individual performance: A handbook in the psychology of the management of organizations* (pp. 69–93). Chichester, UK: Erlbaum.

Parker, S. K., Turner, N., & Griffin, M. A. (2003). Designing healthy work. In: D. A. Hofmann & L. E. Tetrick (Eds), *Health and safety in organizations: A multilevel perspective* (pp. 91–130). San Francisco: Jossey-Bass.

Parker, S. K. and Wall, T. D. (1998). *Job and work design: Organizing work to promote well-being and effectiveness.* London: Sage.

Pearson, C. A. L. (1992). Autonomous teams: An evaluation at an industrial site. *Human Relations, 45*, 905–936.

Probst, T. M. (2004). Safety and insecurity: Exploring the moderating effect of organizational safety climate. *Journal of Occupational Health Psychology, 9*, 3–10.

Reilly, B., Paci, P., & Holl, P. (1995). Unions, safety committees and workplace injuries. *British Journal of Industrial Relations, 33*, 275–288.

Riordan, C. M., & Weatherly, E. W. (1999). Relational demography within teams: An empirical test of a theoretical model. Paper presented at the annual meeting of the Academy of Management, Chicago.

Rocco, E., Finholt, T. A., Hofer, E. C., & Herbsleb, J. D. (2000). *Designing as if trust mattered.* Working Paper. University of Michigan, Ann Arbor, MI.

Rousseau, D. M., & Fried, Y. (2001). Location, location, location: Contextualizing organizational research. *Journal of Organizational Behavior, 22,* 1–13.

Salas, E., Stagl, K. C., & Burke, S. (2004). 25 years of team effectiveness in organizations: Research themes and emerging needs. In: C. L. Cooper & I. T. Robertson (Eds), *International review of industrial and organizational psychology* (Vol. 19, pp. 47–91). Chichester, UK: Wiley.

Sexton, J. B., & Helmreich, R. L. (2000). Analyzing cockpit communications: The links between language, performance, error, and workload. *Human Performance in Extreme Environments, 5,* 63–68.

Shadish, W. R., Cook, T. D., & Campbell, D. T. (2002). *Experimental and quasi-experimental designs for generalized causal inference.* Boston: Houghton-Mifflin.

Simard, M., & Marchand, A. (1995). A multilevel analysis of organizational factors related to the taking of safety initiatives by work teams. *Safety Science, 21,* 113–129.

Simard, M., & Marchand, A. (1997). Teams' propensity to comply with safety rules: The influence of micro-macro organizational factors. *Ergonomics, 40,* 172–188.

Sole, D., & Edmondson, A. C. (2002). Situated knowledge and learning in dispersed teams. *British Journal of Management, 13*(2), 17–34.

Sonnentag, S. (1996). Work team factors and individual well-being. In: M. A. West (Ed.), *Handbook of work team psychology.* Chichester, UK: Wiley.

Sosa, M. E., Eppinger, S. D., Pich, M., McKendrick, D. G., & Stout, S. K. (2002). Factors that influence technical communication in distributed product development: An empirical study in the telecommunications industry. *IEEE Transactions on Engineering Management, 49*(1), 45–58.

Sproull, L., & Kiesler, S. (1986). Reducing social-context cues – electronic mail in organizational communication. *Management Science, 32*(11), 1492–1512.

Sundstrom, E., De Meuse, K., & Futrell, D. (1990). Work teams: Applications and effectiveness. *American Psychologist, 45,* 120–133.

Sundstrom, E., McIntyre, M., Halfhill, T., & Richards, H. (2000). Work teams: From the Hawthorne studies to work teams of the 1990s and beyond. *Team Dynamics: Theory, Research and Practice, 4*(1), 44–67.

The Times. (2000, December 29). BA jumbo plunges as man storms cockpit. Retrieved from: http://www.thetimes.co.uk/article/0,3-59795,00.html.

Tjosvold, D. (1990). Flight crew collaboration to manage safety risks. *Team and Organization Studies, 15,* 11–19.

Townsend, A. M., & Scott, K. D. (2001). Team racial composition, member attitudes, and performance: A field study. *Industrial Relations, 40,* 317–337.

Trist, E. L., & Bamforth, K. W. (1951). Some social and psychological consequences of the long-wall method of coal-getting. *Human Relations, 4,* 3–38.

Trist, E. L., Higgin, G. W., Murray, H., & Pollock, A. B. (1963). *Organizational choice.* London, England: Tavistock Publications.

Trist, E. L., Susman, G. I., & Brown, G. R. (1977). An experiment in autonomous working in an American underground coal mine. *Human Relations, 30*, 201–236.

Tsui, A. S., Egan, T. D., & O'Reilly, C. A. (1992). Being different: Relational demography and organizational attachment. *Administrative Science Quarterly, 37*, 549–579.

Volpe, C. E., Cannon-Bowers, J. A., Salas, E., & Spector, P. E. (1996). The impact of cross-training on team functioning: An empirical investigation. *Human Factors, 38*, 87–100.

Walton, R. E. (1972). How to counter alienation in the plant. *Harvard Business Review*, November/December, *50*(6), 70–81.

Walton Braver, M. C., & Braver, S. L. (1988). Statistical treatment of the Solomon four-team design: A meta-analytic approach. *Psychological Bulletin, 104*(1), 150–154.

Waterson, P. E., Clegg, C. W., Bolden, R., Pepper, K., Warr, P., & Wall, T. D. (1999). The use and effectiveness of modern manufacturing practices: A UK survey. *International Journal of Production Research, 37*, 2271–2292.

Weick, K. E. (1993). The collapse of sensemaking in organizations: The Mann Gulch disaster. *Administrative Science Quarterly, 38*, 628–652.

Wellins, R., Byham, W., & Wilson, J. (1991). *Empowered teams: Creating self-directed work groups that improve quality, productivity and participation.* San Francisco: Jossey-Bass.

West, M. A., Borrill, C. S., & Unsworth, K. L. (1998). Team effectiveness in organizations. In C. Cooper & I. Robertson (Eds.), *International Review of Industrial and Organizational Psychology.* Chichester: John Wiley & Sons.

Wiener, E. L., Kanki, B., & Helmreich, R. (1993). *Cockpit resource management.* San Diego: Academic Press.

Wiener, E. L., Kanki, B. G., & Helmreich, R. L. (1996). *Cockpit resource management.* San Diego, CA: Academic Press.

Wiener, E. L., & Nagel, D. C. (Eds). (1988). *Human factors in aviation.* San Diego, CA: Academic Press.

Williams, K. Y., & O'Reilly, C. (1998). The complexity of diversity: A review of forty years of research. In: B. Staw, & R. Sutton (Eds), *Research in organizational behavior* (Vol. 21, pp. 77–140). Greenwich, CT: JAI Press.

Zohar, D. (2000). A team-level model of safety climate: Testing the effect of team climate on microaccidents in manufacturing jobs. *Journal of Applied Psychology, 85*, 587–596.

Zohar, D. (2002). Modifying supervisory practices to improve sub-unit safety: A leadership-based intervention model. *Journal of Applied Psychology, 87*, 156–163.

Chapter 3

Identity and Identification Processes in Mergers and Joint Ventures

Paul R. Jackson and Ingrid Dackert

Introduction

Mergers and joint ventures are widespread phenomena all over the world, and employee groups in the service and knowledge-based industries have been especially affected Studies of mergers from an economic perspective have, however, shown that the outcomes are disappointing. It has been estimated that at least half of all mergers fail to achieve the expected synergies and economic outcomes (Cartwright & Hudson, 2000). "According to Bain, the global consultancy, 70 per cent of big deals fail to create meaningful value, one to two years after announcement. Some 60 per cent of deals create companies that under-perform their peers and a full 50 per cent actually destroy shareholder value." (*The Financial Times*, February 11, 2005, p. 25) "Employee problems" have been estimated to be responsible for one third to one half of all merger failures (Davy, Kinicki, Kilroy, & Scheck, 1988). It is, however, only relatively recently that research attention has turned to the contribution that psychology can make to a better understanding of the processes involved. A merger is a significant event for both the organisation and its employees and implies a long-term process of change and integration (Cartwright & Cooper, 1990, 1996).

The focus of this chapter is on the importance of identity and identifications in mergers and joint ventures. Mergers and joint ventures are powerful agents for examining cognitive processes and emotional investments. They are particularly powerful agents for examining the emotional investments of social identity processes. Mergers almost always involve the dissolution of prior organisations in favour of the creation of a new entity with an associated new identity. Key issues in this process are likely to arise out of prior identity differences between merger partners and differences in the relative power of the partners during the planning stages and in the merger process itself. Mergers almost certainly involve changes in group memberships, either through the disappearance of an organisation through a merger or through the creation of a joint venture organisation. Mergers also invite social comparisons by increasing the salience either of groups in another merger partner or of an existing group threatened by the merger process. Joint ventures (or strategic alliances) share some of the same characteristics that make identity an important issue, but differ in that the partners involved retain their separate identities while working together to create a separate joint venture organisation (Child & Faulkner, 1998; Dicken, 2003). Identity issues then centre around how partners who are usually competitors also work out how to cooperate. Communication problems can then arise between joint venture partners and also often between the joint venture company and its parents.

The rest of the chapter is divided into two sections. First, we examine the concepts of identity and identification and consider their importance for a good understanding of mergers and joint ventures. In the second part of the chapter we describe cognitive and cultural processes.

Identity and Identifications

There are two broad perspectives in the literature on identity. What might be called the *psychological* perspective focuses on the individual and emphasises personal agency: identity comes from the individual acting on the environment, self esteem arises out of achievement, and identification relates to areas of successful performance. Thus, for example, skilled performances in cookery may lead someone to say "I am a chef". The second *sociological* perspective derives from early work by Cooley (1909) on what he called "the looking glass self", indicating that identity arises out of the reflection of self in social roles. From this perspective, the self is defined by membership of social categories, self-esteem derives from the value afforded by the social category, and identification reflects the extent to which the individual incorporates characteristics of the social category into the self. Thus, individuals might only feel that they can attach to themselves the label of "chef" by acquiring a qualification that gives entry to a professional body or by taking a job with that label (Table 3.1).

Table 3.1: Approaches to identity.

Psychological approaches
  - Origins — agency, acting on the environment
  - Esteem — from achievement
  - Identification — with areas of significant achievement

Sociological approaches
  - Origins — reflection of self in social roles & group memberships
  - Esteem — from status of social group membership
  - Identification — with the social group

Identity and Group Membership

Clearly, both psychological and sociological perspectives are needed if we are to achieve a fully rounded view of identity. Because of the focus in this chapter on mergers and joint ventures involving organisations as social groups, our emphasis here is on the ways in which identity is constructed through role categories and group memberships. A starting point for this discussion is that every individual belongs to multiple role categories, some of which are hierarchically organised. In a given situation, one or other of the possible role categories will be especially salient; and we will show how outcomes differ depending on which category is salient. Social Identity Theory (Hogg & Terry, 2000) examines such issues, and focuses on the role of groups in defining conceptual anchors for behaviour, and also sets out to define the circumstances where groups and differences between them become salient in shaping responses to events. These circumstances include pre-existing differences in identity, dominance of one partner in the change process, threats to identity where one group sees a loss of valued aspects of identity.

Boundaries and Identity

Boundaries are fundamentally important to identity, because they define both personal and social categories (Cross, Yan, & Louis, 2000; Yan & Louis, 1999). That, of course, is why territorial disputes have been so prominent throughout human history. Social boundaries show belongingness by making clear what is and is not a member of a category, and this is a mixed blessing. On the positive side, they reduce uncertainty by allowing categorisation and therefore the allocation of meaning. Once we know what group we belong to, we can more easily interact with others in that group and start to define the identity of the group. However, there is a negative side too, since the very process that makes interaction within the group easier also makes it harder to work across the boundaries. Some areas of the world have "belonged" to a variety of different countries, and where boundaries are drawn is always important. We can see how arbitrary definition of boundaries have been damaging in the history of Africa, where colonial powers (often European) drew boundaries on a map which accorded with the convenience of trade routes and ignored long-lasting tribal boundaries. The histories of both Palestine and Iraq have similarly been made more turbulent by the boundary decisions of colonial powers.

Social role categories matter because their meaning is not intrinsic, but rather it is both personally and socially defined. The personal aspect of roles categories arises from individual meaning systems, which define what it means, for example, to be a manager, an accountant, or a member of a political party. Psychologists and management theorists have long studied these meaning systems in terms of mental models or mind-sets, and we will consider this topic in more detail in a later part of this chapter. The social aspect of role categories emphasise how meanings are not solely individual, but rather are often shared within a society. These shared meanings then become the basis for debate about the characteristics of groups within society, through stereotypes and the exercise of prejudice where supposed attributes to groups are applied to individuals without regard for personal individuality.

All of us belong to more than one role category, and this is where much of the richness of our social life comes from. However, membership of more than one role category carries with it the potential for conflict between their requirements, and there is a large literature within psychology on the negative consequences of role conflict (see Parker, Jackson, Sprigg, & Whybrow, 1998). For example, an active trade unionist who is promoted to a senior management position may experience difficulty in reconciling the interests espoused by the union to which she belongs with the responsibilities of a management position. Most of us have experienced similar difficulties at some time in our lives as we struggle to reconcile the demands of employment with those of family life — so called work-life balance. Tajfel (1982) argues that such multiple role memberships should be kept to a minimum in order to avoid dilution of identities and confusion. He has a point, but the issue for most people is that multiple role memberships are both unavoidable and a valued part of who we are. So, we need to consider how to *manage* conflicting role demands rather than how to *avoid* them. One way to achieve this is through identifying a larger common purpose which can serve to reconcile conflicts between the demands of different roles that the individual occupies.

In most circumstances, boundaries need to be clearly defined if they are to be effective, and psychologists have long recognised that role ambiguity is a potent stressor (Parker, Jackson, Sprigg, & Whybrow, 1998). Most people need to know what is required of them in performing a specific role so that they make sense of the role and be clear about how well they are performing in it. Blurred or porous boundaries can thus be very disturbing and even dangerous. Consider how important it is to have the right dosage of a drug which is administered to a woman following a caesarean section operation to deliver her baby. It is better to have the dosage checked by everyone (physician, midwife, nurse), rather than it be unclear who should do it, with the risk that no one carries out the check.

On the other hand, boundaries, which are too sharply drawn can become prisons that impede effective working and stifle change. Parker, Wall, and Jackson (1997) studied ways in which job performance was enhanced by encouraging workers to adopt flexible work role orientations. Narrowly defined definitions of work roles ("that is not my job") are a traditional way in which workers can express their disapproval of the demands of management. Blurring of boundaries between role categories can also be a most effective element in the armoury of change management options. When organisations merge, the old boundaries can remain in place for many years, and they can provide potent barriers to achieving the benefits which were hoped for. First blurring old boundaries and then shifting them, can form the basis for new categorisations and can challenge the taken-for-granted. We will explore both of these points in a later section of the chapter.

Group Categorisation

One of the most basic forms of group categorisation is the distinction based on relationship to the self: the in-group is the group that I belong to, while the out-group is not (Hogg & Terry, 2000). This distinction is the basis of us-and-them thinking in mergers and joint ventures, and the identification of self with a specific group adds powerful cognitive and emotional forces to identity processes during such organisational events. Categorisations into in-group and out-group tend to polarise perceptions of the characteristics of groups. The self and the in-group will be seen as more similar, and perceived differences between in-group and out-group will be emphasised and enhanced. Groups then become seen in terms of what social psychologists call *prototypes*, organised sets of features, that have two characteristics. First, prototypes are simplifications which emphasise differences rather than similarities between groups, by focusing on those features which most clearly differentiate between groups. Second, the categorisation process leads to a form of depersonalisation: seeing people as embodiments of a group-based prototype and not as unique individuals. Both characteristics of the categorisation process can be potent sources of problems in merger and joint ventures, especially those which involve working across national or cultural boundaries.

However, simplifications imposed by the prototyping process can be subtly dangerous. Consider a quotation from Salk's study (1997) of Basic Co, a German–French joint venture: "The French side is supposed to cheat. The Germans are supposed to do things without subtlety, and that is what is happening" (p. 62). Note two features of this quotation from a French manager. First is the distinction made between two groups based on nationality alone. Second, the groups so defined acquire, as a result of making the distinction, characteristics consistent with national stereotypes, and more potently these distinctions acquire a normative status — each group is *supposed* to behave in this way. Suddenly, individuality is lost and choice disappears with the obligation to act in a particular way. In this way a stereotype perpetuated — through a motivated process of finding ways of explaining the past (culture as a lens through which the world is perceived) and through the imposition of restrictions of choices through what is legitimate (culture as a prison limiting possibilities for action).

Multi-Level Identities — The Importance of Hierarchy

Social systems are hierarchical (Simon, 1996): individuals belong to work groups, groups form organisational units, and organisational units in turn exist within societies. "Groups are open and complex systems that interact with the smaller systems (i.e. their members) embedded within them and the larger systems (e.g. organisations) within which they are embedded". (Arrow, McGrath, & Berdahl, 2000, p. 34) A later chapter in this book (Yeow and Jackson) explores this characteristic of hierarchy in more detail from the perspective of complexity theory. Here, we are concerned with the implications of hierarchy for identity and identification. It is necessary to consider at least three levels:

- *Personal/individual level* — individuals derive their identity in many ways, through their personal achievements and through their occupancy of social roles.
- *Team or group level* — identity at the level of the team or work group is more than and different from the sum of the identities of the constituent individuals. Both structure and collective identity are emergent (Johnson, 2001; Kauffman, 2000) arising out of the interactions among team members, without the necessity of identity being imposed from outside the team.
- *Department or organisational level* — the identity of organisations is an important and growing area of research (e.g. Schultz, Hatch, & Larsen, 2000)

and the main finding is that the corporate brand is very valuable in both achieving an external reputation (Davies, Chun, Da Silva, & Roper, 2002) and promoting the commitment of employees within the organisation (Scott & Lane, 2000).

An important issue that we do not yet understand fully is the relationship among identifications at different levels. We need to learn much more about what happens when they are conflicting, for example when personal values are in conflict with organisational values (Lovell, 2002). We also need to know more about the consequences of focusing on one level of identification (e.g. the organisation) rather than another level (e.g. the team or work group)? What is it that makes one level in a hierarchy salient? What are the consequences for the organisation of individuals withdrawing their commitment to the organisation when they feel let down (McLean Parks and smith explore this using the concept of psychological contract violation in chapter 5)? How does reputational capital at one level (e.g. the reputation of the organisation) become a valued part of an individual's personal identity?

The Dynamics of Identification Processes

Identities are both stable and fluid, as we know from our own experience. At one level, identity is that which is enduring (Albert & Whetten, 1985), but as well as this social identity is dynamic and continually expressed and re-expressed through the daily round of organisational life. For example, Lembke and Wilson (1998) argue that the process of developing a team involves a shift from a focus on the individual to a focus on the team, with associated shifts in ways of thinking and working. In particular, Gersick (1989) noted a change in the character of working in project teams, though this was associated with a shift in emphasis at about the half-way point in a project when the attention of the group shifted to achievement of the project objectives. We would expect to see an increased understanding of shared ways of working and (perhaps) reduced individual differences, as the team develops collective mental models (Klimoski & Mohammed, 1994) which guide their working. Gruenfeld and Hollingshead (1993) studied 22 work groups and found a transition after 5 weeks of a 12-week study from individual efforts to a shared collective effort, based on a change in the kinds of information used and in how information was processed.

Phase shifts have been noted in many areas, and Gersick (1991) describes them in terms of a punctuated equilibrium model of change. Rather than a gradual evolutionary change process, she proposes that we can expect to see periods of steady state working punctuated by fundamental transformations in thinking and feeling.

Promoting Self-Esteem

We now turn to the examination of individuals' identification with social groups and the factors which underpin such identifications. The fundamental driver for group identification processes is the need to protect and promote positive self-esteem, and we will examine in this section four aspects of this process (see Table 3.2).

Preference for groups with positive attributes   The attractiveness of a group depends in part on its *intrinsic characteristics*. Self-esteem enhancement leads people to prefer belonging to groups which have positively evaluated attributes. Most people would probably prefer to work for a successful organisation rather than one which is failing; and would also prefer to work for an organisation whose values and practices are consistent with their own. Early studies used the so-called nominal group technique (Tajfel, 1981) to examine how people enhance the attractiveness of the group to which they belong. Tajfel showed that such enhancement does not depend on objective features, but can be achieved simply by allocating people at random to either the "red" team or the "blue" team. Even when study participants knew that the process was random (and therefore there were no real differences between the characteristics of the groups), they still regarded the in-group (their own) as better than the out-group. We can see therefore a two-way process between individual and group: the group I belong to is better because I am in it, and my self-esteem is enhanced because I belong to a group which is good.

A merger involves an attempt to create a single new organisational entity from at least two previously separate entities. The identity issues therefore involve first the continued existence of old identities either in the institutions of the merged organisation or in the minds of employees, and second the construction of a new identity for the merged organisation. It is not uncommon for old identities to linger for many years. For example, employees involved in the merger of HP and

Table 3.2: Group processes in promoting positive self-esteem.

1. Preferences for group memberships

2. Choice in assertion of identities

3. Choice of comparison groups

4. Position within the group

Compaq in 2003 talked not just about HP and Compaq but also about distinctions between "Compaq people" and "DEC people" after a merger five years earlier.

Terry, Carey, and Callan (2001) examined two characteristics of subjective belief systems which they argue are important in establishing whether a merger is seen by employees as threatening: the status of the groups involved in the merger, and the options available for change. With respect to *status*, the important things are whether there is a perceived difference in status, whether those differences are perceived as legitimate, and whether the status difference is stable or transient. With respect to change possibilities, the issues are whether it is possible to move from one group to another, and how easy it is to change the status evaluations of the groups.

Consider the situation where there is a clear and legitimate difference in status between two merging organisations. Predictions from theory depend greatly on the permeability of boundaries between the groups (Table 3.3). If boundaries are permeable, such that it is easy to move from one group to the other, then lower status partners will see the merger as favourable since they can acquire some of the status of the higher status group. By contrast, members of the higher status group will tend to see the merger unfavourably: the permeable boundary means that they stand to lose some of their esteem. Whether there is a threat to self-esteem depends on initial group membership and on how strongly the group boundaries are maintained after the merger. A different situation arises where status differences are not seen as legitimate, perhaps because one of the merger partners relies on an outdated reputation or is dependent on market advantages which are no longer supportable. In these circumstances, impermeable boundaries serve to preserve differences, which are undeserved and prevent efforts to legitimate

Table 3.3: Boundaries, status, and legitimacy of group differences.

- Groups see merger favourably: Members of *lower status* group, where difference is legitimate and boundaries are permeable — can move to the higher status group
- Groups see merger unfavourably:
  - Members of *lower status* group, where difference is not legitimate and boundaries are not permeable — cannot move to higher status group
  - Members of *higher status* group, where difference is legitimate and boundaries are permeable — lower status members can move and threaten the prior high status

status differences. Thus, lower status group members will tend to regard the merger unfavourably.

Asserting identities   Self-esteem is enhanced through the positive attributes of the groups that individuals belong to, and there is evidence that individuals select the identity to assert in specific circumstances in order to protect and promote their self-esteem. We have already shown that everyone belongs to multiple social categories (gender, ethnic origin, organisational membership, as well as professional affiliation and functional specialism). Individuals select an identity to assert from among these multiple social category memberships in many ways. One simple way is through how we introduce ourselves to others on first meeting them, and in subsequent encounters. Using formal titles emphasises status differences; while using names without titles implies that status is less important. Another way of asserting identities is through seating arrangements in a meeting room. When all members of a merger partner continue to sit together in meetings after a merger, they are asserting their former identity whether they are aware of it or not. Similarly, adopting a specific form of dress is a form of identity assertion. Thus, most people would dress more formally (for example, men wearing a tie) for a selection interview, whether as a candidate or a panel member. When partners in a merger or a joint venture have quite different cultural practices on appearance, individual dress practices can become powerful markers of which group a person chooses to identify with.

Choosing social comparison groups   The attractiveness of a group also depends upon comparisons with other groups: "positive social identity can be achieved, in a vast majority of cases, only through appropriate intergroup social comparison" (Tajfel, 1982, p. 24). Breakwell (1983) and Jetten, Branscombe, and Spears (2002) found that the extent of emotional alignment with a group covaried with the status of the group relative to other groups, as seen either by the group members themselves or by the organisation as a whole. The higher the perceived status of the group, the more likely individuals are to increase their identification with it. They may show this identification in a number of ways: expressing pride in belonging to the group, or putting increased effort into activities that support and develop the group. By contrast, where individuals belong to a group which has low status, they are more likely to reduce their identification with the group. Reduced identification may be reflected in such ways as: keeping quiet about being a member of a group or publicly criticising the group, reducing involvement in activities that support the group, or even in seeking to leave the group in favour of another one which is seen as having higher status (Table 3.4).

Table 3.4: Group status and identification.

- Increased identification through
  - express pride in belonging
  - active efforts to promote the group

- Decreased identification through
  - keeping silent on belonging to the group
  - publicly criticising the group
  - reduce involvement in group activities
  - leaving the group

The starting point for group comparisons and the evolution of working cultures in international mergers and joint ventures is likely to be the social identities from the national cultures of origin of the senior management team members. Salk (1997) points out that there will generally be dominance of one partner in the IJV in forming the working culture of the IJV organisation. One factor which can create dominance is the location of the JV itself (Killing, 1983) — the partner whose country is the base for the JV will be more familiar with the legal frameworks, labour market practices, and social norms which are prevalent. Another source of dominance can be a function of differences in the degree of dependence of the JV company on one or other of the parents for resources or specialist expertise. Such dependency relationships could easily create divided loyalties for organisational members.

Identity threats through new organisational memberships can spill over in negative impacts on other aspects of life — collateral damage. For example, loss of status following a work re-organisation after a merger can lead individuals to reduce their pro-social/citizenship behaviours in other areas of work life. Turnley and Feldman (1999) showed that psychological contract violations are related to exit, voice, loyalty, and neglect behaviours. Such violation is particularly likely in mergers and IJVs since they are very likely to challenge established expectations about rights and obligations (see the chapter by Sparrow, this book).

Marginality and centrality   In this section we consider two aspects of marginality: the position of an individual in the group relative to others, and the position of the group's values relative to the values of the organisation.

Position of the individual within the group   A strong contributor to the individual's emotional investment in the group is the degree of centrality of the individual within the group. Being a central player in a high status group

Table 3.5: Marginality as opportunity after a merger.

- Central position — potential threat to self-esteem
- Marginal position — opportunity to enhance self-esteem
    - junior role in a core group
    - senior role outside the operating core of the organisation

is presumably a strong contributor to self-esteem. Key members of a high status group are likely to work hard to maintain their status within the new organisation, and this can be a powerful restraining factor in achieving fundamental change. If a high status group disappears as part of a change process (for example through a plant closure, or through changes in technology or company product lines), the threat to individual self-esteem is likely to be high (Table 3.5).

On the other hand, the formation of a merged organisation or a joint venture provides opportunity for those who were marginal in a prior organisation, perhaps because they were in a relatively junior position or to achieve a more central position through the formation of a new organisation. Such changes are less likely to threaten self-esteem for individuals who were previously marginal. Marginal individuals can thus become important players in the successful formation of new organisations through mergers or joint ventures.

Position of group values within the merged organisation   The extent of emotional threat posed by mergers and joint ventures will also vary according to whether they involve a change in the values which were espoused by the partners involved. Efforts to change values (through culture-change programmes, for example) that are central to a group's identity will constitute greater risk to the success of the new enterprise, while marginal aspects are more likely to be given up (or allowed to evolve or compromise) in order to evolve new organisational forms.

Cognitive and Cultural Processes

The Construction of Meaning

It is an accepted commonplace that we deal with the world (and especially the social world of organisations) not as an objective reality but on the basis of an internal representation of it. How we see something will influence our understanding and how we respond; and differences in seeing lead to differences in response to the same event or circumstance. This presupposition is the basis of Kelly's personal construct theory (Kelly, 1955) which views people as scientists, engaged in actively exploring their world, experimenting with it, and building "theories" of how it works. Personal constructs are the building blocks of people's mental representations of the environment, and these representations are used to "fit over the realities of which the world is composed" (Adams-Webber, 1970, p. 31). It is assumed that people apply their personal constructs to forecast events and to test their predictive efficiency after the event has occurred. While Kelly emphasised the uniqueness of construct systems (they are made up from "personal" constructs), it would be difficult for us to live together without some elements of commonality in our ways of construing the world. Thus, meanings are partly idiosyncratic and partly shared.

Another slant on the construction of meanings is offered by Karl Weick (1995) in his elaboration of *sensemaking*, the process whereby people in organisations make sense of information, especially that which is ambiguous. The construction of meaning involves interpretations of past events, expectations of future events, and especially story telling to create narratives for inventing and re-inventing the past. In organisational change processes such as mergers or the formation of joint ventures, the people involved will try to make sense of events, and their actions will result from active cognitive processes based on stored mental representations (James & James, 1989). Weick describes two elements of sensemaking: scanning and interpreting.

Scanning refers to the process of gathering information from the external and internal environment which might influence future performance. Given how complicated the world is, scanning is inevitably a process of sampling, and this involves selectivity in what is attended to. Moreover, selectivity is not random, but rather is motivated. For example, we do not notice adverts for particular types of product (for example, car insurance or hair treatment products) until we are "in the market" for them; then we are surprised how many there are. In an important sense, selectivity in scanning the environment is constrained by our cognitive frameworks. These frameworks make it possible to see some things, but also create blind spots that make it impossible to see other things (just as a colour-blind person sees red and green as the same colour).

Weick (1995) gives the startling example of the Battered Child Syndrome which was first described by John Caffey (a radiologist) in 1946. This report was ignored for many years by paediatricians because it was not published in a paediatrics journal (the not-invented-here syndrome). There were six reported cases in 1946; 749 cases in 1961; and later estimates were of 7,000 cases (1967), 60,000 cases (1972), and 500,000 cases (1976). The increase in reported cases presumably reflects not a sudden growth in the damaging actions of parents but rather a growing recognition of the syndrome by professionals and better reporting channels. In other words, experts were blind to something that had always been happening, presumably because their sensemaking of intimate relationships within families could not conceive of harm done by those closest to a child. They then resisted evidence because it came from a source outside their own professional field; but over time became sensitive to the phenomenon and started to scan the cases they dealt with from day to day.

The second element of sensemaking is *interpreting*, the process of ascribing meaning by developing or applying ways of comprehending the meaning of information. Bartlett (1932) showed how people's understanding and memory for events is shaped by their expectations. When he asked them to recall a story that they had heard, their reconstructions often included things which were not present in the original so that the story they told "made sense". They used different words from those in the original in order to capture the sense of a story. They changed the order of events to give more coherence to their own narrative than perhaps there was in the original. They added elements to the story to reflect associations from their own memories of similar events. They left out elements of the story that seemed not to be important. All in all, our memory does not record events as does a camera. Rather, memory is orderly in that we see organisation in events even where it is not there; memory is motivated in that we see what we choose to see. Furthermore, memory is active in that we construct our interpretive world from what we see and from our own existing memories. At the individual level, this process of constructing our interpretive world has been described in various ways (Table 3.6, adapted from Eysenck & Keane, 2000). Each captures a different facet of the process of meaning-making, but they all have these key features in common.

Table 3.6: Ways of thinking about ways of thinking.

- *Mental models* — an organised network for describing the relationships between concepts
- *Frames of reference* — putting events into frameworks
- *Schemas* — structured clusters of concepts for people or events
- *Implicit personality theories, prototypes* — theories about the behaviour of self and others
- *Scripts* — a time-based pattern for expected ways of behaving in social situations

---

Source: Adapted from Eysennck and Keane (2000).

Cognitive Tasks During Organisational Change

Isabella (1990) developed a model of the cognitive processes associated with organisational change. She found evidence for four stages and argues that each stage has a construed reality, an interpretative task and a predominant frame of reference. The *construed reality* includes facts, rumours, gossip, conventional explanations, past events, symbols, all of which are used by organisational members as evidence in making sense of their experience. The second element is the *interpretative task* and this varies through the change process. Before a change, the major task is one of conceiving of alternative futures, and anticipating potential gains and losses. During the change itself, the major task is one of reconstructing ways of thinking to take account of altered organisational realities. After the change, the task involves evaluation of the change itself and reflection on its personal and organisational impact. The third element is the *predominant frame of reference* which is a coherent picture for evaluating and interpreting information. Isabella (1990) says that as change unfolds, the frame of reference shifts. This means that people "involved in a change need to undergo an alteration of their cognitive structures". Through interviewing managers about key organisational events, such as acquisitions, relocations, and reorganisation, she found that interpretations unfold in four stages (see Table 3.7).

The four distinctive stages — anticipation, confirmation, culmination, and aftermath — were linked to the process of change. In the *anticipation* phase before change occurs, the construed reality is one of rumours, and partial knowledge which is scattered and incoherent. Early in the change process itself, the *confirmation* phase is characterised by the way in which events are explained by those experiencing them in terms of familiar or conventional explanations with reference to past similar events. Next, the *culmination* phase involves a process of reconstructing interpretations of events with exposure to both past experiences and new ones. Finally, the *aftermath* phase concentrates attention on the consequences of change, with a new frame of reference which accounts for strengths and weaknesses in the post-change environment, in a construed reality of winners

Table 3.7: Four stages in organisational change processes.

- *Anticipation* — rumours of what might happen
- *Confirmation* — explaining the past in terms of the familiar
- *Culmination* — reconstructing interpretations of events
- *Aftermath* — reflections on a new frame of reference

Source: After Isabella (1990).

and losers. A trigger event initiate the transition from one stage to another and are fuelled by the manager's personalisation of the event. The model show how the process of managerial interpretations shift and how the construed reality change as new events, facts or questions arise (Isabella, 1990).

Attributional Processes

Within an organisation or work group, construction of reality and interpretations arise from interaction processes. A socio-cognitive model of organisational culture has been used by Silvester, Anderson, and Patterson (1999) to understand the dynamic and collective process of sensemaking in organisations and groups. The basic element of their approach is an analysis of individuals' causal attributions. Attributions are causal explanations which explain an event in terms of prior causal agents. Attributions vary in their character (see Table 3.8): they vary in their breadth of impact (global versus specific), in their degree of enduringness (stable versus unstable), in whether they originate within the person or the environment (internal versus external), and in how much they are open to influence by the individual or group (controllable versus uncontrollable). Silvester et al. argue that causal attributions like these are fundamentally important parts of human meaning-making. When people encounter novel or potentially threatening events they make causal attributions which are stored as schemas in long-term memory. The character of the attributions people make will have very powerful consequences for the process of change. People tend to attribute positive events to their own achievements ("I'm a competent person" — an internal attribution), while they will tend to attribute negative events to situational characteristics ("the photocopier broke down" — an external attribution). The situational attribution for negative events serves to deflect blame from the individual, and this defensive strategy might be very important in an organisation where blame is the predomi-

Table 3.8: Dimensions of causal attributions.

- *Global* versus *specific*: the breadth of impact of the perceived cause across the organisation
- *Stable* versus *unstable*: how enduring the cause is perceived to be
- *Internal* versus *external*: the origin of causes, either within the person or group (internal) or within the environment (external)
- *Controllable* versus *uncontrollable*: how much the cause can be controlled by the person or group

nant mode of managing (a so-called blame culture). However, such attributional styles can be potent barriers to achieving change, since external attributions for negative events devolve the individual of responsibility for achieving a different outcome the next time. Achieving individual acceptance of responsibility for mistakes without allocating blame is fundamental to real change during mergers.

Although attributions take place at an individual level, they will be communicated to other members in a group so that they become part of a shared reality and a common understanding of causes of events can be created. Silvester et al.'s study found evidence for shared attributions that had become part of the organisational culture, the construed reality (Isabella, 1990) of taken-for-granted causal explanations for past events which are then applied to new circumstances. They also found that cultures are not homogeneous: stakeholder groups in the organisational change process differed considerably in their causal attributions. Most disturbingly, they found that the main change agents (the trainers in a company-wide culture-change programme) were most negative in their attributions about the potential for change.

Cognitive Aspects of Identity Processes

Identity processes can work both retrospectively and prospectively. *Prospectively*, expectations guide future choices and decisions, and can be powerful as self-fulfilling prophecies. Thus, expectations of what might be can blind organisational actors to alternative possibilities such that they can unwittingly prove themselves right by bringing to pass what they expect to happen. *Retrospectively*, identity processes can be potent explanations for the past — a means of understanding where we have been and making sense of it (Weick, 1995).

Looking forwards: Expectations as drivers for behaviour   Interpretations and expectations are important as they provide the basic elements of schemas for making sense of the organisational environment (Thomas, Clark, & Gioia, 1993; Weick, 1995). The processes involved in sensemaking proposed by Weick (1984) will be grounded on the employees existing cognitive structures. The gathering of information, interpretation of new information and the following actions will all be driven by how the employees attach meaning to the organisations.

We can illustrate these processes through an example of the merger of the two regional head offices of the Old(a) and the Old(b) organisations responsible for social insurance in the south of Sweden. The personal construct theory was applied to study the employees expectations of the merger by Dackert, Jackson, Brenner, and Johansson (2002). A person's construction system is composed of a finite number of dichotomous constructs concerning specific elements. The elements in the merger context was the two old organisations and the expected new organisation. The constructs were elicited through letting representative individuals compare the three organisations in dyads repeatedly. Accordingly, the construct will be built up of the individuals own words and reflect their mental representations. Many of the elicited constructs were similar, and it was possible to extract a set of constructs that covered the universe of meaning for the individuals involved in the merger of head offices. Further exploration of these constructs generated four dimensions — people-centredness, effectiveness, decentralised control, and workload demand — as relevant in the employee interpretation and expectation of the change process.

The two employee groups agreed in their expectations of the new merged organisation to be significantly different from the Old(b) organisation and to be more like Old(a) with regard to people-centredness. In terms of efficiency, the merged organisation was expected to be more like the Old(a) organisation particularly by the Old(a) employees. In centralised control and workload demand the same pattern was partly found. The result showed that the new merged organisation in most aspects was expected to share characteristics of both the original organisations and that, as a whole, the Old(a) organisation was expected to be dominant in the merger process.

Study participants based their view of the expected dominance of Old(a) in the relationship on three factors. Firstly, the larger size of the Old(a) organisation was emphasised. Although Larson and Lubatkin (2001) found no evidence that the relative size of the merging organisations affected the integration, participants in this study clearly expected the difference in size to be important. Secondly, the integration process and in particular the outcome of the earlier merger involving Old(a) was brought up. Interviewees described Old(a) as having "swallowed" its former merger partner seven years earlier. Finally, the fact that the Old(a) director was appointed director for the new merged organisation and his leadership style was stressed. In this respect, the expectations of the study participants are in accordance with literature suggesting that post-merger integration is critically dependent on the ways in which this process is managed.

To conclude, the employees' expectations of the new merged organisation was based on their perceptions of the two merger partners. Further, the employees expected one of the organisations to be dominant in the integration process. A question that has to be asked then is if these expectations will shape perceptions and behaviour in the coming integration process. Following Weick (1984) and James (1989), we can conclude that they probably do as the employees' sensemaking of further information and events are based on their expectations.

Looking back: constructing the past as a guide to the future A large body of research shows that making sense of the past is just as important as expectations about the future; indeed Weick has argued that all sense-making is retrospective. Explanations and attributions are not self evident; they are the result of motivated cognitive processes. Consider the negotiations between individuals from two companies (a Japanese engineering company and a British potential customer) seeking to reach agreement on a joint venture. When a difficulty arises in a negotiation over a decision to be made, there are always choices for how to account for that difficulty. Given that every individual is a member of multiple social categories, attributions made by someone might be based on a number of alternatives, including gender, ethnic origin, professional or organisational group membership. All of these attributions are examples of *de-personalisation* (Hogg & Terry, 2000) in so far as they account for individuals' behaviour on the basis that they act not as an individual but as a member of a social category. Such attributions serve powerful purposes — they make the past understandable and they give a basis for making the future predictable (even when the attributions are wrong). In both ways, they give a mechanism for managing uncertainty and this is important to most people.

Cartwright and Cooper (1996) found that an initially positive attitude to the merger was soon transformed into a them-and-us attitude. Similarly, Buono, Bowditch, and Lewis (1985) found that soon after a merger the two employee groups began to perceive their merger partner as an invading enemy and became increasingly nostalgic for their prior organisation. These findings are replicated elsewhere (Terry et al., 2001; Terry, Giessner, McKimmie, & Doherty, 2003) and indicate very strongly how difficult it is to overcome positive regard for the past (even when the reality was not so rosy) in favour of benefits of a merged organisation. However, there is room for optimism from a study by Gaertner, Dovidio, and Bachman (1996) of a bank merger. They found that intergroup bias was reduced by contact between partners of equal status, by the creation of positive interdependence between groups, and by the presence of many opportunities for interaction.

Nahavandi and Malekzadeh (1988) studied adaptation processes in mergers using an adapted version of an acculturation model from cross-cultural psychology developed by Berry (1980). They define acculturation as "changes induced in (two cultural) systems as a result of the diffusion of cultural elements in both directions" (p. 217). Similarly, Larsson and Lubatkin (2001) proposed that acculturation is the outcome of a process which forms a jointly determined culture. Four kinds of change can be distinguished (see Table 3.9) which vary in the extent of change involved and in the relative influence of each merger partner in the change process. Both *integration* and *assimilation* involve a high degree of change: integration involves change for both partners, while assimilation reflects one partner incorporating the other. The other two modes are scarcely change at all. *Separation* implies a coming together of two organisations, but a merger in name only where the original partners continue to work independently in their own ways. Finally, *deculturation* implies a destructive process where merger dismantles prior cultures without replacing them in any constructive way.

Vaara (2002, 2003; Vaara & Tienari, 2002) use a narrative approach to understanding the processes underlying post-merger integration. Following the work of Isabella described earlier, he and colleagues argue for the role of success and failure stories constructed by organizational members as powerful determinants of the extent of integration following a merger. Narrative stories build new identities because they give organisational actors alternative ways of defining their different pasts that can then form the basis for their common future reflecting the merged organisation rather than the perspectives that they did not share in the past. Such story-building becomes particularly important when difficulties are encountered in a merger or a joint venture. Thus, Vaara (2002) reports interviews from senior managers involved in eight Finnish–Swedish mergers, and gives a number of examples of the discourses which actors employ in accounting for failure. Three discourses in particular are of interest here. In the *cultural* discourse, actors are identified with different sides representing nationalities, cultures or organisational sub-cultures. Merger becomes an exercise in national or cultural rivalry, and in one instance is compared explicitly to an ice-hockey game where "we (the Finnish managers) tried to make sure that the Swedes would not win" (p. 231). The *role-bound* discourse attributes blame to major players in the merger adopting (or failing to adopt) specific roles which constrained their actions, or led them to act in ways which were inappropriate.

Table 3.9: Acculturation modes during a merger.

- *Integration* — assimilation of structures with neither side dominating the other
- *Assimilation* — one organisation willingly adopts the culture and systems of the other
- *Separation* — the two organisations maintain their own culture and systems, and continue to function independently
- *Deculturation* — partners value neither their own culture, practices and systems nor the other's ➔ breakdown of the cooperation

---

Source: Adapted from Nahavandi and Malekzadeh (1988).

Finally, the *individualistic* discourse appealed to personality or other attributes of the person.

The cultural discourse described by Vaara is based on a rather unconventional way of thinking about culture itself. Traditional approaches such as that of Hofstede (1980, 1991) tend to reify culture leading to the view expressed by, for example, Cartwright and Cooper (1993a, 1993b) who argue that the failure of mergers can be accounted for by incompatibility between the cultures of merger partners. What we propose here is that cultural characteristics are not forces which act to either aid or hinder mergers and joint ventures. Instead, they are cognitive constructions which serve motivational purposes in allowing organisational members to use culture as an explanation for events. Salk (1997) develops the concept of culture as explanation in her work on social identity in relation to IJVs: "attributions are more usefully seen as socially negotiated constructs, used by informants in defining their relationship to the venture setting and its members." (pp. 69–70) Managers in IJVs have choices in which identities they bring to bear on interpreting situations and enacting identities within the JV. Especially early in the encounter stage of forming a joint venture, actors are likely to engage in stereotyping: using national culture as an explanation for the behaviour of others. She gives an example of this in a British–Italian JV where the explanations offered by members of both organisations clearly did not fit the behaviour that they were describing.

What social categories people use as explanations for past events or justifications for their actions can be very important. For instance, a powerful way of saving face after failure of an activity can be an explanation in terms of stable attributes of others or of the situation (and therefore factors which could be expected to difficult to change). An appeal to national cultural differences can also serve this purpose. The power of cognition in accounting for behaviour is such that some authors have suggested that culture (national and organisational) may not be important in the traditional way often found in the literature. By contrast, Salk (1997) suggests that we must "entertain the possibility that use by the social actors of terms related to "culture" may have little or nothing to do with measurable or independently observable differences in member values or behaviours" (p. 53).

In this perspective, culture is continuously enacted by organisational members and the concept is calculatedly mobilised in support of specific organisational purposes in order to account for successes or failures. In a particularly striking study, Wilkof, Brown, and Selsky (1995) describe accounts by staff from two joint venture partners of specific critical incidents within a relationship which had been very troubled. The stories involved elaborate explanations for the troubled relationship which made reference to alleged national characteristics, and contained specific elements which had acquired deep significance in the explanations offered. However, "not only did the stories not match most of the time, it did not even sound like people were talking about the same incident or the same companies." (p. 377) In this way, culture became a convenient peg on which to hang the partners' justifications for the failure of their partnership, rather than a causal factor responsible for that failure.

Conclusion

In this chapter, we have dealt with social identity processes to shed light on the "employee problems" that has been said to contribute to the failure of many mergers and joint ventures. Identity is to a large extent constructed through social categorisation and group membership, according to Social Identity Theory (Hogg & Terry, 2000). Mergers involves changes in group membership and key issues are likely to arise out of the differences in prior identity in relation to the creation of a new identity. Social boundaries are fundamental to identity by making clear belongingness to a group or an organisation. During mergers and joint ventures old boundaries has to be shifted to form the basis of a new categorisation. An us-and-them thinking has to be replaced of a we-thinking. However, characteristics of the categorisation process can hinder such integration through focusing on features that differentiate between the groups and seeing people as typifying a group and not as unique individuals. On the individual level, the group identification processes are fundamental in order to protect and to promote self-esteem. The changes in group membership can be perceived as threatened by the employees depending on the relative status of the groups and the possibility to move from one group to another. Members of an organisation that is seen as high-status may be threatened if members from an organisation perceived having lower status can move to their group. On the other hand, members from the low-status organisation may see the merger as favourable if they can higher their status and self-esteem through moving to the high-status group.

Cognitive processes as construction of meaning accompanying the identity processes. People involved in a merger or joint venture try to make sense of what happens through interpretation of the event and the process in light of their past experiences. Mental representations is built up which is partly personal and partly shared by the members in a group or organisation. The construction of reality is an ongoing process during the change and imply that the people involved need to alter their cognitive structure. In the construction process people use past experience to form expectations of what will happen in the future and looking back through constructing the past as a guide for the future. Differences in culture is often stressed as a source of failure, especially in international mergers and joint ventures, of both employees and in traditional approaches to culture research (Cartwright & Cooper, 1993a, 1993b). The incompatibility between the cultures is seen as the cause of failure. However, cultural characteristics can also be seen as cognitive constructions that is used of the people involved in the merger in accounting for failure (Vaara, 2002). The tendency to emphasise cultural differences has been suggested to be a part of the creation of social identities (Salk, 1997). From that point of view the use of national cultures, often in a stereotyping way, has more to do with social identity and self-esteem than with actual differences and behaviour of the groups.

Finally, some practical implication can be drawn from an identity perspective on mergers and joint ventures. To pave the way for new categorisations it seems important to blur the old borders between the organisations before shifting them. Otherwise the old boundaries may remain within the new organisation. Pre-merger contacts can also reduce in-group bias and facilitate the construction of a new common identity. However, power issues have to be considered and dealt with in the interaction between the groups in order to minimise threats to personal and social identity.

References

Adams-Webber, J. R. (1970). Actual structure and potential chaos: Relational aspects of progressive variations within a personal construct system. In: D. Bannister (Ed.), *Perspectives in personal construct theory* (pp. 32–46). London: Academic Press.

Albert, S., & Whetten, D. A. (1985). Organizational identity. In: B. M. Staw, & L. L. Cummings (Eds), *Research in organizational behavior* (Vol. 14, pp. 179–224). Greenwich, CT: JAI Press.

Arrow, H., McGrath, J. E., & Berdahl, J. L. (2000). *Small groups as complex systems: Formation, coordination, development, and adaptation.* Thousand Oaks: Sage.

Bartlett, F. (1932). *Remembering: A study in experimental and social psychology.* Cambridge: Cambridge University Press.

Berry, J. W. (1980). Social and cultural change. In: H. C. Triandis, & R. W. Brislin (Eds), *Handbook of cross-cultural psychology. Social psychology* (Vol. 5, pp. 211–299). Boston: Allyn & Bacon.

Breakwell, G. M. (1983). Identities and conflicts. In: G. M. Breakwell (Ed.), *Threatened identities.* Chichester: Wiley.

Buono, A. F., Bowditch, J. L., & Lewis, J. W. (1985). When cultures collide: The anatomy of a merger. *Human Relations, 38*(5), 477–500.

Cartwright, S., & Cooper, C. L. (1990). The impact of mergers and acquisitions on people at work: Existing research and issues. *British Journal of Management, 1*, 65–76.

Cartwright, S., & Cooper, C. L. (1993a). The psychological impact of merger and acquisition on the individual: A study of building society managers. *Human Relations, 46,* 299–326.

Cartwright, S., & Cooper, C. L. (1993b). The role of cultural compatibility in successful organisational marriage. *Academy of Management Executive, 7*(2), 57–69.

Cartwright, S., & Cooper, C. L. (1996). *Managing mergers, acquisitions and strategic alliances: Integrating people and cultures.* Oxford: Butterworth-Heinemann.

Cartwright, S., & Hudson, S. L. (2000). Coping with mergers and acquisitions. In: R. J. Burke, & C. L. Cooper (Eds), *The organization in crisis. Downsizing, restructuring, and privatization* (pp. 269–283). Oxford: Blackwell Publishers.

Child, J., & Faulkner, D. (1998). *Strategies of cooperation: Managing alliances, networks, and joint ventures.* Oxford: Oxford University Press.

Cooley, C. H. (1909). *Social organisation: A study of the larger mind.* New York: Schribner.

Cross, R. L., Yan, A. M., & Louis, M. R. (2000). Boundary activities in 'boundaryless' organizations: A case study of a transformation to a team-based structure. *Human Relations, 53*(6), 841–868.

Dackert, I., Jackson, P. R., Brenner, S. O., & Johansson, C. R. (2002). Eliciting and analysing employees' expectations of a merger. *Human Relations, 56,* 705–725.

Davies, G., Chun, R., Da Silva, R., & Roper, S. (2002). *Corporate reputation and competitiveness.* London: Routledge.

Davy, J. A., Kinicki, A., Kilroy, J., & Scheck, C. (1988). After the merger: Dealing with people's uncertainty. *Training and Development Journal, 42,* 56–62.

Dicken, P. (2003). *Global shift* (4th ed.). London: Sage.

Eysenck, M. W., & Keane, M. T. (2000). *Cognitive psychology: A student's handbook.* Hove: Psychology Press.

Gaertner, S. L., Dovidio, J. F., & Bachman, B. A. (1996). Revisiting the contact hypothesis: The induction of a common ingroup identity. *International Journal of Intercultural Relations, 20,* 271–290.

Gersick, C. J. G. (1989). Marking time; predictable transitions in task groups. *Academy of Management Journal, 32,* 274–309.

Gersick, C. J. G. (1991). Revolutionary change theories: A multilevel exploration of the punctuated equilibrium paradigm. *Academy of Management Review, 16*(1), 10–36.

Gruenfeld, D. H., & Hollingshead, A. B. (1993). Sociocognition in work groups: The evolution of group integrative complexity and its relation to task and performance. *Small Group Research, 24*(3), 383–405.

Hofstede, G. (1980). *Culture's consequences: International differences in work-related values.* Newbury Park, CA: Sage.

Hofstede, G. (1991). *Culture and organisations: Software of the mind.* Maidenhead: McGraw-Hill.

Hogg, M. A., & Terry, D. J. (2000). Social identity and self-categorization processes in organizational contexts. *Academy of Management Review, 25*(1), 121–140.

Isabella, L. A. (1990). Evolving interpretations as a change unfolds: How managers construe key organisational events. *Academy of Management Journal, 33*(1), 7–41.

James, L. A., & James, L. R. (1989). Integrating work environment perceptions: Explorations into the measurement of meaning. *Journal of Applied Psychology, 74*, 739–751.

Jetten, J., Branscombe, N. R., & Spears, R. (2002). On being peripheral: Effects of identity insecurity on personal and collective self-esteem. *European Journal of Social Psychology, 32*(1), 105–123.

Johnson, S. (2001). *Emergence: The connected lives of ants, brains, cities and software.* London: Allen Lane The Penguin Press.

Kauffman, S. (2000). *Investigations.* Oxford: Oxford University Press.

Kelly, G. A. (1955). *Principles of personal construct psychology.* New York: Norton.

Killing, J. P. (1983). *Strategies for joint venture success.* London: Croom Helm.

Klimoski, R. J., & Mohammed, S. (1994). Team mental model: Construct or metaphor? *Journal of Management, 20*(2), 403–437.

Larsson, R., & Lubatkin, M. (2001). Achieving acculturation in mergers and acquisitions: An international case survey. *Human Relations, 54*(12), 1573–1607.

Lembke, S., & Wilson, M. G. (1998). Putting the "team" into teamwork: Alternative theoretical contributions for contemporary management practice. *Human Relations, 51*(7), 927–944.

Lovell, A. (2002). Ethics as a dependent variable in individual and organisational decision making. *Journal of Business Ethics, 37*(2), 145–163.

Nahavandi, A., & Malekzadeh, A. R. (1988). Acculturation in mergers and acquisitions. *Academy of Management Review, 13*, 79–90.

Parker, S. K., Jackson, P. R., Sprigg, C. A., & Whybrow, A. C. (1998). *Organisational interventions to reduce the impact of poor work design.* London: HSE Publications.

Parker, S. K., Wall, T. D., & Jackson, P. R. (1997). "That's not my job": Developing flexible employee work orientations. *Academy of Management Journal, 40*, 899–929.

Salk, J. (1997). Partners and other strangers: Cultural boundaries and cross-cultural encounters in international joint venture teams. *International Studies of Management and Organisation, 26*, 48–72.

Schultz, M., Hatch, J. M., & Larsen, M. H. (Eds). (2000). *The expressive organisation: Linking identity, reputation and the corporate brand.* Oxford: Oxford University Press.

Scott, S. G., & Lane, V. R. (2000). A stakeholder approach to organisational identity. *Academy of Management Review, 25*, 43–62.

Silvester, J., Anderson, N. R., & Patterson, F. (1999). Organizational culture change: An inter-group attributional analysis. *Journal of Occupational and Organizational Psychology, 72*, 1–23.

Simon, H. A. (1996). *The architecture of complexity* (3rd ed.). Cambridge, MA: MIT Press.

Tajfel, H. (1981). *Human groups and social categories: Studies on social psychology.* Cambridge: Cambridge University Press.

Tajfel, H. (1982). Social psychology of intergroup relations. *Annual Review of Psychology, 33*, 1–39.

Terry, D., Giessner, S., McKimmie, B., & Doherty, N. (2003). Responses to a merger: The effects of premerger group status and integration pattern. *Australian Journal of Psychology, 55*, 64–64.

Terry, D. J., Carey, C. J., & Callan, V. J. (2001). Employee adjustment to an organizational merger: An intergroup perspective. *Personality and Social Psychology Bulletin, 27*(3), 267–280.

Thomas, J. B., Clark, S. M., & Gioia, D. A. (1993). Strategic sensemaking and organizational performance — linkages among scanning, interpretation, action, and outcomes. *Academy of Management Journal, 36*(2), 239–270.

Turnley, W. H., & Feldman, D. C. (1999). The impact of psychological contract violations on exit, voice, loyalty, and neglect. *Human Relations, 52*(7), 895–922.

Vaara, E. (2002). On the discursive construction of success/failure in narratives of post-merger integration. *Organization Studies, 23*(2), 211–248.

Vaara, E. (2003). Post-acquisition integration as sensemaking: Glimpses of ambiguity, confusion, hypocrisy, and politicization. *Journal of Management Studies, 40*(4), 859–894.

Vaara, E., & Tienari, J. (2002). Justification, legitimization and naturalization of mergers and acquisitions: A critical discourse analysis of media texts. *Organization, 9*(2), 275–304.

Weick, K. (1984). Management of organizational change among loosely coupled elements. In: P. Goodman (Ed.), *Change in organizations*, (pp. 375–408). San Francisco: Jossey-Bass.

Weick, K. E. (1995). *Sensemaking in organisations.* Thousand Oaks, CA: Sage.

Wilkof, M., Brown, D., & Selsky, J. (1995). When the stories are different: The influence of corporate culture mismatches on interorganizational relations. *Journal of Applied Behavioral Science, 31*(3), 373–388.

Yan, A., & Louis, M. R. (1999). Migration of organizational functions to the work unit level: Buffering, spanning, and bringing up boundaries. *Human Relations, 52*(1), 25–47.

Chapter 4

Global Human Resource Management

Paul Sparrow

The Nature of Global Human Resource Management

The aim of this chapter is to provide a review of the current psychological knowledge in some key areas of global human resource management (HRM) and to illustrate the applicability of this knowledge to organisations. In this chapter, I shall

- outline the main territory of global HRM based upon a recent research project;
- signal areas of important academic development that lie at the intersection of HRM and other fields of study;
- provide a framework in which to consider traditional work that relates national culture to HRM (this topic is covered in more detail by Bond, this volume);
- introduce some new developments around the topic of international mindset; and
- signal the changing focus of work around the development of international management teams and the need to change our analytical frames.

First, we must understand the territory to which psychological knowledge must contribute. Global HRM is a rapidly changing field. A couple of years ago, the Chartered Institute of Personnel and Development commissioned research to study the impact of globalisation on the HR profession. Globalisation processes may be studied at the level of industry, firm and function. Studies of industry-level globalisation direct attention at factors, such as levels of international trade, intensity of international competition, product standardisation, presence of international competitors in geographic markets, cost drivers and location of value-adding activities (Johansson & Yip, 1994; Makhija, Kim, & Williamson, 1997; Morrison & Roth, 1992). Firm-level globalisation studies consider factors, such as foreign subsidiary

Developments in Work Organizational Psychology
Copyright © 2006 by Elsevier Ltd.
All rights of reproduction in any form reserved
ISBN: 0-08-044467-9

sales, export sales, level of foreign assets, number of foreign subsidiaries, and level and dispersion of top manager's international experience (Ramaswamy, Kroeck, & Renforth, 1996; Sullivan, 1994, 1996). Functional-level globalisation studies concentrate on different mechanisms of people, information, formalisation or centralisation-based integration, organisation design features and the development of attitudinal orientations (Kim, Park, & Prescott, 2003; Malbright, 1995). The CIPD research examined primarily function level phenomena inside organisations (see Sparrow, Brewster, & Harris, 2004; Brewster, Sparrow, & Harris, 2005, for an overview of the findings). The project examined the differences between international HRM (IHRM) and HRM in a domestic context and the extent to which IHRM is more closely linked to the business agenda than domestic HRM. It asked if we could build on existing models of IHRM in order to better capture the complexity of modern approaches to the topic? In order to build appropriate insights, the methodology utilised four inter-linked approaches:

- Seven longitudinal process case studies aimed at revealing *within-firm processes* associated with globalisation, involving 63 interviews over an 18-month period with HR directors, business managers and service providers, attendance at key HR strategy workshops within the organisations, use of internal documentation and external press search. Fieldwork was conducted in the UK, France, Belgium, the Netherlands and Singapore.
- Web-based questionnaire of 732 HR professionals designed to examine the level of "role internationalisation" and associated knowledge requirements.
- Survey of senior HR practitioners in 64 of the Times top 200 companies to explore *across-firm factors* associated with globalisation by examining international strategy, structure and HR policies pursued.
- Seven design, research-sharpening and policy validation workshops with other firms and institutional bodies.

One of the central findings of the research was that an underlying shift in global thinking can be seen in the actions of several leading multinational and domestic firms. They are being driven by the need to remain innovative in what may be contracting and rationalising markets, or markets that are being shaken up by new entrants and new competitive behaviour. Initiatives aimed at improving temporal, functional or financial flexibility are being introduced side by side with integrated programmes intended to link work practices to the need to deliver radical cost improvements. In increasing flexibility, firms also want to change the nature of employee identification and their sense of involvement, and this changed identity knows few national borders. The seven firm-level contexts examined reveal the issues typically being dealt with by HRM functions in a global context. They are pursuing several different models of IHR organisation and their IHR functions face a number of challenges. In particular, IHR functions have to help their firms manage the

- consequences of global business process redesign, the pursuit of a global centre of excellence strategy and the global re-distribution and re-location of work that this often entails;
- absorption of acquired businesses, merging of existing operations on a global scale, the staffing of strategic integration teams, and attempts to develop and harmonise core HR processes within these merged businesses;
- rapid start-up of international operations and organisation development as they mature through different stages of the business life cycle;
- changing capabilities of international operations with increased needs for up-skilling of local operations and greater complexity;
- need to capitalise on the potential that technology affords the delivery of HR through shared services, on a global basis, while ensuring that local social and cultural insights are duly considered when it is imperative to do so;
- changes being wrought in the HR service supply chain as the need for several intermediary service providers is being reduced, and as web-based HR provision increases;
- articulation of appropriate pledges about the levels of performance that can be delivered to the business by the IHR function, and the requirement to meet these pledges under conditions of cost control;
- learning about operating through formal or informal global HR networks, acting as knowledge brokers across international operations, and avoiding a "one best way" HR philosophy;
- offering a compelling value proposition to the employees of the firm, and understanding and then marketing the brand that the firm represents across global labour markets that in practice have different values and different perceptions; and
- identity problems faced by HR professionals as they experience changes in the level of decentralisation/centralisation across constituent international businesses. As knowledge and ideas about best practice flow from both the centre to the operations and vice versa, it is not uncommon for HR professionals at all levels of the firm to feel that their ideas are being overridden by those of other nationalities or business systems.

Sparrow, Brewster, and Harris (2004) drew two key conclusions about the role of the HR function in international firms. First, it is clear that the added value of the HR function in an international firm lies in its ability to manage the delicate balance between overall co-ordinated systems and sensitivity to local needs, including cultural differences, in a way that aligns with both business needs and senior management philosophy. Second, it is clear that there is a distinction to be made now between IHRM and global HRM. Traditionally, IHRM has been about managing an international workforce — the expatriates, frequent commuters, cross-cultural team members and specialists involved in international knowledge transfer. Global HRM is not simply about covering these staff around the world. It concerns managing IHRM activities through the application of global rule-sets. Attention needs to be devoted to understanding the ways in which the HR function itself contributes to the process of globalisation.

As Malbright (1995, p. 119) pointed out, inside firms "… Globalisation occurs at the level of the function, rather than the firm". However, the problem is that the HR function is not the one that can be considered, currently, as being highly globalised. Indeed, a range of researchers has found that other departments are much more globalised (Hansen, Nohria, & Tierney, 1999; Kim et al., 2003; Yip, 1992). If other functional activities are being better connected across geographical borders through flows of information that are intended to enhance levels of innovation and learning, then the HR functions that service them are themselves going to be forced to become more globalised. The future of the global HR function will be both heavily dependent upon and will be shaped by the globalising activity of two contiguous functions: information systems and marketing or corporate communications (Sparrow, Brewster, & Harris, 2004). By implication, the syllabus that we must teach and the knowledge base that we must develop will be influenced by thinking that crosses over the "borders" between these fields of knowledge (see Figure 4.1 for an outline of areas of overlapping interests).

Ulrich (2000) has argued that the development of organisational capability — the means through which the firm implements policies and procedures — is a pressing challenge in several areas of international management. In addition to the topics traditionally associated with the management of people, this requires IHR professionals to understand economic and financial capability, strategic/marketing capability and technological capability.

Claiming Expertise in Academic Debates that Cut Across Fields of Study

To illustrate the point, I provide an example of recent work that provides both opportunity and threat to work psychologists from each of the interfaces. The first area of intersection concerns the HRM and Information Systems interface. The increased availability of computing and communication technologies has enabled more geographically dispersed transfer (or export) across the knowledge infrastructure that exists inside firms. Firms have therefore begun to seek better ways

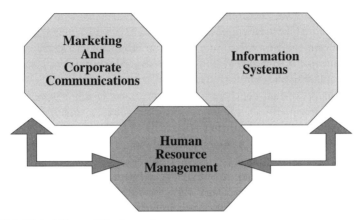

Figure 4.1: The positioning of the global HR function and key power threats/
alliances. Copyright Sparrow et al. (2004).

to invest, manage and harvest their intellectual capital. As such, they have broadly
responded on two fronts (Hodgkinson & Sparrow, 2002). First, they have used
E-commerce initiatives to foster greater efficiency in their transaction processes,
linking internal transactional systems and processes to the outside world, using
different models such as business-to-business or business-to-consumer. Second,
they have used knowledge management initiatives to leverage their intellectual
capital. This has turned attention away from the pursuit of streamlined internal
transactions towards a focus on internal collaborative endeavours that facilitate
the sharing of information and knowledge. The latter endeavour has witnessed the
development and operationalisation of global knowledge management processes.
This has seen a convergence of interest between two fields of study: information
systems and HRM. Unfortunately, however, there has been little discussion about
the phenomenon of global knowledge management between the psychology, economic and knowledge engineering research communities typically active in the
area. Consequently, our understanding of the field is fragmented, full of much
prescription that does not work outside the narrow applications on which the prescription was based, and many analyses are distinctly subject-biased.

Work psychologists, therefore, need to bring their skills to bear on specific issues that they are best equipped to understand, while also relating this to the broader management debate, but clearly have an important role to play in helping understand the role of knowledge management in global firms. Above and beyond better understanding and summation of the different perspectives that exist in the firm (work on individual cognitions is explored later in this chapter) attention must also be given to the integration mechanisms (and the underlying organisational capabilities to manage these effectively) that lead to more effective knowledge acquisition and creation, capture and storage and diffusion and transfer. Sparrow (2005) has discussed the issues associated with centres of excellence, knowledge management systems, expatriates and their advice networks, globally distributed teams and global-expertise networks.

As firms change their design in response to the need to build more international capability, then as part of their natural development they often establish dedicated organisational forms to facilitate this. These include specialised and network-based structures. A series of terms have been used to describe this process of progressive global knowledge transfer: centres of excellence, centres of competence, centres of expertise or communities of practice. I shall adopt the first term here, as it has gained prominence in the global HRM literature. Centres of excellence have a strategic remit to leverage or disseminate knowledge to other parts of the firm (Holm & Pedersen, 2000). In order to succeed their role has to reach beyond local undertakings, must be tightly integrated with their surrounding technical or professional communities, and the centres have both high competence and high use of their competence throughout surrounding units. There is an exciting research agenda surrounding this development, for although there is a growing body of anecdotal evidence to suggest that the phenomenon is increasing among the world's globalising firms, this evidence also suggests that firms are struggling with the managerial issues involved (Frost, Birkinshaw, & Prescott, 2002). Therefore, helping the firm to understand the role, design, competence and leadership needs of its own Centres of Excellence (COEs) is a major challenge and opportunity for global HR functions as understanding of the managerial issues involved is rudimentary. Researchers now need to answer a series of questions. What activities, processes and capabilities might constitute a centre of excellence, how should such organisational forms be mandated (i.e. what has to happen in terms of the capability building investments needed, decision-making autonomy, requisite levels of connectivity to other sources of competence inside the firm, leadership and processes of knowledge management?)

The second area of intersection concerns the marketing/corporate communications and HRM interface. This is an area of study that is proving to be fertile ground. The context of global HRM has drawn attention to the need for firms to attract and retain talent on a global basis, the impact that corporate social responsibility can have on the image and brand of the firm, and the need to find new ways of engaging employees. It has led to the development of employee value propositions — HRM policies that cut across the whole employment experience by treating employees as consumers and asking "why would a highly talented person work in my organisation?" and then developing a tailored proposition that captures the most meaningful experiences for employees and the ability of the firm to satisfy needs, expectations and aspirations (Sparrow & Cooper, 2003).

In practice then, global HRM revolves around the ability of firms to find concepts like this that have "relevance" to managers and employees across several countries — despite the fact that these staff have different values embedded in different national cultures and despite the reality that the global themes pursued by firms may end up being operationalised with some local adaptation. Firms use these *super-ordinate themes* to provide a degree of consistency to their people management worldwide and also as an attempt to socialise employee behaviour and action. Sparrow, Brewster, and Harris (2004) found four themes: the use of strategic performance management processes, the development of global capability or competency-based HR systems, the pursuit of global talent management strategies, and the identification of corporate and global employer brands. It is to the last of these areas that I turn, for this development is bringing the work of marketing and HRM/work psychology academics into closer alignment. Global HR functions have realised that as the world gets smaller, they need to make sure that the way in which they are perceived as a firm is similar wherever they go. What do their consumers want from them, what do current employees think? Firms are now thinking about their external brand image and corporate reputation, and the ways in which their employees can identify with and actively support the brand (Harris & de Chernatony, 2001; Hatch & Schultz, 2001; Davies, Chun, Da Silva, & Roper, 2003; Martin & Beaumont, 2003). Building or defending the corporate brand or reputation has become a major concern in many industries and the financial implications of damage to this brand are significant. The marketing literature has established a connection between brand advantage, customer service and the style of people management in the firm and this has forced firms to think about their external brand image and how their employees can actively support this brand. This has led to the development of interest in *Employer branding* — management of the image of the firm as seen through the eyes of internal and external stakeholders and the creation of consistency and uniformity in the delivery of the brand identity. Employees sit at the interface between the internal and external interface of the firm with its environment and can, through their actions and behaviours, exert a powerful influence on the perception of the brand offering and the corporation (Harris & de Chernatony, 2001).

Currently, we still know little about the linkages between HR and marketing in the brand management process, despite increasing awareness that the HR function is now becoming involved in this work on an international scale, but the agenda is now beginning to emerge.

Martin and Beaumont (2003) note that brands convey a series of strategic advantages for firms in that they: reduce the effort needed by consumers in their search for high quality products; convey psychological rewards such as a sense of belonging and social inclusion; can be infused with emotional values (a personality); can be used to develop a relationship between the consumer and this perceived personality; and the clusters of values that they represent can be used to help an organisation extend into new international markets with related values. The overlapping interests between marketing specialists and work and organisational psychologists is both obvious and (potentially — if there proves to be limited dialogue between the academic disciplines) horrifying. Here people are talking about (and also measuring and managing) things like:

- corporate personalities (climates and cultures),
- processes of organisational identification,
- processes of engagement and emotional attachment, and
- processes of values-fit.

These are all central areas of knowledge to work and organisational psychology. Yet this topic, with a few exceptions, has become the domain of marketing specialists. The advice that work psychologists can give on the above processes is surely of fundamental importance to firms pursuing this agenda.

Insight into Individual Psychological Processes

There is a very wide range of issues to which work psychologists can apply their particular knowledge and expertise. Many of these are covered by other chapters in this book, but it is worth briefly reinforcing two connections. First, the issues of cross-cultural management and the insights that stem from social psychology in this regard (see Bond, this volume) have relevance for many phenomena that are associated with the globalisation of HRM. Second, the psychological contract (see McLean Parks, this volume) has also begun to be studied from a cross-cultural perspective (see for example Sparrow, 1998; Rousseau & Schalk, 2000; Westwood, Sparrow, & Leung, 2001; Kirkul, Lester, & Belgio, 2004).

The factors that lead to distinctive national and local HRM solutions have typically been examined and explained to managers from four frames of reference (Sparrow & Hiltrop, 1997). These are the evolution of the business system and the structure of labour markets; institutional influence on the employment relationship; competence and role of HRM decision-makers; and the influence of national culture on policy preferences. Each framework requires detailed insights. In the field of comparative HRM, psychologists have begun to move beyond the traditional paradigm based in the main on country-level studies towards an examination of some more important questions concerning culturally related behavioural dynamics within individuals.

Within the field of work psychology, this has led to the development of a *new cultural paradigm research tradition* that treats cultural dimensions as quasi-individual difference characteristics (Farh, Earley, & Lin, 1997). Individual-level data show that while people can share or endorse a given cultural value or belief, there is enough natural variability within a country for it to be treated as an important individual difference (Earley & Mosakowski, 1995). Studying individuals within firms, this stream of research has shown how, when measured as an individual-difference variable, cultural values significantly impact three things: the effect of established antecedents on HRM-related behaviour, the actual preferences for the design and conduct of specific HRM practices, and a range of important HRM-related outcomes such as commitment or job involvement. A question that soon began to emerge from this work concerned the relative strength of the effect of cultural value orientations as an individual difference variable. Put simply, just how important are cultural value orientations in relation to other factors? Even if they predict the desirability of a wide range of HRM practices or outcome behaviours, there are lots of other individual factors that can shape the extent to which employees will behave this way. There seems to be some difference in the predictive power of cultural values at the individual level depending on the context within which individuals are studied. Kirkman and Shapiro's (2001) study of teams in two US multinationals found that 9–23% of variance in organisational commitment could be attributed to value orientations. When cultural values have been looked at within indigenous firms in non-US countries, once various demographic factors (age, service, gender and grade) and a range of ways of fitting the person to the organisation were controlled for, it has been found that an individuals' cultural values by themselves explained 16% of organisational commitment of Taiwanese employees (Sparrow & Wu, 1998), from 10 to 16% of the attractiveness (or not) of various HRM practices to them (Nyambegera, Sparrow, & Daniels, 2000) and 19% of the variance in job involvement (Nyambegera, Daniels, & Sparrow, 2001). In order to understand the influence of national culture on HR policy preferences, the links are to be found through a series of mechanisms, including (Sparrow & Hiltrop, 1997).

1. The attitudes and definitions of what makes an effective manager, and the implications of this differential understanding for the qualities and competencies subsequently built into recruitment, training and development systems. Insights

from cross-cultural psychology coupled with knowledge from organisational sociologists about the nature of national business systems, tell us much about our need to understand not just how such HR systems have to be made to operate in a fair way across cultures, but also the extent to which it is possible for firms to internationalise these processes.

2. The conduct and rules governing face-to-face interactions. Any HR process dependent upon the giving of face-to-face feedback is dependent upon cultural factors, such as levels of power distance and uncertainty avoidance. This has implications for the conduct of the process and opens up the need to understand the impact of specific cultural dynamics on practices and processes such as recruitment interviews, communication, negotiation and participation.

3. The expectations of the manager–subordinate relationship. This has significant implications for the design and conduct of performance management systems and expectations about the effectiveness of subsequent motivational processes. These clearly differ across cultures.

4. The operation of pay systems, which are designed around fundamentally different principles across countries, and require us at the individual level to understand the role of factors such as differential concepts of distributive justice and attitudes about socially healthy pay and the individualisation of reward.

5. Mindsets (cognitions) that international managers use to think about strategic issues such as organisational structures, competitive dynamics of their industry, cause-and-effect consequences of specific HR interventions and so forth.

Global HRM managers will then have to become very sophisticated. Each of the above perspectives form part of the context that they must understand if they are to correctly interpret the mindset and actions of local employees (Smith & Meiksins, 1995). Direct links between each set of factors and the HRM policies and practices have been demonstrated. However, two additional complexities are added. First, we are told that we cannot understand the character of these national patterns of HRM unless we also understand the social systems that shape them. Therefore, academic analyses highlight the complex set of interactions between HRM practices and factors such as the role of the market, employment relationship, economic mode of production and labour process, historical and cultural traditions. Second, we are warned to avoid the tendency to ignore the impact of social and organisational action when we analyse national differences. The best way of understanding social systems is to see how they arise out of the activities of firms.

International Mindsets

The agenda is huge and far too broad for a chapter such as this, so I focus attention on the last, but central issue, i.e. the development of an international mindset. Anthropologists and psychologists have begun to examine two central issues within global firms in this regard, which are now considered in more detail:

- the development of an international mindset and knowledge sharing at the individual level, and
- processes of mutual adjustment.

What have we learned about cognitions in the context of the development of an international mindset? Attention has been directed to two main areas:

- the role of expatriates as a mechanism for knowledge transfer and the nature of the international mindset, and
- the nature of culturally embedded knowledge.

The earliest debates on international management strategy argued that strategic capability is ultimately dependent on the "cognitive processes" of international managers and the ability of firms to create a "matrix in the minds of managers" or a transnational mentality (Bartlett & Ghoshal, 1989, p. 195). There are two aspects or components to this mentality (as noted later there is considerable debate about the level of connectiveness between the two):

- Attitudinal/values
- Cognitive structures.

The first component has been described as representing an "attitudinal attribute" of an international orientation. This attitude is assumed to correlate with both the extent and the quality of international experience (Kobrin, 1994). Researchers have attempted to develop measures that correspond to the core dimensions of a managers' thinking about international strategy and international organisation and have then shown how this mindset changes over time. As an example of this kind of work, Murtha, Lenway, and Bagozzi (1998) conducted a study of cognitive change towards a more global mindset in 410 managers over a three-year period within a single multinational organisation. They identified a core value-set or logic that was associated with global operations.

Global managers also need to have a "good" *mental model of how knowledge and information is shared* across the people with whom they need to interact if they are to deliver an important global business process, product or service (Hodgkinson & Sparrow, 2002). In this regard, expatriates have been seen as an important mechanism for knowledge capture and transfer inside global firms.

Recently we have seen both more empirical study and detailed theorising about this phenomenon. Theoretical work includes the application of knowledge transfer theory to the topic of expatriation (Bonache & Brewster, 2001) and modelling of how expatriates help diffuse HRM practices across international borders (Cerdin, 2003). Empirical work has examined: the spread of tacit knowledge within top management teams through "advice networks" (Athanassiou & Nigh, 2000); factors that mitigate against the international transfer of knowledge through expatriates (Smale & Riusala, 2004); the "social capital" that accrues to international managers as a consequence of their boundary spanning roles (Kostova & Roth, 2003); and knowledge sharing through interpersonal cross-border relationships (Makela, 2004).

Attention has then focused on the role played by both social networks and also superior cognitive processes possessed by expatriates. As researchers, we need richer and more complex tools to help both expatriates and members of international teams to be effective. Athanassiou and Nigh (1999, 2000, 2002) argue that this means conceptualizing, measuring, and analysing the complexity of interpersonal processes within global firms by using new methodologies. In their empirical study of 450 employees in 20 global account management teams in a large professional services firm, they looked at the teams through the lens of social capital theory which they operationalised as the assets contained in relationships among people, and the social networks, or configurations of relationships, that hold and carry the social capital (Borgatti, Candace, & Everett, 1998; Lin, 2001) and argued that we must build new models of decision-making processes to facilitate the various modes for global expansion.

A number of researchers, such as Sackmann (1991, 1992) and Zack (1999) have argued that we have to unravel different kinds of cultural knowledge:

- Declarative (or dictionary) knowledge, concerning the way that managers define what something is and how they classify objects.
- Directory (or process or procedural) knowledge, concerning the information that describes how things are done.
- Prescriptive (or recipe) knowledge, concerning information on how things should *preferably* be done.
- Axiomatic knowledge, reflective of fundamental beliefs and attributed causes (why something happens) that cannot be reduced any further.

By implication, an international mindset must display insight into each of these forms or types of knowledge. Not surprisingly, research at the individual level tends to demonstrate the deep persistence of nationality and considerable stickiness in the transfer of knowledge from one culture to another. First, even within an apparently like-minded cadre, team or network, there are often different logics at play. For example, when HR professionals are asked about the perceived relevance of specific HR practices to the competitive advantage of their firms, there is a clear imprint of nationality. Sparrow and Budwhar (1997) analysed the practices of HR professionals around the world. Analysis of the original IBM/Towers Perrin dataset was based on rankings of 38 core HR practices by over 3000 HR practitioners in firms from 12 countries: the U.S., Canada, Australia, U.K., France, Germany, Italy, Japan, Korea, Brazil, Argentina and Mexico (Sparrow, Schuler, & Jackson, 1994). HR practitioners rated the importance of each practice in delivering competitive advantage to their firm. Additional data for 137 Indian HR practitioners were then added by Sparrow and Budwhar (1997). Analysis of the responses across the 13 countries showed that respondents "packaged" HR practices into a series of *recipes* (prescriptions of how they believed things should be done). These recipes concerned: the range of practices that created a sense of empowerment through changes to organisation structure; the range of practices that accelerated the pace at which human resources could be developed within the firm; the practices to develop employee welfare; an efficiency orientation; and a long-term perspective. As noted above, these recipes are the product of a complex range of causal factors including such things as the role of the state, financial sectors, national systems of education and training, labour relations systems and the influence of cultural value orientations (Whitley, 1999) but clearly HR managers had created their unique logics of action that guide management practice in each country. The challenge for work psychologists is to understand which parts of the *recipe knowledge* adopted can be influenced by individual level factors, or more to the point, changed once the manager operates outside the context of their national business system.

The second and equally complex problem is that even when managers apparently agree about the importance and relevance of a particular practice or intervention, there may in practice be very different cognitive maps within the group about the resultant cause-and-effect processes inherent in any intervention. Their axiomatic knowledge, or beliefs, is reflective of very different assumptions about fundamental cause and effect. There are, for example, marked differences in the perceptions around any best practice, i.e. why such a practice might be important and the outcomes anticipated. To explore this, Budwhar and Sparrow (2003) examined the logics and cognitive maps of 48 British and Indian HR professionals around the issues of integration of HR with the business strategy and devolvement of HR to line managers using visual card sorting. Analysis of their causal belief structures, using transcribed data from the interviews and Comparative Cause Mapping Version 2 (CMAP-2) (Laukkanen, 1994, 1996, 1998) identified 571 natural language units, 303 from Indian managers and 268 from British managers for the theme of which there were 432 standard causal units shared by both Indian and British managers. The study showed that at a "macro" level, managerial thinking about the topic of HRM, especially with regard to strategic concepts such as integration and devolvement, was converging. However at a "micro" level there was still a strong divergence in managerial thinking about HRM practices. Although in surveys both sets of HR professionals had rated these policies as being extremely important, when cognitive mapping techniques were used to reveal why they were important and what the assumed cause-and-effect outcomes would be, the professionals were working to fundamentally different logics.

Understanding that there are different logics at play and unravelling the content of such is clearly just the first contribution that work psychologists can help make at this level. In the context of global management, Baba, Gluesing, Ratner, and Wagner (2004) argue that we now must consider deeper issues. Does the evidence suggest that *knowledge (procedural, directory and recipe)* and *belief (i.e. axiomatic knowledge)* should be considered as separate, or must be considered as being intertwined? There are competing views on this question among the cognitive scientists, let alone among international management researchers. Work on team cognition considers that knowledge and belief can be separated out from each other, such that knowledge may be considered as objective and beliefs as more subjective. Set against this, a more social-constructionist perspective considers that all four forms of knowledge noted above *are built into cognitive structures.* The latter perspective assumes that there are complex networks of associations between cognitive schema that reflect actual experience and memory. These cognitive structures are then connected to beliefs, and the beliefs in turn are "validated" by cultural experiences.

This is not just some quaint academic debate. Depending on the answer, firms might be advised by work psychologists to adopt very different tools, techniques, processes and mechanisms. Baba et al. (1994) demonstrated this by questioning the efficacy of globally distributed teams as a vehicle for knowledge sharing. Global teams have created an explosion in the quantity and complexity of inter-relationships among the various national systems that exist inside international firms. Their study however challenges some assumptions about the performance gains that might arise from this co-ordinating mechanism. They examined the process through which the cognitive structures of globally distributed team members became more similar to one another over time, using a longitudinal and ethnographic research method. They studied six teams in a US manufacturing multinational from 1993 to 2001, reporting on a 14-month tracking of one of these teams — a 20 person team operating across one US and six European and Asian sites. Their findings showed that four things were necessary for effective change in cognitions — all of which they argued were missing from global teams (thereby reinforcing the persistence of cognitive differences):

1. observation of others at work,
2. conversations that include joint problem solving,
3. testing of ideas, and
4. resolving of discrepancies.

They showed that beliefs about overall business models were culturally grounded. These beliefs contradicted each other and meant that team members rejected certain aspects of knowledge held by the other (especially declarative and procedural types of knowledge). Knowledge sharing processes in themselves do not produce shared cognitions. Rather, team members have to undergo separate but parallel learning experiences in a common context. Hidden knowledge in remote sites has to be surfaced, often by third party mediators or knowledge brokers. Issues of self-interest and power (historical, cultural and linguistic issues can be exploited by team leaders to further their own agendas) have to be shifted towards more collaborative and task-interdependence work processes. In a cross-cultural context, sharing of knowledge has to include the beliefs upon which evaluative knowledge is based. Using a biological and genetic metaphor, Baba et al. (2004) argue that evaluative knowledge acts as a control gene and regulates whether other forms of more structural knowledge will be switched-on (accepted and integrated into the team's cognitive structure) or switched-off (rejected). It would be nice to see more testing of such a proposition.

In effect, in order to facilitate better global management, we have to help top teams and those individuals involved in the eventual execution of a global strategy to understand the basis of their views. This requires the development of what Martin and Beaumont (2001) and previous researchers have called strategic discourses inside firms — institutional changes that serve to "sediment" messages about any particular change into the mindset of local employees and habitualise other parts of the firm towards a new strategy.

International Teams and Networks

As part of this process of habitualisation, as work psychologists our attention is being directed to a different level of analysis — that of teams, networks and mutual adjustment processes. Social capital theory and social network theory are crucial to our understanding of the management of global knowledge transfer through expatriate networks (Wang & Kanungo, 2004). For an expatriate, the actors in the network can be individuals, such as peer expatriates, local working partners and local friends. These network ties serve as channels for social resources, such as informational, emotional, instrumental and appraisal support (Wang & Kanungo, 2004). Network size, network cultural diversity, network closeness and contact frequency have all been found to influence expatriate psychological well-being (Reagans & McEvily, 2003). For the global HR function, this suggests a change in emphasis away from traditional concerns with expatriate skill and international management competencies towards the need to assist expatriates in the development and quality of their social network.

Research is drawing clear lines of distinction now between global teams and global networks. Global teams — defined as semi-permanent groups that are assembled to facilitate co-operation and communications between headquarters and subsidiaries — have become a central aspect of global organisation operation (Harvey & Novicevic, 2002). Global teams perform three key roles (Mohrman, Cohen, & Mohrman, 1995): collaborative global project initiation; headquarters-subsidiary conflict mediation; and mobilising support in the headquarters for co-operation with a subsidiary. Global networks however are a much more loosely connected group of people or units that interact on a regular but more informal basis. Although these are potentially a far more powerful vehicle for global knowledge management, we still know little about how they can be managed and co-ordinated effectively (Sparrow, 2005).

Global teams have created an explosion in the quantity and complexity of interrelationships among the various national systems that exist inside international firms. As researchers, we need richer and more complex tools to help them be effective and this means conceptualising, measuring and analysing the complexity of interpersonal processes within multinational firms by using new methodologies (Athanassiou & Nigh, 1999, 2000, 2002). In their empirical study of 450 employees in 20 global account management teams in a large professional services firm, they looked at the teams through the lens of social capital theory which they operationalised as the assets contained in relationships among people, and the social networks, or configurations of relationships, that hold and carry the social capital (Borgatti, Candace, & Everett, 1998; Lin, 2001) and argued that we must build new models of decision-making processes to facilitate some of the new modes of global expansion. One of the implications of this is the need to examine mutual adjustment and learning processes, rather than (as psychologists often want to do) directing attention to just within-person processes.

Mutual Adjustment Processes

Most research by work psychologists still seem to adopt a traditional definition of international adjustment (Black, Mendenhall, & Oddou, 1991). From a theoretical perspective, expatriate adjustment models can be classified as being driven by assumptions about learning, stress coping, developmental and personality (Mendenhall, Kűhlman, Stahl, & Osland, 2002). Learning models assume that since expatriate adjustment has to do with learning new skills and techniques of adaptation, the impact of the "other" culture can be seen as a change in behavioural reinforcement contingencies. The major task facing expatriates is to adjust their social skills such that they can learn the salient characteristics of the new environment in terms of new roles, rules and norms of social interaction. Cross-cultural training was designed on the principle that the rules and values of a new culture had to be learned (and a repertoire of cognitive and behavioural schema and responses developed) before adjustment could take place (Black, Mendenhall, & Oddou, 1991). Stress-coping models are based on the assumption that feelings of anxiety, confusion and disruption associated with culture shock are akin to individual stress reactions under conditions of uncertainty, information overload and loss of control. The adjustment reaction is characterised by a variety of symptoms of psychological distress associated with any critical life event. Stress management (coping strategies), rather than stress avoidance is necessary in order for expatriates to engage in necessary behaviours (Aycan, 1997).

Developmental models tend to highlight phases of adjustment (for example contact, disintegration, reintegration, autonomy and independence) that reflect progressive stages of cultural awareness (Adler, 1983). Individuals undertake adaptive activities only when environmental challenges threaten their internal equilibrium. Processes of periodic (rather than linear) disintegration, regrouping/regeneration then higher maturation (progressive inter-cultural sensitivity often also associated with global leadership competence) are an inevitable consequence of exposure to other cultures. In a rare qualitative study of returned expatriate stories, Osland (1995) adapted the metaphor of heroic adventures to note the importance of personal transformations that accompany adjustment processes. Finally, personality-based models argue that such development can in part be predicted by a set of generalisable attitudes and traits, such as adaptation, cross-cultural and partnership skills (Kealey, 1996) or personality variables that are associated with model cross-cultural collaborators. The importance of these pre-requisites depends on the nature of the position and task variables, firm characteristics and host country. Empirical support is however still weak, and again there may be contradictions between what is required for interaction adjustment and work adjustment. Moreover, as Stahl (1998) found in his study of German expatriates assigned to work in Japan and the US, each country may present different problems and conflicts to the expatriates, each requiring different personality-related coping strategies.

In terms of global workforce planning researchers often now prefer to talk about international employees (IEs) rather than the more traditional idea of expatriates and categorisation of international assignee, parent country national, host country national or third country national. International employees include international commuters, employees on long-term business trips, assignees on short term or intermediate term foreign postings, permanent transferees or permanent cadre, international transferees (moving from one subsidiary to another), immigrants, returnees, contract expatriates or virtual international employees in cross-border project teams.

In addition to an increasingly diverse set of international employees, global firms are composed of many diverse, interdependent work groups, such as new product development teams and manufacturing planning teams, all of which have unique decision domains, and develop unique perspectives in response to differential tasks, goals and environments. Although managers can act autonomously within each of these decision domains, they are affected increasingly by each other's actions (Scarbrough, Swan, & Preston, 1999; Staples, Greenaway, & McKeen, 2001). Research attention is therefore shifting to the study of work teams with multi-cultural members (Snow, Snell, Davidson, & Hambrick, 1996). Topics under study include cross cultural communication and team performance (Matveev & Nelson, 2004), emotional conflict (von Glinow, Shapiro, & Brett, 2004) and the role of face-to-face interaction in virtual team performance (Kirkman, Rosen, Tesluk, & Gibson, 2004).

A recent review of work on expatriate adjustment by Mendenhall et al.(2002, p. 169) noted "… most empirical research in the field examines the expatriation process from a one-sided perspective, focusing solely on accounts of expatriate managers. Few empirical studies have included the host country perspective". Researchers have commonly regarded expatriate adjustment as a unidirectional process of one individual adjusting to a foreign environment. However, if we are to move beyond our currently limited views of expatriate adjustment, then we need more research that employs longitudinal designs and that includes the host country perspective on the determinants, processes and outcomes of adjustment. We need more cross-border research regarding what occurs when two diverse groups begin interacting with one another.

We must then conceptualise adjustment as part of a process of mutual adjustment for two reasons:

1. On their assignment expatriates increasingly have to cooperate with host country nationals, and therefore frequently have to rely on their assistance (Zimmermann, Holman, & Sparrow, 2003). Moreover, expatriates often have to work as part of an international team both within the subsidiary, and across different countries.

2. Not all employees on foreign assignment today can be considered as traditional expatriates. For example, Briscoe and Schuler (2004) note that in Dow Chemical Company at any one point in time 1000 employees out of 62,000 are on assignment outside their country of origin, of which 175 are US employees based abroad, 175 are non-US nationals inside the US and 650 are non-US employees based in international locations (transferees). They note: "… the tradition of referring to all international employees as expatriates — or even international assignees — falls short of the need for international HR practitioners to understand the options available … and fit them to evolving international business strategies" (Briscoe & Schuler, 2004, p. 223).

Zimmermann, Sparrow and Holman (2004) have attempted to respond to this challenge. They argued that differences between team members in international teams tend to focus on understanding of work practices (reflecting the work outlined earlier on differences in recipe knowledge across nationalities) and also in the interaction styles associated with cultural differences. These differences may cause difficulties in team collaboration, requiring mutual adjustments in order for the team to function well. Adjustment processes should not then be examined in the isolated context of an expatriate, but should be understood as a dynamic, complex series of mutual interactions. In order to understand mutual adjustment we must study the process by which members of different nationalities achieve a fit and reduced conflict between each other, with regard to their differences in work practices and interaction styles.

116 managers in 11 bi-national teams were studied over a period of one year in two German companies, a bank and an electronics company. The teams consisted of four different combinations of nationalities. At the bank, two German-English teams took part, who were responsible for international business management and for implementing IT systems, respectively. In the electronics company, five German-Indian, two German-Japanese, and two German-Austrian teams were examined. They were tasked with developing software functions for electronic control units to be used in car engines. The findings from in-depth interviews and team observations revealed the mechanisms of mutual adjustment at the level of cognitive processes, attitudes and behaviours of team members. The study also highlighted the special importance of the interaction processes that were identified as the "internal adjustment components", namely, certain types of communication, a change of views through different information sources, evaluations of differences, adjustment attitudes and teaching and control. Once more, this is ripe territory for further exploration and theoretical development.

Conclusion

In this chapter, we have attempted to explore and signal the range of work that does involve — or should involve — work psychologists around the topic of global HRM. I have argued that developments within the field are presenting a rich agenda for research. At the firm level, there are important processes that surround the resultant strategies based on merger, acquisition, organisational redesign and knowledge transfer. Firm-level initiatives are leading to the development of activity that crosses traditional academic boundaries. I used work on knowledge management as an example of interests that cut across the information systems/HRM interface and work on employment branding that cuts across the marketing/corporate communications/HRM interface. The opportunity in such areas is for renewed theoretical development and interesting research work that brings together quite different perspectives. The risks, from the standpoint of the work psychologists, are that organisational interventions be designed around work that is sadly deficient in terms of its psychological base and validity. We must influence the research and practitioner agendas in these areas. At the level of HR practices there is a large agenda of work related to the need to understand how societal and national values influence the design of, signals sent by, perceived messages and enactment of HR policies and interventions. This requires work around international resourcing, development and rewards. It also requires more research on the role of values as an individual variable — an identification of what may be sensibly developed within individuals and what might remain a powerful source of individual difference. We know much about how people differ across countries and the imprint that this leaves upon work practices. We need to know more about what this means for the management of these practices in a more global context. This implies that we must consider in more detail how the psychological dynamics that lead to important employee outcomes operate across different cultural contexts and indeed whether the causal pathways that we have inferred from study of western populations may be generalisable to other work groups. Once we enter this agenda of understanding cross-cultural dynamics, we find that the next important question is to unravel what is really implied by an international mindset. This requires us to bring together our understanding of cognitions and different forms of knowledge with our knowledge about attitudinal and value structures. Put simply, what do I need to know about your world for me to be able to manage you out from my world and how might greater transfer of insight truly be managed? Finally, in this chapter it has been argued that in line with the individual-level attention to what is involved in an international mindset, we need as work psychologists to redirect our attention to the team, network and mutual processes that are necessary to habituate a greater sense of global connectivity in work and inside organisations.

References

Adler, N. J. (1983). Cross-cultural management research: The ostrich and the trend. *Academy of Management Review, 8,* 226–232.

Athanassiou, N., & Nigh, D. (1999). The impact of company internationalisation on top management team advice networks: A tacit knowledge perspective. *Strategic Management Journal, 19*(1), 83–92.

Athanassiou, N., & Nigh, D. (2000). Internationalisation, tacit knowledge and the top management team of MNCs. *Journal of International Business Studies, 31*(3), 471–488.

Athanassiou, N., & Nigh, D. (2002). The impact of the top management team's international business experience on the firm's internationalisation: Social networks at work. *Management International Review, 42*(2), 157–182.

Aycan, Z. (1997). Expatriate adjustment as a multifaceted phenomenon: Individual and organisational level predictors. *The International Journal of Human Resource Management, 8*(4), 434–456.

Baba, M. L., Gluesing, J., Ratner, H., & Wagner, K. H. (2004). The contexts of knowing: Natural history of a globally distributed team. *Journal of Organisational Behaviour, 25*(5), 547–587.

Bartlett, C. A., & Ghoshal, S. (1989). *Managing across borders: The transnational solution.* Boston, MA: Harvard Business School Press.

Black, J. S., Mendenhall, M., & Oddou, G. (1991). Towards a comprehensive model of international adjustment: An integration of multiple theoretical perspectives. *Academy of Management Review, 16,* 291–317.

Bonache, J., & Brewster, C. (2001). Knowledge transfer and the management of expatriation. *Thunderbird International Business Review, 43*(1), 145–168.

Borgatti, S. P., Candace, J., & Everett, M. (1998). Network measures of social capital. *Connections, 21*(2), 27–36.

Brewster, C., Sparrow, P. R. & Harris, H. (2005). Towards a new model of globalising human resource management. *International Journal of Human Resource Management, 16*(6), 953–974.

Briscoe, D., & Schuler, R. S. (2004). *International human resource management* (2nd ed.). New York: Routledge.

Budwhar, P. S., & Sparrow, P. R. (2003). Strategic HRM through the cultural looking glass: Mapping the cognition of British and Indian managers. *Organisation Studies, 23*(4), 599–638.

Cerdin, J.-L. (2003). International diffusion of HRM practices: The role of expatriates. *Beta: Scandinavian Journal of Business Research, 17*(1), 48–58.

Chandrakumara, A., & Sparrow, P. R. (2004). Exploring meaning and values of work orientation as an element of national culture and its impact on HRM policy-practice design choices: Lessons from Sri Lankan domestic and foreign-invested firms. *International Journal of Manpower, 25*(6), 564–589.

Davies, G., Chun, R., Da Silva, R. V., & Roper, S. (2003). *Corporate reputation and competitiveness.* London: Routledge.

Earley, P. C., & Mosakowski, E. (1995). A framework for understanding experimental research in international and intercultural context. In: B. J. Punnett, & O. Shenkar (Eds), *Handbook of international management research*, London: Blackwell.

Farh, J. L., Earley, P. C., & Lin, S. C. (1997). Impetus for action: A cultural analysis of justice and organisational citizenship behavior in Chinese society. *Administrative Science Quarterly*, *42*, 421–444.

Frost, A., Birkinshaw, J. M., & Prescott, C. E. (2002). Centers of excellence in multinational corporations. *Strategic Management Journal*, *23*(11), 997–1018.

Hansen, M. T., Nohria, N., & Tierney, T. (1999). What is your strategy for managing knowledge? *Harvard Business Review*, *77*(2), 106–116.

Harris, F., & de Chernatony, L. (2001). Corporate branding and corporate brand performance. *European Marketing Journal*, *35*(3/4), 441–456.

Harvey, M., & Novicevic, M. H. (2002). The co-ordination of strategic initiatives within global organisations: The role of global teams. *International Journal of Human Resource Management*, *13*(4), 660–676.

Hatch, M. J., & Schultz, M. (2001). Are the strategic starts aligned for your corporate brand? *Harvard Business Review*, *79*(2), 129–134.

Hodgkinson, G. P., & Sparrow, P. R. (2002). *The competent organisation: A psychological analysis of the strategic management process*. Milton Keynes: Open University.

Holm, U. I. F., & Pedersen, T. (2000). *The emergence and impact of MNC centre of excellence*. London: MacMillan.

Johansson, J. K., & Yip, G. S. (1994). Exploiting globalisation potential: U.S. and Japanese strategies. *Strategic Management Journal*, *15*(8), 579–601.

Kealey, D. J. (1996). The challenge of international personnel selection. In: D. Landis, & R. S. Bhagat (Eds), *Handbook of intercultural training* (2nd ed.). Thousand Oaks: Sage.

Kim, K., Park, J.-H., & Prescott, J. E. (2003). The global integration of business functions: A study of multinational businesses in integrated global industries. *Journal of International Business Studies*, *34*, 327–344.

Kirkman, B. L., Rosen, B., Tesluk, P. E., & Gibson, C. B. (2004). The impact of team empowerment on virtual team performance: The moderating role of face-to-face interaction. *Academy of Management Journal*, *47*(2), 175–192.

Kirkman, B. L., & Shapiro, D. L. (2001). The impact of cultural values on job satisfaction and organisational commitment in self-managing work teams: The mediating role of employee resistance. *Academy of Management Journal*, *44*, 557–569.

Kirkul, J., Lester, S. W., & Belgio, E. (2004). Attitudinal and behavioural outcomes of psychological contract breach. *International Journal of Cross Cultural Management*, *4*(2), 229–252.

Kobrin, S. J. (1994). Is there a relationship between a geocentric mind-set and multinational strategy? *Journal of International Business Studies*, *25*(3), 493–511.

Kostova, T., & Roth, K. (2003). Social capital in multinational corporations and a micro–macro model of its formation, *Academy of Mangement Review*, *28*(2), 297–317.

Laukkanen, M. (1994). Comparative cause mapping of organisational cognitions. *Organisation Science*, *5*, 322–343.

Laukkanen, M. (1996). Comparative cause mapping of organisational cognitions. In: J. R. Meindl, C. Stubbart, & J. F. Porac (Eds), *Cognition within and between organisations.* London: Sage.

Laukkanen, M. (1998). Conducting causal mapping research: Opportunities and challenges. In: C. Eden, & J.-C. Spender (Eds), *Managerial and organisational cognition.* London: Sage.

Lin, N. (2001). Building a network theory of social capital. In: N. Lin, K. Cook, & R. S. Burt (Eds), *Social capital: Theory and research* (pp. 3–29). New York: Aldine de Gruyter.

Makela, A. K. (2004). The social capital of expatriates and repatriates: Knowledge sharing through interpersonal cross-border relationships. Paper presented at EIASM workshop on expatriation, Brussels (October 18–19).

Makhija, M. V., Kim, K., & Williamson, S. D. (1997). Measuring globalisation of industries using a national industry approach: Empirical evidence across five countries and over time. *Journal of International Business Studies, 28*(4), 679–710.

Malbright, T. (1995). Globalisation of an ethnographic firm. *Strategic Management Journal, 16,* 119–141.

Martin, G., & Beaumont, P. (2001). Transforming multinational enterprises: Towards a process model of strategic human resource management change. *International Journal of Human Resource Management, 12*(8), 1234–1250.

Martin, G., & Beaumont, P. (2003). *Branding and people management: What's in a name?* London: Chartered Institute of Personnel and Development.

Matveev, A. V., & Nelson, P. E. (2004). Cross cultural communication competence and multicultural team performance: Perceptions of American and Russian managers. *International Journal of Cross Cultural Management, 4*(2), 253–270.

Mendenhall, M. E., Kűhlman, T. M., Stahl, G., & Osland, J. S. (2002). Employee development and expatriate assignents. In: M. J. Gannon, & K. L. Newman (Eds), *Handbook of cross-cultural management.* London: Blackwell.

Mohrman, S., Cohen, S., & Mohrman, A. (1995). *Designing team-based organisations.* San Franscisco, CA: Jossey-Bass.

Morrison, A. J., & Roth, K. (1992). A taxonomy of business-led strategies in global industries. *Strategic Management Journal, 13*(6), 399–418.

Murtha, T. P., Lenway, S. A., & Bagozzi, R. P. (1998). Global mind-sets and cognitive shift in a complex multinational corporation. *Strategic Management Journal, 19,* 97–114.

Nyambegera, S., Daniels, K., & Sparrow, P. R. (2001). Why fit doesn't always matter: The impact of HRM and cultural fit on job involvement of Kenyan employees. *Applied Psychology: An International Review, 50*(1), 109–140.

Nyambegera, S., Sparrow, P. R., & Daniels, K. (2000). The impact of cultural value orientations on individual HRM preferences in developing countries: Lessons from Kenyan organisations. *International Journal of Human Resource Management, 11*(4), 639–663.

Osland, J. (1995). *The adventure of working abroad: Hero tales from the global frontier.* San Francisco, CA: Jossey-Bass.

Ramaswamy, K., Kroeck, K. G., & Renforth, W. (1996). Measuring the degree of internationalisation of a firm: A comment. *Journal of International Business Studies, 27*(1), 167–177.

Reagans, R., & McEvily, B. W. (2003). Network structure and knowledge transfer: The effects of cohesion and range. *Administrative Science Quarterly, 48*, 240–267.

Rousseau, D. M., & Schalk, R. (2000) (Eds.). Psychological contracts in employment: Cross-national perspectives. Thousand Oaks, CA: Sage.

Sackmann, S. A. (1991). *Cultural knowledge in organisations: Exploring the collective mind.* Newbury Park, CA: Sage.

Sackmann, S. A. (1992). Culture and sub-cultures: An analysis of organisational knowledge. *Administrative Science Quarterly, 37*, 140–161.

Scarbrough, H., Swan, J., & Preston, J. (1999). *Knowledge management: A literature review.* London: Chartered Institute of Personnel and Development.

Smale, A., & Riusala, K. (2004). Predicting stickiness factors in the international transfer of knowledge through expatriates. Paper presented at EIASM workshop on expatriation, Brussels, October 18–19.

Smith, C., & Meiksins, P. (1995). System, society and dominance effects in cross-national organisational analysis. *Work, Employment and Society, 9*(2), 241–267.

Snow, C. C., Snell, S. A., Davidson, S. C., & Hambrick, D. C. (1996). Use transnational teams to globalise your company. *Organisational Dynamics, 32*(4), 20–32.

Sparrow, P. R. (1998). Re-appraising psychological contracting: Lessons for employee development from cross-cultural and occupational psychology research. *International Studies of Management and Organisation, 28*(1), 30–63.

Sparrow, P. R. (2005). Knowledge management in Global organisations. In: I. Bjorkman, & G. Stahl (Eds), *Handbook of research into international HRM*. London: Edward Elgar.

Sparrow, P. R. & Budwhar, P. (1997). Competition and change in India: Mapping transitions in HRM. *Journal of world Business, 32*(3), 224–242.

Sparrow, P. R., & Cooper, C. L. (2003). *The employment relationship: Key challenges for HR.* London: Butterworth-Heinemann.

Sparrow, P. R., & Hiltrop, J. M. (1997). Redefining the field of European human resource management: A battle between national mindsets and forces of business transition. *Human Resource Management, 36*(2), 1–19.

Sparrow, P. R., & Wu, P. C. (1998). How much do national value orientations really matter? Predicting HRM preferences of Taiwanese employees. *Employee Relations: The International Journal, 20*(1), 26–56.

Sparrow, P. R., Brewster, C., & Harris, H. (2004). *Globalising human resource management.* London: Routledge.

Sparrow, P. R., Schuler, R. S., & Jackson, S. (1994). Convergence or divergence: Human resource policies and practices for competitive advantage worldwide. *International Journal of Human Resource Management, 5*(2), 267–299.

Stahl, G. K. (1998). *Internationaler einsatz von fuhrungskräften.* Munich: Oldenbourg.

Staples, D. S., Greenaway, K., & McKeen, J. D. (2001). Opportunities for research about managing the knowledge-based enterprise. *International Journal of Management Reviews, 3*(1), 1–20.

Sullivan, D. (1994). Measuring the degree of internationalisation of a firm. *Journal of International Business Studies*, *25*(2), 325–342.

Sullivan, D. (1996). Measuring the degree of internationalisation of a firm: A reply. *Journal of International Business Studies*, *27*(1), 179–192.

Ulrich, D. (2000). From eBusiness to eHR *Human Resource Planning, 20*(3), 12–21.

von Glinow, M. A., Shapiro, D. L., & Brett, J. M. (2004). Can we talk, and should we? Managing emotional conflict in multinational teams. *Academy of Management Review, 29*(4), 578–592.

Wang, X. Y., & Kanungo, R. N. (2004). Nationality, social network and psychological well-being: Expatriates in China. *International Journal of Human Resource Management, 15*(3), 775–793.

Westwood, R., Sparrow, P. R., & Leung, A. (2001). Challenges to the psychological contract in Hong Kong. *International Journal of Human Resource Management, 12*(4), 621–651.

Whitley, R. D. (1999). *Divergent capitalisms: The social structuring and change of business systems*. Oxford: Oxford University Press.

Yip, G. S. (1992). *Total global strategy*. Englewood Cliffs, NJ: Prentice-Hall.

Zack, M. (1999). Managing codified knowledge. *Sloan Management Review, 40*(2), 45–58.

Zimmermann, A., Holman, D., & Sparrow, P. R. (2003). Unravelling adjustment mechanisms: Adjustment of German expatriates to intercultural interactions, work, and living conditions in the People's Republic of China. *International Journal of Cross Cultural Management, 3*(1), 45–66.

Zimmermann, A., Sparrow, P. R., & Holman, D. (2004). Mutual adjustment processes in international teams: Lessons for the study of expatriation. 4th Workshop on expatriation, European institute for advanced studies in management, Brussels, October 18–19.

Chapter 5

Ghost Workers: Implications of New Workforce Realities for Organizations and Their Workers

Judi McLean Parks and faye l. smith

> And you have all these people say, 'When are you going to get a
> real job?' I mean, you're going through all the motions of a real
> job. I mean, you're showing up at a place between eight and five.
> And technically, you're probably doing as much as anyone else
> who works there ... You know? But you're just sort of this ghost.
> And you don't have a real life (Helen).[1]

> ghost (ghöst), n. A faint semblance; a faint trace; an unwanted sec-
> ondary image[2]

In the field of organizational behaviour, our models of work relationships have
been grounded in implicit assumptions that there is a "traditional" full-time
worker, who represents the norm of the employment relationship. Just as the perspective of the "traditional" family portrayed in the 1950s and 1960s popular culture and television now seems somewhat out of touch with reality (e.g. "The
Donna Reed Show", "Leave it to Beaver", "The Adventures of Ozzie and
Harriett", or "Father Knows Best" in the US, or "Die Familie Hesselbach", "Die
Familie Schoelermann", "Mrs. Dale's Diary" and "The Jimmy Clitheroe Show"

---

[1]Quoted in Henson (1996, p. 1).
[2]Webster's New World Dictionary (1970, p. 216).

Developments in Work Organizational Psychology
Copyright © 2006 by Elsevier Ltd.
All rights of reproduction in any form reserved
ISBN: 0-08-044467-9

in Europe), similarly, the perspective of the "traditional" worker also appears to lack the reality of today's workplace. Just as the 1950s and 1960s, popular characterization of "traditional" families may not have recognized the full diversity of family relationships, the research in organizational behaviour similarly has not recognized the diversity in work relationships. As a result, little if any real attention has been paid to the legions of "ghost" workers who work day in and day out, go through all the motions of a "real" job, assume all the same responsibilities and perform all the same duties as their more "corporeal" colleagues. By and large, these ghost workers have been invisible to organizational scholars.

Work relationships have shifted away from the "traditional" worker with presumed lifetime employment, who worked 9:00–5:00 and who was "an organization man [*sic*]" (White, 1956). This shift has moved towards relationships with workers who pack their own parachutes (Hirsch, 1987), work when work is available, retrain for new skill sets in a revolving door economy and may have no strong affiliation with any given organization regardless of technical or professional skills. In some senses, these workers have become the non-organizational workers, as contrasted to the "organization man [*sic*]" of yesteryear. Organizations have embraced this new worker for reasons of cost and convenience, and like the gigolo, appear to be averse to committing to any specific relationship.

As a result of increasing complexity in a global economic environment, a number of worker categories have evolved, including the "traditional" workers as well as a myriad of alternative work arrangements (McLean Parks, Kidder, & Gallagher, 1998), such as temps, floats, contract workers or seasonal workers (see Table 5.1). To grasp how untraditional "traditional" work arrangements have become, one only has to look at the rise and heft of the contingent work institutions themselves. In the United States, Manpower Temporary Services eclipses Walmart in the number of people employed (Klein, 2002),[3] and the US labour force is nearly one-third contingent (BLS, 1995). France is now the 2nd largest temp market, generating 30% of temp revenues worldwide (the US comprises the largest percentage). Eighty-six percent of new hires in France are on short-term contracts (Cooper & Kamm, 1998). Taken together, non-"traditional" work arrangements may range anywhere from 20% to 60% of a nation's workforce (International Confederation of Temporary Work Businesses, 1998). Yet such figures may, in fact, understate the number of temporary workers. Klein (2002, p. 248) notes that, "Every day, 4.5 million workers are assigned to jobs through temp agencies in Europe and the US, but since only 12.5% of temps are placed on

---

[3]Given that Manpower's workers' employment is sporadic, on any given day, Walmart clocks in more workers. Never-the-less, the numbers are striking: 800,000 workers work for Manpower and 720,000 for Walmart (Klein, 2002, p. 472).

a given day, the real number of temporary workers in Europe and the US is closer to 36 million people". More over, it is no longer just the clerical worker or receptionist that is a "temp" or other form of non-"traditional" worker. Increasingly, accountants, chemists, computer programmers, customer service representatives, engineers, managers, nurses, and medical staff join the ranks of the temporary worker. "Outsourcing ... has expanded through virtually every industry as companies rush to shed staff in everything from human resources to computer systems" (Bernstein, 1995). IBM alone has shed more than 15,000 workers through outsourcing (Dobbs, 2004), and Europe will lose over a million jobs to offshore outsourcing by 2010, with the UK losing 760,000 jobs by 2015 (Treanor, 2004).

We contend that the existing theory and research in the organizational behaviour has not captured the nuanced differences in the attitudes, values, behaviours and concerns of these amorphous ghosts of organizational research. Further, we contend that existing research, for the most part, has not attempted to do so. Yet, there are likely to be important differences that impact our understanding of work relationships and the attitudes and behaviours of the workers themselves. By ignoring this more nuanced view of the work relationship, we fail to consider the increasing complexity of the workplace and the dynamic nature of the work relationship, as well as its impact on our theoretical frameworks and empirical results. The inclusion of an unacknowledged yet different type of worker introduces potentially important unspecified variables and increased error variance into our empirical studies. Further, the prescriptions suggested by our research risk the propagation of recommendations or panaceas that at best are unfounded and at worst are damaging. The unacknowledged and unmeasured diversity of work relationships in organizations creates new paradoxes, tensions and concerns that we ignore at our own risk.

In this paper, we use key questions to guide our exploration into issues related to the changing work relationship, not only for us as researchers but also for the organizations and workers that we study. The questions — as well as the implications — that are our focus are those that we find particularly important and interesting. These questions and implications are not meant to be exhaustive, but rather to provoke the interest and thoughtful rumination of researchers interested in work relationships and the implications of new workforce realities. Given these realities, these questions and their implications must not only be understood but also incorporated into our theorizing and empirical work.

Specifically, we ask:

- Who is inside and who is outside the organizational boundaries?
- What is the impact of different norms of reciprocity for "traditional" and non-"traditional" work arrangements?
- What is the impact of the different currencies (resources) of exchange?

Table 5.1: Non-"traditional" work arrangements (modified from McLean Parks et al., 1998).

Exemplar categories	Definition	Membership in organization when boundaries defined as				
		Bureaucracies	Nexus of contracts	Physical	Shared cultures	Production process
"Traditional"	Permanent full- and part-time workers with either an implicit or explicit understanding that employment will be continuous or ongoing	Yes	Yes	If tasks completed inside structure	Yes	Yes
Non-"traditional" *Non-"traditional" workers, employed by they company in a continuing relationship, but not at the same location each day*						
Floats	Full-time employees who are moved around within different departments or divisions within the organization as a regular part of their job	Yes	Yes	If tasks completed inside structure	Yes	Yes
Networked	Individuals whose work is performed outside the boundaries of their home organization	Yes	Yes	No	Yes	Yes

Non-"traditional" workers, hired directly by the company into temporary positions

| In-house temporaries | Workers hired by the organization to meet variable scheduling needs, listed in a "registry" (i.e. performs function of temporary agency) | Yes | Yes | If tasks completed inside structure | No | Yes |
| Direct-hire or seasonal temporaries | Workers for whom organizations advertise and recruit for the purpose of filling position vacancies as needed | Yes | Yes | Yes | No | Yes |

Non-"traditional" workers, employed by a different company from that where the execute obligations and their performance is monitored

Leased workers	Employee leasing company effectively "rents" an entire workforce to a client employer	No	Yes	If tasks completed inside structure	No	Yes
Temporary firm workers	The temporary firm is the employer, rather than the client organization who utilizes the workers	No	Yes	If tasks completed inside structure	No	Yes
Subcontracted workers	Work is transferred to another organization whose employees perform tasks on or off the premises of the client company	No	Yes	No	No	Yes
Consultants	Organization either contracts with a professional consulting firm or independent consultants for the completion of project	No	Yes	If tasks completed inside structure	No	Yes

(Continued)

Table 5.1 (Continued)

Exemplar categories	Definition	Membership in organization when boundaries defined as				
		Bureaucracies	**Nexus of contracts**	**Physical**	**Shared cultures**	**Production process**
Independent Contractors	Brought into the firm to supply specific skills, from manual labour such as plumbing to software and other engineering applications	No	Yes	Yes	No	Yes
Non-workers						
Those who are involved in the production process but who are not workers						
Customers	Customers who are involved directly in the production process, for example, in a service organization or a purchaser of a custom designed or specialized product	No	No	If tasks completed inside structure	No	Yes
Regulatory	Regulators involved in the production process, such as inspectors for compliance with codes	No	No	If tasks completed inside structure	No	Yes
Volunteers	Unpaid/remunerated workers who volunteer to complete tasks under the direction of the organization	No	No[a]	If tasks completed inside structure	Yes	Yes

[a]Actually it depends on whether or not "consideration" has been exchanged—for example, ideological currency (Thompson & Bunderson, 2003) would make the relationship with a volunteer contractual.

Who is Inside and Who is Outside Organizational Boundaries?

The realities of today's workforce include an increasingly non-"traditional" worker base. As a result, it has become more difficult — for researchers as well as organizations and workers — to identify who is inside and who is outside organizational boundaries. Given the diversity of work arrangements in today's economy, it is possible that some workers may never have put foot in the organization nor ever have received a paycheck from it (McLean Parks et al., 1998). Yet, these workers may regard themselves, and others may view them, as members.

Rafaeli (1997) notes the difficulty of specifying who is or is not a member of an organization, due in part to different conceptual delineations of organizational boundaries. Specifically, Rafaeli (1997) notes that organizational boundaries differ depending on whether the organization is seen through the lens of the *bureaucratic model* (Weber, 1947), the *nexus of contracts* (Jensen & Meckling, 1976), the *production process* (Bowen & Schneider, 1988; Chase & Erickson, 1988; Lele, 1986), as a *shared culture* (Morgan, 1986), or as delimited by *physical boundaries* (Oldham, Cummings, & Zhou, 1995; Tushman, 1977). Each of these perspectives varies in terms of who is or is not considered a member of the organization. For example, organizations conceived of as *bureaucracies* (Weber, 1947) would not include leased workers, subcontracted workers, temps, consultants, independent contractors, customers, regulators or volunteers; a *nexus of contracts* perspective (Jensen & Meckling, 1976) omits customers, regulators and volunteers; the perspective of the organization as a *production process* (Bowen & Schneider, 1988; Chase & Erickson, 1988; Lele, 1986) includes all of these work relationships (see Table 5.1).

Workers — whether they execute their task through "outsourcing" or under the direction of the bureaucratic manager — may be considered by themselves or others as part of the organization and as representing, in some sense, the organization and its values (McLean Parks & smith, 2000, 2004). Hence their skills, abilities, attitudes and behaviours, as well as their relationships with other workers and organizational constituencies can be important determinants of the success of the organization and of how the organization is seen by its various constituencies.

This blurring of the organization's boundaries has become more pronounced in recent years, with the increased reliance on emergent and non-"traditional" work relationships. If viewed from the perspective of an organization as a *production process*, then customers actually may be considered organizational members (Rafaeli, 1997). This is the perspective emphasized by the company Steak n Shake™ in a recent marketing campaign in the United States. In a TV advertisement, a Steak n Shake™ server explained,

A workaurant is a place where you work your way through the line
… work to see the menu, work to carry your tray and fill your
drink, work to balance your tray and drink while you get your
condiments, work to find a place to sit, and work to clean your
own table … . At Steak n Shake™ we're a restaurant. You sit,
while I do the work. (Cebyrznski, 2003, emphasis added)

Although perhaps a tongue in cheek depiction of "workaurants" and "restaurants", organizations viewed as production processes would classify both the
server and the customer in this example as organizational members in the
"workaurant". Yet other classification schemes would categorize customers as
non-members and servers as members, or perhaps even broaden the boundaries to
include even more entities as members under the organization's umbrella
(Rafaeli, 1997). For example, Jensen and Meckling's (1976) classic nexus of contracts would include employees, vendors, suppliers and independent contractors
as members of the organization. Weber's bureaucratic model (1947), which relies
on authority structures to define who members are or are not, by virtue of their
appearance on an organizational chart (Rafaeli, 1997), would not include the customer but would include the server within the boundaries of the organization. If
organizational boundaries are defined on the basis of shared cultures where common experiences shape common norms (Morgan, 1986), then physicians at different clinics may be seen as co-workers in the same organization through the
shared culture of their medical values. However, these same physicians may not
be considered as belonging to the same organization as that of the janitor who
cleans their office or the accountant who tracks their billing. In this case, professional values are shared and given Morgan's (1986) perspective, these shared values
would include those who shared these values as members. However, if the values
were different from those of a given hospital or unit, then through the lack of a
shared culture, a given physician would not be a member. A view of organizations
as bounded by physical structures and geography (Oldham, Cummings, & Zhou,
1995; Rafaeli, 1997) with a distinct external boundary (Tushman, 1977) would
again include customers, but not employees who "telecommute" (see Table 5.1).
This complexity, as Rafaeli notes, "suggests that it may be most accurate to define
and describe [organizational] membership as a profile, rather than a dichotomy"
(p. 132, emphasis added). In viewing membership as a profile of membership
characteristics (e.g. distal in terms of membership based on production process,
less distal in terms of membership based on bureaucratic reporting lines), the
work relationship becomes a matter of salience, indicating the degree to which
different types of workers are "vested" in the organization, as perceived by self or
others.

The blurring of the boundary of the organization and the integration of emergent forms of work relationships is important to the organizations from a number of perspectives. The first of these perspectives is member **identification** with the organization (e.g. Ashforth & Mael, 1989). Identification with the organization has been shown to impact worker motivation and a variety of other attitudes and behaviours that can improve organizational performance, and thus may be an important tool for organizations to cultivate. The second of these perspectives is that of the organization's **identity**. At a very pragmatic level, a worker can be seen as an organizational member by any number of constituencies. Even if not included as a member by the organization itself, such a worker can become a *de facto* representative of the organization and its values, creating an organizational identity (McLean Parks & smith, 2000, 2004). The third perspective is the categorization of workers into **in- and out-groups** on the basis of the type of work relationship. Finally, we will also explore the impact of the blurring or organizational boundaries on **worker identity**.

Organizational Identification

Organizations have long capitalized on the benefits of a host of worker attitudes and behaviours derived from strong organizational identification, such as high levels of commitment (e.g. Van Dick et al., 2004), cooperation (e.g. Kramer, 1993; Polzer, 2004), loyalty (Adler & Adler, 1988; Van Vugt & Hart, 2004), motivation (e.g. Van Dyne, Graham, & Dienesch, 1994), increased performance (e.g. Kilcullen, Mael, Goodwin, & Zazanis, 1999), trust (e.g. Brashear, Boles, Bellenger, & Brooks, 2003) and, importantly, the willingness to perform extra-role or organizational citizenship behaviours (e.g. Bergami & Bagozzi, 2000; Feather & Rauter, 2004; O'Reilly & Chatman, 1986). The importance of these behaviours is most clearly evident in illustrations in the extreme, for example, through volunteers or workers in volunteer organizations. Parent volunteers provide assistance in the public school classrooms, and civilian auxiliaries view themselves as essential members of the military (Cheng, 1996). EarthWatch, active in many parts of the globe, is known for placing volunteers in the field where they can assist research scientists conducting field work. The volunteers become part of the research team, working alongside the scientific community, while developing the skills and an understanding of the environmental and social contexts in which they work (EarthWatch, 2004). In essence, these volunteers become research assistants who are not only unpaid, but also who contribute financially to the research projects. This is possible because of the strong identification that the volunteers have with the studies in which they are engaged, including ecology, zoology and archaeology. In other words, the organization is salient and congruent with the volunteers' personal identities, allowing them to invest in and enact identities that are important to them in a concrete and meaningful manner.

Identification with an organization and its identity has important implications. The information provided through an organization's identity impacts how and to what degree identification (e.g. Ashforth & Mael, 1996; Mael & Ashforth, 1992, 1995) or dis-identification (Elsbach & Bhattacharya, 1998) with the firm occurs. In addition, an organization's identity facilitates motivation and commitment among workers (e.g. Feather & Rauter, 2004), as well as increased loyalty from consumers (e.g. Fullerton, 2003; McLean Parks & smith, 2000, 2004) and stockholders (e.g. McLean Parks & smith, 2000, 2004). Further, an organization's identity can be a strategic advantage, hence it must be managed for all stakeholder groups, including managers, employees, customers, investors, suppliers and the public (Dukerich & Carter, 2000; Hatch & Schultz, 2000). If damaged, the organization's identity must be repaired (Dukerich & Carter, 2000).

Organizational Identities

Organizational identities communicate that which is central, enduring and distinctive about a given organization (Albert & Whetten, 1985). Organizational identities function to create meanings that guide action (Daft & Weick, 1984), by articulating what is valued, expected behaviours and important benchmarks (Barker, 1993; Bullis & Tompkins, 1989; Cheney, 1983; Simon, 1976; Tompkins & Cheney, 1985). According to McLean Parks and smith (2000, 2004), these identities can be communicated by organizational members or their representatives, or by <u>perceived</u> organizational members or representatives. Further, the identities created may be neither intentional nor wanted.

Organizations, in attempting to manage their identities and capitalize on the potential benefits of a positive identity, should not ignore the workers of different types or forms that can become unintended representatives of the organizations and communicators of organizational identity. For example, Martha Stewart, the domestic maven, is the supplier of a brand of domestic products (e.g. Martha Stewart sheets and towels), does not work at K-Mart and her products represent only a fraction of the products sold by K-Mart. When she was convicted of lying about why she sold nearly 4000 shares of Imclone stock the day before a negative Imclone announcement, plunging Imclone's stock, K-Mart's sales fell (McClam, 2004; Madore, 2005). However incorrectly, her name — as a supplier for K-Mart — was seen by consumers as part and parcel of the K-Mart brand. Perhaps anticipating negative spillover onto their products, both McDonald's and Nutella astutely dropped Kobe Bryant — the Lakers basketball star — as a celebrity endorser of their brands shortly after he was charged with rape (Kimball, 2005). Although Kobe did not work for these companies, as an endorser, consumers would have seen him as a representative. Had they not dropped Kobe as a celebrity endorser, it could have negatively impacted their brands. At a more mundane level, the customer whose service call is transferred to an overseas worker will be left with the impression made by that worker as a representative of the company — regardless of the fact that the worker receives no pay check from the company and has no direct affiliation other than as a worker in a call centre that provides outsourced services.[4] Yet, to the customer, the actions of the overseas worker — as representative of the company — convey information about the perceived (accurate or not) identity of the organization. If the worker is seen as rude or unhelpful, the customer may infer that this is a company that is uncaring and unworthy of customer loyalty. As these three examples suggest, Martha, Kobe and the outsourced worker each may be seen as an organizational member, whose actions reflect on the organization and convey elements of that organization's identity to various constituencies. These identities thus are communicated by representatives who may or may not have been intended as representatives by the organization and further, the identity conveyed may or may not be the identity the organization wished to communicate.

The emergent forms of work relationships and associated blurring of organizational boundaries is also important from the workers' perspective, who, regardless of whether or not others may consider them as within organizational boundaries, may consider <u>themselves</u> to be members of the organization. Although there may be a number of implications, here we focus on just two, both related to identity: the creation of in- and out-groups based on the worker categorization, and the formation and potential dismantling of workers' personal identities.

In-groups and Out-groups

As the research on social identity (e.g. Tajfel, 1981; Tajfel & Turner, 1986) has suggested, individuals categorize themselves and others in their social environments — including their work environments — into in-groups (associated with oneself) and out-groups, by using available categories and distinctions, categories and distinctions which may be provided by the context, as well as categories and distinctions that the individuals themselves provide. Members of in-groups, or the group to which one belongs, are differentiated from members of out-groups, made of individuals who are not part of one's own group categorization. In work

---

[4]Credit goes to Paul Jackson for this example.

environments, we might expect these potential categories to include the type of work relationship, for example, core or temp workers. As new work relationships emerge, categorizations into in- and out-groups along these lines may be inevitable, and the consequences potentially significant. These categorizations will be more salient and implications more pronounced when workers belonging to these different categories converge on the same work location.

Over 30 years of research has clearly demonstrated that this categorization process results in various types of in-group favouritism (Brewer, 1979; Mullen, Brown, & Smith, 1992). For example, people prefer (their own) in-groups (Perdue, Dovidio, Gurtman, & Tyler, 1990), are more lenient towards in-group members (Duncan, 1976) and more willing to excuse in-group members' unacceptable behaviours (Hewstone, 1990). Moreover, out-group members are more likely to believe that coercion is an effective influence tactic (Rothbart & Hallmark, 1988). In addition, in-group members assess and evaluate each other more positively (Scaillet & Leyens, 2000), while derogating or denigrating out-group members (Brewer, 1979; Fein & Spencer, 1997; Branscombe & Wann, 1994), and are likely to be disadvantaged in the distribution of resources (e.g. Hodson, Dovidio, & Esses, 2003). Certainly, anecdotal evidence suggests the disparity between the types of workers doing the same job can be substantial, and at times could be interpreted as ill treatment. For example, in order to ensure a given legal employment status, Microsoft, temps are "barred from all extracurricular company functions, including taking part in late-night pizza meals and after-hour parties" (Klein, 2002, p. 251). Although perhaps not the intent, such practices make the non-"traditional" workers into Microsoft social pariahs.

Worker Identity

In addition to such in/out-group effects, workers' personal identities may have lost an element of what formerly was an important part of "self" (especially in achievement cultures such as the United States, Great Britain and Japan (Hofstede, 1980), in contrast to ascriptive cultures such as Mexico or Saudi Arabia (Hofstede, 1980)). Perhaps the first to articulate the importance of one's job to identity, Erikson (1956, 1993 (1959)) noted that jobs are at the core not only of the individual's identity, but also of their communal culture. When important components of one's identity change, then the continuity of identity is threatened (Breakwell, 1986).

Baumeister differentiated among destabilized, diluted and deficient identities. *Destabilized* identities are those in which the identity fails to provide continuity or stability, where the present, past and anticipated future selves are separate and lack a sense of unity (Baumeister, 1986, p. 122); a *diffused or diluted* identity lacks sufficient substance to provide commitment to values and goals; finally, identity *deficit* is an "inadequately defined self" (Baumeister, 1986, p. 199), per- haps resulting from a destabilized or diluted identity. Such destabilization may be particularly critical when identity needs have been consolidated around occupa- tional or work capacities (Erikson, 1968 (1956)), and may ultimately result in an identity crisis derived from identity deficit (Baumeister, 1986). Identity deficit can leave one without a clear set of values or image of one's personal control over one's actions or how to relate to others. For example, by using buyouts and early retirement to cut the costs of older workers (Gallagher, 2005), some workers may suffer from identity deficit, as they find themselves without the job that has defined them for a quarter of a century or more. However, <u>if</u> such workers can reframe their identity such that it no longer includes a labour market worker iden- tity, transitions to early retirement may not result in an identity deficit (Jackson & Taylor, 1994). A key difference is the level to which one is vested in the work identity, and whether or not it is possible to reframe one's identity or to lessen the emphasis on the former work identity.

New workforce realities, then, may easily result in a destabilized identity, espe- cially for non-"traditional" workers. As a result of the "pack your parachute" (Hirsch, 1987) mentality, workers may go through continuous cycles of employ- ment and unemployment and while employed, may work in a variety of companies, locations and with different skill sets. As a consequence of these cycles, work iden- tities may become diluted. Identity deficit may be one outcome of this identity destabilization and dilution. At the extreme, the loss or degradation of one's iden- tity through work can induce a sense of shame (Tangney & Dearing, 2002), which in turn can trigger violence (Baumeister, 1996) at work (Baxter & Margavio, 1996) or at home (Hornung & McCullough, 1981; Hornung, McCullough, & Sugimoto, 1981; Ingalls, 1999), or even suicide (e.g. Magnier, 2001; Fusé, 1980).

Unemployment, or even under-employment, represents much more than the loss of an income, especially if they are highly involved (Jackson, Stafford, Banks, & Warr, 1983; McLean Parks & Kidder, 1994). McLean Parks and Kidder (1994, p. 113) noted that "… [t]he more involved employees are in their jobs and the more their identities are tied up in their jobs, the more they will feel the effect of a lay- off. For these employees, a layoff is more than a loss of income. It is often equated with the *actual loss of their reason for being*" (emphasis in the original). We con- tend a variety of mechanisms — including alternative work arrangements — neg- atively impact or marginalize the identity of a once proud worker. One can easily imagine the disaffection of the computer programmer — who returned to school to learn new programming skills — who now finds their job outsourced and must become an unwilling and underpaid consultant just to put food on the table. Is this an unreasonable scenario? In just one anecdotal example, Bernstein (1995) reported that when American Airlines outsourced its ticket agents, workers who had previously earned $40,000 were offered their old jobs back for $16,000. "When viewed in this light, violence committed by such individuals is no longer an irrational, random event. It becomes [a] logical consequence of … loss" (Stuart, 1992, p. 74). Perhaps it is not so surprising that workplace violence has become one of the three most common causes of occupational death in the United States since 1992 (BLS, 2002). Disconcertingly, violence is the number one cause of occupational death among female workers in the United States (BLS, 2002).

Flannery (1995) identified five types of workplace assailants, including workers, customers, the mentally ill, abusers in domestic disputes and criminals. Identity destabilization and loss may be one contributing factor for at least two, if not more, of these assailants: the worker and domestic abuser. For the worker, destabilization and loss may result in either suicide or aggression towards customers or other workers. In Japan, the economic slump of the previous decade has resulted in record high unemployment, where suicides have linked to job losses (AP Wire Service, 2003). Catalano, Dooley, Novaco, Wilson, and Hough (1993) found that the risk of violent behaviour is greater among workers in industries where layoffs are occurring. At the time of their study, the economic environment was primarily impacted by layoffs. In today's work environment, under-employment is quite likely to be added to the mix. Many of the current forms emergent work relationships are employed to cut the organization's costs, making it reasonable to expect that these cost-cutting emergent relationships will result in various degrees of under-employment. Thus, we contend that the marginalization of workers through outsourcing and other new arrangements may also increase aggression in the workplace. Quite simply, for one's job can be the very essence of a worker's identity.

Domestic violence is also a social problem that impacts workplace productivity, morale and costs (Johnson & Gardner, 1999), where victims can include not only the intended targets but also co-workers and bystanders (Johnson & Gardner, 1999; Popham, 1998). Domestic violence becomes an issue at work because that is where abusers can most easily find their victims. Job loss and inconsistent gender-stereotypic work realities (e.g. female as family breadwinner) are both related to identity, and both have been identified as major causes of domestic violence (Hornung & McCullough, 1981; Hornung et al., 1981; Ingalls, 1999). Hornung et al. (1981) explored the link between spousal assault and status inconsistencies between spouses, finding that rates of violence were higher when a woman's occupational status was greater than her husband's. Further, the more a woman's resources (e.g. pay check) exceed her husband's, the more likely domestic violence is to occur (Allen & Strauss, 1980). Regardless of relative resources, domestic abuse increases when husbands are less able to fulfil the provider role (Rodman, 1968). Thus, husbands whose jobs are lost or who suffer under-employment get a double dose of identity destabilization and loss — both as provider and as valued employee.

For previous generations of workers, job loss may have been the primary cause underlying identity destabilization and identity loss in such cases. Although still a factor, we can add to that mix the emerging workforce realities that clearly will contribute to identity destabilization and identity loss through not only job loss, but also through status inconsistency, which in turn can lead to domestic violence — where violence at home spills over into the workplace. The potential costs are significant: in the United States, it is estimated that domestic violence costs organizations between $3 and $5 billion per year (Scalora, Washington, O'Neil, Casady, & Newell, 2003). In the case of workplace violence (other than the spillover from domestic abuse) and workplace suicide, in the United States these costs easily exceed $4.2 billion annually in financial costs, with additional costs to co-workers, 88% of whom report that they are psychologically affected by the threat of workplace violence (Miller, 1999).

In sum, in this section we have explored the implications of the blurring of organizational boundaries and the integration of emergent forms of work relationships. First, we suggested that organizational identification will vary in predictable ways for workers classified, however arbitrarily, as members or non-members. For example, we have suggested that volunteers, typically classified as non-members, may have high levels of identification with the organization. Second, we explored the implications on organizational identity, suggesting that workers who may ("traditional" employees) or may not (outsourced workers) be organizational members can none-the-less be seen as organizational members by consumers and other constituency groups, whether or not the organization intends that they be seen as such, and may convey an organizational identity that may or may not be the one the organization wishes to communicate. Third, we have suggested that workers may classify themselves along the lines of their relationship with the organization into in- and out-groups, which may result in in-group favouritism and the marginalization of some types of workers. Fourth, we have suggested that the blurring or organizational boundaries may impact the identities of the workers themselves, and that the loss of a valued identity may be one predictor of workplace violence.

What is the Impact of Different Norms of Reciprocity for "Traditional" and Non-"Traditional" Work Arrangements?

All models of exchange relationships are grounded in reciprocity. Norms of reciprocity prescribe what is considered appropriate and inappropriate behaviour in exchange relationships, and are the bedrock for judgments about justice and fair play. By prescribing appropriate and inappropriate behaviour, reciprocity norms create expectations that, if breached, create a sense of violation (Sheppard, Lewicki, & Minton, 1992).

There has been an enormous amount of research examining reciprocity since the groundbreaking studies of Malinowski (1922) from a wide variety of fields, including sociology, economics and anthropology. Reciprocity, as the basis of all exchange, is fundamental also to our models of work relationships. Early research by Sahlins (1972) described reciprocity as an expectation of a mutual exchange, and as a continuum that ranges from negative to balanced to generalized reciprocity (Sahlins, 1972). The reciprocity engendered by a relationship has implications for the effectiveness of the control and governance mechanisms, as well as the likelihood that the parties will engage in benevolent behaviour. *Negative reciprocity* is characterized by relationships in which getting something for nothing — or perhaps in doing harm to another — is germane, and frequently is found in relationships where the relationship is not expected to continue. When a work relationship is grounded in negative reciprocity, trust will be ineffective as a form of control or governance. In contrast, *balanced reciprocity* is similar to the general notion of economic transactions. If perfectly balanced, the exchange is equitable. If balanced reciprocity is subscribed to, then failure to reciprocate can result in the termination of the relationship. Finally, *generalized reciprocity* refers to exchange relationships that are "putatively altruistic" (Sahlins, 1972, p. 191), characterized by acting in the interest of another with no explicit obligation for reciprocation. Failure to reciprocate under generalized reciprocity does not dissolve the relationship, because there is no explicit expectation of a like exchange (McLean Parks, 1990). Sahlins (1972) suggests that the parties in an exchange relationship will be more likely to engage in a pro-social behaviour when exchange is governed by norms of generalized reciprocity, and that different reciprocity norms will be encouraged by different social or economic circumstances. For example, increased "kinship" distance may lead to the reduction of generalized reciprocity, as generalized reciprocity is found primarily among parties with close relationships (Sahlins, 1972).

Sahlins' depiction of kinship distance seems quite applicable to the "distance" of a "traditional" versus non-"traditional" worker (see Figure 5.1). Portrayed as three concentric circles, the innermost circle represents those who are closely related. In Sahlins' work, the close, inner circle relationships represented close kin, perhaps blood relatives. For our purposes, the innermost circle would represent close work relationships, perhaps by virtue of close physical proximity, being members of the in-group, and through strong identification with the organization. In contrast, the outermost circle represents those who are only distally tied to one another, lack a common identity and identification with the organization, and are members of the out-group. As one moves from the innermost circle of closely aligned and related workers to the outer circle, the norm of reciprocity, which governs the exchange, will move from generalized to balanced to negative reciprocity (McLean Parks, 1990; Sahlins, 1972). Further, as Gouldner (1960) noted, norms of reciprocity are marked by their immediacy, or the time frame in which reciprocation is required. The "revolving door" of more distal workers will inhibit the formation of trust between the workers and the organization, with the shortened time span associated with the greater immediacy requirements of these more distal workers. Thus, once again, as one moves from the inner to the outer circle (from core to distal/peripheral worker), immediacy moves from a more indefinite or unspecified time frame to immediate or instantaneous (see Figure 5.1).

In close relationships, relational currency represents a type of long-term savings account from which withdrawals can be made at any time,[5] and thus immediacy is not a concern. Long term relationships in a sense are self-enforcing, where the emotional costs incurred by violating trust are assumed to be greater than the potential gains (Luhmann, 1979). However, in more distal relationships, reciprocity demands immediacy, as one moves away from the more stable, longer term work relationships. The extreme distal relationship might be exemplified by a one-shot prisoner's dilemma where the potential for exploitation is high. However, in more ongoing relationships, a tit for tat strategy will punish exploiters and reward those who cooperate (Axelrod, 1984). Thus in longer term relationships, immediacy concerns are relaxed, as the potential for exploitation is reduced. Further, in close relationships, one may not need a favour every time a favour is given, where trust in the other party allows delayed gratification. Yet, over the long run, the exchange of favours is likely to even out. For example, in the Chinese Guanxi, where mutual obligations are fundamental, relationships are enduring and may, at the extreme, encompass a lifetime.[6] Guanxi perhaps is best characterized by a friendship with overtones of an unlimited exchange of favours (Pye, 1982). Favours may be exchanged one for one, or one member may provide a favour and not demand one in return. Yet members of one's Guanxi network recognize that obligations and favours can be called at any time.

---

[5]Thanks to Paul Jackson for this analogy and making the connection to Guanxi.

[6]Guanxi is focused on relationships between specific individuals, and is the exchange of obligations and favours between the specific individuals. In contrast, the Japanese principle of Wa refers to group loyalty and consensus, where obligations are created for the collective, rather than the individuals within the collective. Thus, for Guanxi, reciprocation is expected by the individual obligated, yet for Wa, reciprocation can be demanded of any individual in the collective (Alston, 1989). This example raises the interesting issue of the importance of "who" it is that reciprocates in the fulfilment of obligations.

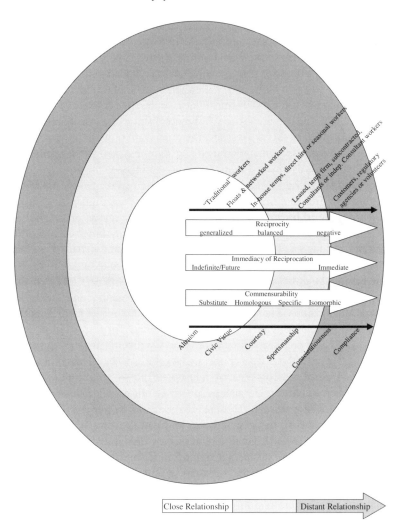

Figure 5.1: Reciprocity norms, immediacy, commensurability, extra-role behaviours and work relationships.

Given the characterization of negative, balanced and generalized reciprocity and the mapping of reciprocity on to the various work relationships, immediacy will be a priority for those who are more distal from the core "traditional" workers. One implication is in the realm of extra-role or organizational citizenship behaviours (Van Dyne, Cummings, & McLean Parks, 1995). Generally used to describe behaviours, which go beyond delineated role requirements, extra-role behaviour, in the aggregate, is critical to the functioning of the organization (Barnard, 1938; Katz & Kahn, 1978; Organ, 1988). The most researched dimensions of extra-role behaviour include compliance (e.g. conformance with job requirements, such as attendance), conscientiousness (e.g. conscientious conformance, perhaps a superior attendance record or extra diligence in executing one's task), sportsmanship (e.g. focusing on what is right at work, and avoiding complaining), courtesy (e.g. keeping co-workers informed or taking active steps to prevent problems), civic virtue (e.g. active participation in training opportunities) and altruism (e.g. helping other workers complete their tasks). Intuitively, these behaviours, from the "task oriented focus of compliance to the proactive supportiveness of altruism", appear to be arranged along a continuum, "from the least to the most intensely focused on helping the organization — from a minimum to a maximum level of effort and contribution" (McLean Parks & Kidder, 1994). Although the degree to which each of these extra-role behaviours represents a facet of required performance is the subject of some debate (e.g. Van Dyne et al., 1995), the behaviours from conscientiousness to altruism seem to be more than simply a quid pro quo, and the line demarking in-role from extra-role behaviour is blurred. This blurring of the line encourages those whose work relationship is characterized by negative reciprocity to engage only in compliance or even mere compliance. In contrast, those whose work relationship is characterized by generalized reciprocity, with its lower immediacy, are more likely to engage in altruism, such as helping other workers complete their tasks (see Figure 5.1). Thus, by implication, the new workforce realities may discourage more non-"traditional" workers from engaging in critical extra-role behaviours, workers whose need for immediacy in reciprocation and under-developed trust in the organization may make them unwilling, if not unable, to go beyond mere requirements.

Four Principles of Reciprocity

Another important facet of reciprocity was suggested by Gouldner (1960), who noted that reciprocity norms prescribe first that one is expected to help those who have either helped in the past or are expected to do so in the future, and second that one is expected to forbear from harming those who have helped in the past or are expected to do so in the future (McLean Parks, 1997). Sahlins (1972) and Mitchell's (1988) focus on negative reciprocity (doing harm) suggests two additional principles, that thirdly, one is expected to forebear from helping those who have harmed or are expected to harm in the future, and fourth, one is expected to harm those who have harmed or are expected to harm in the future. Fulfilling these expectations, however onerous or inconvenient, can form the basis for an exchange of obligation (Malinowski, 1922).

Importantly, these four principles of reciprocity are characterized by restraint or dispensation (see Figure 5.2), differentiated by whether they are comprised of acts of omission (restraint) or acts of commission (dispensation). By integrating these four principles of reciprocity not only with the extra-role behaviours discussed above but also with potential retributive behaviours — perhaps by ignoring malfunctioning equipment or by active sabotage — suggest that it would be normatively acceptable to help those who have helped you or to avoid harming them, as well as to avoid helping those who have harmed you or even to harm them (McLean Parks, 1997). Because greater culpability is attached to acts of commission than acts of omission (e.g. Baron & Ritov, 1994), the breach or violation of these expectations will be judged more harshly, all else equal, when breached through an act of commission than if breached through an act of omission (McLean Parks, 1997). How harshly such breaches or violations are judged will impact responses to the violation, for example, whether or not the violated worker engages in sabotage (McLean Parks, 1997), is silent or exits the relationship (Turnley & Feldman, 1988), or is neglectful (McLean Parks, 1997; Turnley & Feldman, 1988).

These principles of reciprocity suggest that not only will non-"traditional" workers be less inclined to engage in extra-role behaviours, but that, if feelings of mistreatment or a loss of control arise, may engage in retributive behaviours. The need for retribution can be a response to frustration (Dollard, Doobs, Miller, Mowrer, & Sears, 1939) or injustice (da Gloria, 1984), to a sense of losing control (Thompson, 1983) or to the loss of identity previously discussed. Workers

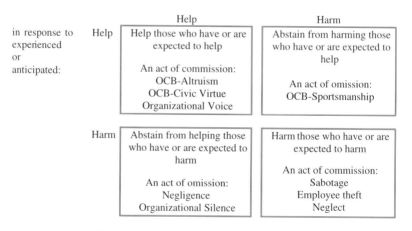

Figure 5.2: Four principles of reciprocity.

have engaged in sabotage when they have believed themselves to be overworked (Giacalone, 1990) or in retaliation for management practices and policies (Crino & Leap, 1989) — reporting feelings of alienation and exploitation. Sabotage is one way that workers can regain control (Thompson, 1983) and is a leading cause of computer failures (Ferelli & Trowbridge, 1990). Workers who have seen the jobs of their colleagues, if not themselves, outsourced may understandably feel exploited, experiencing feelings of alienation and a loss of control. In relating reactions to negative work relationships, Smith (1913), the raconteur from the early 20th century noted, "… Next morning upon visiting the work the farmer was surprised to find that 1000 young trees had been planted upside down, their roots waving in the breeze …" (p. 15).

What is the Impact of Different Currencies of Exchange?

In this section, we explore how the currency used in the exchange between the organization and the worker — whether transactional currency, relational currency (Rousseau & McLean Parks, 1993; McLean Parks & smith, 1998; McLean Parks et al., 1998), or ideological currency (Edwards & Bunderson, 2003) varies in different types of work relationships, and the implications of different currencies. The "what" of an exchange relationship is a critical component for two reasons. First, it is important because the commensurability of the resources can vary; second, it is important because the nature of the resources themselves may vary in different types of work relationships.

At its heart, **commensurability** refers to the metrics that a worker may use to determine the "value" of the resource exchanged, particularly when the resources are not of the same type, or when no normative "exchange rate" has evolved. For example, a worker who gives weekend or vacation day to complete a project by a deadline may be compensated by the organization with a day off at a later point in time. These two resources would seem to be commensurate to all intents and purposes. It may not be so simple, however, if the worker must devote extra hours — perhaps at the time that the worker's spouse is receiving a community award. All of a sudden, a day off at some point in the future does not seem to be equivalent recompense for what was lost. It is no longer commensurate, and the exchange relationship is no longer balanced. The commensurability of different resources has implications for how different types of non-"traditional" workers may "value" the resources exchanged, and whether or not, for example, they believe that their psychological contracts — the reciprocal entitlements (pay, opportunities for advancement, job security, fair treatment) and obligations (role requirements, attendance, loyalty to the company) perceived by the worker (e.g. Rousseau & McLean Parks, 1993) — may have been violated.

Pruitt (1981) described specific, homologous and substitute forms of compensation, which vary based on the realm of need that is satisfied and the coin or resource used to satisfy the need. In brief, *specific* compensation satisfies a specific need in a coin or resource that differs from the need itself (from what was given up). For example, workers who steal from the organization in response to wage cuts are providing themselves specific compensation (McLean Parks, 1997). The coin is different (wages versus stolen product), in this case. However, the same need — to feed one's children — has been satisfied, whether by stolen bread or higher wages. Similarly, a busy executive may hire a concierge service to run dry cleaning to the cleaners and pick up children after soccer practice. In this case, the need — time to complete parental responsibilities — has been fulfilled within the home realm, but with a different coin (paying for services rather than using up one's own time). This is an exchange of like for nearly like, and thus is specific compensation. *Homologous* compensation comprises resources of a like kind (e.g. a romance novel for a text book) where the resources, although alike (e.g. books) satisfy different needs (e.g. pleasure reading versus learning). *Substitute* compensation comprises different types of resources and is exchanged in different domains, fulfilling different needs. McLean Parks (1997) provides the example of purchasing Papal indulgences for sins committed against others in the early Catholic Church. Neither the need nor the coin are equivalent. These three relationships can be seen in Figure 5.3. Specific, homologous and substitute compensation are accounted for in existing theory, but the absence of a form of compensation in which both the need and the coin are identical is a glaring omission.

Filling this gap, Sparrowe, Dirks, Bunderson, and McLean Parks (2004) add to Pruitt's (1981) three categories by suggesting a fourth category, *isomorphic* compensation occurs when "like for like" resources are exchanged that satisfy the same need (e.g. paper money for the same amount of money in coins) in the same domain. Further, they note that this exact matching may be quite important. In our

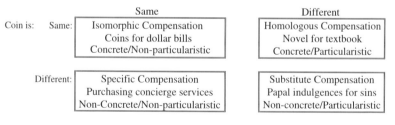

Figure 5.3: Commensurability and resource exchange.

first example — working through a weekend — one can see the complexity inherent in determining the resources. Being compensated by a day off would be isomorphic compensation, if it were just the time that had been lost. But if the time lost represents participating in an important event for one's spouse, then it is no longer isomorphic compensation, a distinction that, as we shall see, may be quite important (see Figure 5.3).

Returning to our previous discussion of kinship distance (see Figure 5.1), we now note that commensurability can also range along a continuum that moves from closely aligned and related workers to more distal workers, which parallels the movement from generalized to negative reciprocity. Specifically, we would argue that when substitute compensation is used, since neither the resource nor the need are the same, it is more difficult to calibrate the exchange and to ensure fairness. Thus, substitute compensation may be most easily used and less likely to result in a breach or violation in close relationships with generalized reciprocity, where the parties trust one another and may, perhaps, be counted on to be fair. At the other extreme, isomorphic compensation may be the only acceptable compensation in more distal relationships where a more direct matching is needed in order to guard against exploitation. Homologous and specific compensation would lie between these two extremes. A vivid example of the potential for exploitation when resources and needs fulfilled cannot be matched is the undocumented but colourful legend of how Manhattan Island was purchased from the Native American tribes for $24 worth of beads. Accepting the legend as true, the resources exchanged were obviously different — land versus beads. The needs met by each resource also were different — land provided homes and food while beads provided decoration. The legendary inequity resulting from the substitute compensation exchanged exemplifies the potential for exploitation when neither the need nor the resource are the same, and hence commensurability is difficult to ascertain.

This brings us to the topic of the actual currencies exchanged.

Currencies

The extant literature, in particular that in the psychological contracts area, has emphasized the importance of the type and nature of the resources exchanged (e.g. McLean Parks et al., 1998; Rousseau & McLean Parks, 1993). Extreme transactional contracts are those in which the primary mode of exchange is economic or monetized, while the extreme relational contract includes the exchange not only of economic resources, but also socio-emotional resources (Rousseau & McLean Parks, 1993; McLean Parks & smith, 1998). Edwards and Bunderson (2003) added a third currency to those of the transactional and relational: ideological currencies, which are the "credible commitments to pursue a valued cause or principle (not limited to self-interest) that are implicitly exchanged at the nexus of the individual-organization relationship" (Edwards & Bunderson, 2003, p. 574). The ideological currency concept taps into the values that workers may hold near and dear, and that are likely to serve as a primary motivator for the time they devote to both work and other activities. In this case, the worker has internalized the values espoused by the organization (Edwards & Bunderson, 2003), and is attached to the organization by virtue of a common cause. For example, animal rights advocates may be bound to a cosmetic company because it does not engage in animal testing — it is the common ideology that binds the worker and it is contributions towards that ideology (by not testing on animals) that is the coin of the exchange.

Foa and Foa (1971, 1975) argued that resources can be described in terms of: (1) how particularistic they are, and (2) how concrete or tangible they are. *Particularistic* resources are those in which the identity of the parties' matters — for example, who gives you a kiss. Non-particularistic resources are fungible, and can be substituted for one another, for example, 100 pennies exchanged for a dollar. *Concrete* resources are those that can generally be unambiguously interpreted by outsiders (McLean Parks & smith, 1998). In an exchange of money (my dollar for your 100 pennies) it is easy to see that the exchange has been fair, and most people would probably agree that the exchange was like for like, and resulted in a fair outcome for both parties. Relationships in which concrete resources are exchanged, then, are much easier to monitor (McLean Parks & smith, 1998). As argued by McLean Parks and smith (1998) transactional relationships will focus on concrete and non-particularistic resources — an arm's length transaction where identity is relatively unimportant and the outcomes are easily monitored and matched like for like, ideally isomorphic compensation. In contrast, the socio-emotional aspects of the more relational work relationship — such as loyalty and friendship — are more likely to be particularistic and less concrete. This makes them more difficult to monitor, and simultaneously makes judgments subjective and more prone to misinterpretation or mis-calibration.

As one might imagine, concrete and tangible resources, at least in part because of the ease with which they can be monitored, are easier to calibrate, insuring commensurability, and incorporate into either isomorphic or specific compensation (see Figure 5.2). Similarly, non-particularistic resources will be easier to calibrate, while particularistic resources will be quite difficult to calibrate. Is my kiss worth more than yours? Difficulty in calibrating resources is quite likely to lead to misunderstandings, perceptions of inequity, possible exploitation and violated psychological contracts (McLean Parks, 1997). Ideological currencies require isomorphic compensation (Shore et al., 2004). For ideological currencies, no other coin will do (Edwards & Bunderson, 2003). Neither can another need be substituted because ideologies are both particularistic and lack concreteness. By definition, the particularistic character of an ideology suggests that no other need can be substituted. Further, because ideologies lack concreteness, their compensation is neither easily monitored nor calibrated. Consequently, for ideological currencies, the only way to ensure a fair exchange is isomorphism. For example, an animal rights advocate will not be ideologically attached to an organization that supports Habitat for Humanity, but which has no engagement in animal rights issues — other social issues simply will not do. This creates a paradox, as isomorphism lends itself most clearly to the concrete and non-particularistic, yet ideologies are non-concrete and particularistic (see Figure 5.3).

In sum, concrete and non-particularistic resources are more easily calibrated, monitored and compared to ensure against exploitation. The more distal the relationship, the more likely that concrete and non-particularistic resources will be used. Non-concrete and particularistic resources, such as social relationships, will be more commonly exchanged when relationships are close. Yet the exchange of resources differentially among the various types of workers, such as pizza parties for core workers, is likely to result in social comparisons, feelings of marginalization and relative deprivation (Crosby, 1976). Like the paradox of ideological currencies, these comparison processes may be particularly prone to a breach of violation of the relationship.

Conclusions

Work relationships are changing. Just like the idealistic view of family relationships from the 1950s has changed, so too has the work relationship. With the exception of papers comparing one class of worker to another (e.g. temps to "traditional" workers), little if any real attention has been paid to the legions of "ghost" workers who are part of the new global economy. As a consequence, our existing theory and empirical results have little that is reliable to say about these workers' attitudes, values and behaviours, and how their presence in the workforce — in ever increasing numbers — will impact not only other workers, but also the organizations in which they work. We have suggested that three broad areas ripe for theorizing and exploring the impact of these diverse work relationships. We have explored the blurring of organizational boundaries and its impact on organizational identification, on in-groups and the identity of both the workers and of the organization. We have delved into issues associated with the norms of reciprocity that are the bedrock of all exchange relationships, and explored the relationship between these reciprocity norms and their immediacy with diverse work relationships, and suggest that they may be particularly important in determining the willingness to engage in extra-role behaviour, but also reactions to alienation and perceived mistreatment at work. Finally, we have explored how the actual currency exchanged in these diverse work relationships and the importance of the issue of commensurability. It is our hope that this paper stimulates a more careful consideration and analysis of the new paradoxes, tensions and concerns that arise when we recognize the largely unacknowledged and unmeasured diversity of work relationships in organizations.

Acknowledgment

We would like to thank Li Ma and Sammy Showail for their help with the literature review. Support of for this project of a research grant from the Boeing Center for Technology, Information & Manufacturing (BCTIM) is gratefully acknowledged.

References

Adler, P., & Adler, P. (1988). Intense loyalty in organizations: A case study in college athletics. *Administrative Science Quarterly, 33*, 401–417.

Albert, S., & Whetten, D. (1985). Organizational identity. In: L. Cummings, & B. Staw (Eds), *Research in organizational behaviour* (Vol. 7). Greenwich, CT: JAI Press.

Allen, C., & Strauss, M. (1980). Resources, power, and husband–wife violence. In: M. Straus, & G. Hotaling (Eds), *The social causes of husband–wife violence* (pp. 188–208). Minneapolis, MN: University of Minnesota.

Alston, J. (1989). Wa, Guanxi and Inwa: Managerial principles in Japan, China and Korea. *Business Horizons*, March/April, *32*, 26–31.

AP Wire Service. (2003). Suicides over tough economic times hit record high in Japan, July 26.

Ashforth, B., & Mael, F. (1989). Social identity theory and the organization. *Academy of Management Review, 14*, 20–39.

Ashforth, B., & Mael, F. (1996). Organization identity and strategy as a context for the individual. *Advances in Strategic Management, 13*, 19–64.

Axelrod, R. (1984). *The evolution of cooperation*. New York: Basic Books.

Barker, J. (1993). Tightening the iron cage: Concertive control in self-managing teams. *Administrative Science Quarterly, 38*, 408–437.

Barnard, C. (1938). The functions of executive. Cambridge, MA: Harvard University Press.

Baron, J., & Ritov, I. (1994). Reference points and omission bias. *Organizational Behaviour and Human Decision Processes, 59*, 475–498.

Baumeister, R. (1986). *Identity: Cultural change and the struggle for self*. New York: Oxford University Press.

Baumeister, R. (1996). *Evil: Inside human violence and cruelty*. New York: Henry Holt and Company.

Baumeister, R. (1997). Identity, self concept, and self esteem: The self lost and found. In: R. Hogan, J. Johnson, & S. Briggs (Eds), *Handbook of personality psychology* (pp. 681–710). San Diego, CA: Academic Press.

Baxter, V., & Margavio, A. (1996). Assaultive violence in the US post office. *Work and Occupations, 23*(3), 277–296.

Bergami, M., & Bagozzi, R. (2000). Self-categorization, affective commitment and group self esteem as distinct aspects of social identity in the organization. *British Journal of Social Psychology, 39*, 555–577.

Bernstein, A. (1995). Outsourced — and out of luck. *Business Week*, July 17, 60–61.

Bowen, D. & Schneider, B. (1988). Services marketing management: Implications for organizational behavior. In: B.M. Straw & L.L. Cummings (Ed.) *Research in Organizatinal Behavior*. Greenwich, Ct. JAL.

Bureau of Labour Statistices (1995). Contingent and alternative employment arrangement, Report 900, United States Department of Labor, Washington, DC.

Bureau of Labor Statistics (BLS). (2002). US Department of Labor, Bureau of Labor Statistics. *Census of Fatal Occupational Injuries.*

Branscombe, N. & Wann, D. (1994). Peripheral ingroup membership status and public negativity toward outgroups. *Journal of Personality and Social Psychology, 68*(1), 127–137.

Brashear, T., Boles, J., Bellenger, D., & Brooks, C. (2003). An empirical test of trust building processes and outcomes in sales manager–sales person relationships. *Journal of the Academy of Marketing Science, 31*(2), 189–200.

Breakwell, G. (1986). *Coping with threatened identities*. London: Methuen.

Brewer, M. (1979). Ingroup bias in minimal intergroup situation: A cognitive-motivational analysis. *Psychological Bulletin, 19*, 381–388.

Brewer, M. (1991). The social self: On being the same and different at the same time. *Personality and Social Psychology Bulletin, 7*, 475–482.

Bullis, C., & Tompkins, P. (1989). The forest ranger revisited: A study of control practices and identification. *Communication Monographs, 56*, 287–306.

Catalano, R., Dooley, D., Novaco, R., Wilson, G., & Hough, R. (1993). Using ECA survey data to examine the effect of job layoffs on violent behaviour. *Hospital & Community Psychiatry, 44*(9), 874–879.

Cebyrznski, G. (2003). The secret's out: Steak n Shake TV ads rock to a simple tune. *Nation's Restaurant News*, May 12 (http://www.findarticles.com/p/articles/mi_m3190/is_19_37/ai_101860235).

Chase, R. & Erickson, W. (1988). The service factory. *Academy of Mangement Executive, 2*, 191–196.

Cheney, G. (1983). On the various and changing meaning of organizational membership: A field study of organizational identification. *Communication Monographs, 50*, 342–362.

Cheng, C. (1996). Uniform, symbols, and "old me": A symbolic interactionist ethnography of the social construction of hegemonic masculinity. Paper presented at the SCOS conference, UCLA, Los Angeles, CA (as cited in Rafaeli, 1997).

Cooper, H. & Kamm, T. (1998). Europe firms lift unemployment by laying off unneeded workers, *Wall Street Journal*, June 3.

Crino, M., & Leap, T. (1989). What HR managers must know about employee sabotage. *Personnel, 66*(5), 31–38.

Crosby, F. (1976). A model of egoistical relative deprivation. *Psychological Review, 83,* 85–113.

da Gloria, J. (1984). Frustration, aggression and a sense of injustice. In: A. Mummendey (Ed.), *Social psychology of aggression: From individual behaviour to social iteraction* (pp. 127–141). New York: Springer.

Daft, R., & Weick, K. (1984). Towards a model of organizations as interpretation systems. *Academy of Management Review, 9*(2), 284–295.

Dobbs, L. (2004). *Exporting America: Why corporate greed is shipping American jobs overseas.* New York: Warner Business Books.

Dollard, J., Doobs, L., Miller, N., Mowrer, O., & Sears, R. (1939). *Frustration and aggression.* New Haven, CT: Yale University Press.

Dukerich, J., & Carter, S. (2000). Distorted images and reputation repair. In: M. Hatch, & M. Schultz (Eds), *The expressive organization: Linking identity, reputation and the corporate brand* (pp. 97–114). Oxford: Oxford University Press.

Duncan, B. (1976). Differential social perception and attribution of intergroup violence: Testing the lower limits of stereotyping Blacks. *Journal of Personality and Social Psychology, 34,* 590–598.

Dutton, J., Dukerich, J., & Harquail, C. V. (1994). Organizational images and member identification. *Administrative Science Quarterly, 39,* 239–263.

EarthWatch. (2004). http://www.earthwatch.org/aboutew/mission.html, http://www.earthwatch.org/expeditions/faq.html#1.

Edwards, J., & Bunderson, J.S. (2003). Violations of principle: Ideological currency in the psychological contract. *Academy of Management Review, 28,* 571–586.

Elsbach, K., & Bhattacharya, C. (1998). Organizational dis-identification. Paper presented at the Annual meetings of the academy of management. Boston, MA.

Erikson, E. (1993 [1959]). The problem of ego in identity. In: G. Pollock (Ed.), *Pivotal papers on identification* (pp. 265–303). Madison, CT: International Universities Press.

Erikson, E. (1968 [1956]). *Identity: Youth and crisis.* New York: W.W. Norton.

Feather, N., & Rauter, K. (2004). Organizational citizenship behaviours in relation to job status, job insecurity, organizational commitment and identification, job satisfaction and work values. *Journal of Occupational & Organizational Psychology, 77*(1), 81–94.

Fein, S., & Spencer, S. (1997). Prejudice and self-image maintenance: Affirming the self through derogating others. *Journal of Personality and Social Psychology, 73,* 31–44.

Ferelli, M., & Trowbridge, D. (1990). People are the security problem, not computers. *Computer Technology Review, 10,* 8–9.

Flannery, R. (1995). *Violence in the workplace.* New York: Crossroads.

Foa, U. (1971). Interpersonal and economic resources. *Science, 171,* 345–351.

Foa, U., & Foa, G. (1975). *Resource theory of social exchange.* Morristown, NJ: General Learning Press.

Fullerton, G. (2003). When does commitment lead to loyalty? *Journal of Service Research, 5*(4), 333–344.

Fusé, T. (1980). Suicide and culture in Japan: A study of seppuku as an institutionalized form of suicide. *Social Psychiatry, 15*(2), 57–63.

Gallagher, J. (2005). Class action suits likely to increase as companies cut older workers. *Knight Rider/Tribune News Service*, January 15, page 1.

Giacalone, R. (1990). Employee sabotage: The enemy within. *Supervisory Management, 37*(7), 6–7.

Gouldner, A. (1960). The norm of reciprocity: A preliminary statement. *American Sociological Review, 25*, 161–177.

Hatch, M., & Schultz, M. (2000). Scaling the tower of Babel: Relational differences between identity, image and culture in organizations. In: M. Hatch, & M. Schultz (Eds), *The expressive organization: Linking identity, reputation and the corporate brand* (pp. 11–35). Oxford: Oxford University Press.

Henson, D. (1996). Just a Temp. Philadelphia, PA: Temple University Press.

Hewstone, M. (1990). The ultimate attribution error: A review of the literature on intergroup causal attribution. *European Journal of Social Psychology, 10*, 222–226.

Hirsch, P. (1987). *Pack your own parachute: How to survive mergers, takeovers, and other corporate disasters*. Reading, MA: Addison-Wesley.

Hodson, G., Dovidio, J., & Esses, V. (2003). In-group identification as a moderator of positive–negative asymmetry in social discrimination. *European Journal of Social Psychology, 33*(2), 215–233.

Hofstede, G. (1980). *Culture's consequences*. London: Sage.

Hornung, C., & McCullough, B. (1981). Status relationships in dual-employment marriages: Consequences for psychological well-being. *Journal of Marriage and the Family, 43*(2), 125–141.

Hornung, C., McCullough, B., & Sugimoto, T. (1981). Status relationships in marriage: Risk factors in spouse abuse. *Journal of Marriage and Family, 43*(3), 675–692.

Ingalls, R. (1999). *A matter of class: A narrative analysis of working class masculine identities*. Unpublished doctoral dissertation, *Dissertation Abstracts International*.

Jackson, P., Stafford, E., Banks, M., & Warr, P. (1983). Unemployment and psychological distress in young people: The moderating role of work involvement. *Journal of Applied Psychology, 68*, 525–535.

Jackson, P., & Taylor, P. (1994). Factors associated with employment status in later working life. *Work, Employment and Society, 8*, 553–567.

Jensen, M., & Meckling, W. (1976). Theory of the firm: Managerial behaviour, agency costs, and ownership structure. Journal of Financial Economics, *3*, 305–360.

Johnson, P., & Gardner, S. (1999). Domestic violence and the workplace: Developing a company response. *Journal of Management Development, 18*, 590–597.

Katz, D. & Kahn, R. (1978). The Social Psychology of Organizations. NY: Wiley.

Kilcullen, R., Mael, F., Goodwin, G., & Zazanis, M. (1999). Predicting US Army Special Forces field performance. *Human Performance in Extreme Environments, 4*(1), 53–63.

Kimball, G. (2005). Kobe has his out: Silence. *The Boston Herald*, March 3, p. 94.

Klein, N. (2002). *No logo*. New York: Picador USA.

Kramer, R. (1993). Cooperation and organizational identification. In: J.K. Murnighan (Ed.), *Social psychology in organizations: Advances in theory and research* (pp. 244–268). Englewood Cliffs, NJ: Prentice-Hall.

Lele, M. (1986). How service needs influence product strategy. *Sloan Management Review*, 28(1), 63–70.

Levens, J., Paladino, P., Rodriguez-Torres, R., Vaes, J., Demoulin, S., Rodriguez-Perez, A., & Gaunt, R. (2000). The emotional side of prejudice: The attribution of secondary emotions to ingroups and outgroups. *Personality & Social Psychology Review*, 4(2), 186–197.

Luhmann, N. (1979). *Trust and power*. New York: Wiley.

Madore, J. (2005). Less loyal to Martha's brand. *Newsday*, March 1, p. A39.

Mael, F., & Ashforth, B. (1992). Alumni and their alma mater: A partial test of the reformulated model of organizational identification. *Journal of Organizational Behaviour*, 13, 103–123.

Mael, F., & Ashforth, B. (1995). Loyal from day one: Biodata, organizational identification, and turnover among newcomers. *Personnel Psychology*, 48, 309–333.

Magnier, M. (2001). Japan's suicide rate. *Los Angeles Times*, December 15, p. A1.

Malinowski, B. (1922). *Argonauts of the Western Pacific*. London: Routledge & Keagan Paul.

McClam, E. (2004). Martha Stewart to begin serving prison term in weeks, aiming to soon regain "good life." *Associated Press State & Local Wire*, September 16.

McLean Parks, J. (1990). *The contracts as a control metaphor for relationships in organizations: The effects of social distance and contractual specificity*. Unpublished doctoral dissertation, University of Iowa.

McLean Parks, J. (1997). The fourth arm of justice: The art and science of revenge. In: R. Lewicki, B. Sheppard, & B. Bies' (Eds), *Research on negotiation in organization* (pp. 113–144). Greenwich, CT: JAI Press.

McLean Parks, J., & Kidder, D. (1994). Trends: Till death us do part: The changing nature of organizational contracts and commitments. *Journal of Organizational Behaviour, Trends*, 1, 111–136.

McLean Parks, J., Kidder, D., & Gallagher, D. (1998). Fitting square pegs into round holes: Mapping the domain of contingent work arrangements onto the psychological contract. *Journal of Organizational Behaviour*, 19, 697–730.

McLean Parks, J., & smith, f. (1998). Organizational contracting: A "rational" exchange? In: J. Halpern, & R. Stern (Eds), *Debating rationality: Nonrational aspects of organizational decision making* (pp. 168–210). Ithaca, NY: Cornell University Press.

McLean Parks, J., & smith, f. (2000). Organizational identity: The ongoing puzzle of definition and redefinition. Paper presented at the 2000 Academy of Management meetings. Managerial and Organizational Cognition Division, Toronto, CA, August.

McLean Parks, J., & smith, f. (2004). A tapestry of meaning: Articulating organizational identity through identity frames. *Organization Science*, under revision.

Miller, L. (1999). Workplace violence: Prevention, response and recovery. *Psychotherapy: Theory, Research, Practice, Training*, 36(2), 160–169.

Mitchell, W. (1988). The defeat of hierarchy: Gambling as exchange in Sepik society. *American Ethnologist*, 15(4), 638–667.

Morgan, G. (1986). *Images of organizations*. Thousand Oaks, CA: Sage.

Mullen, B., Brown, R., & Smith, C. (1992). Ingroup bias as a function of salience, relevance and status: An integration. *European Journal of Social Psychology, 22,* 103–122.

Oldham, G., Cummings, A., & Zhou, J. (1995). The spatial configuration of organizations: A review of the literature and some new research directions. *Research in Personnel and Human Resources Management, 13,* 1–37.

O'Reilly, C., & Chatman, J. (1986). Organizational commitment and psychological attachment: The effects of compliance, identification, and internalization on prosocial behaviour. *Journal of Applied Psychology, 71,* 492–499.

Organ, D. (1988). Organizational Citizenship behavior: The Good Soldier Syndrome. Lexington Books. Lexington, MA.

Perdue, C., Dovidio, J., Gurtman, M., & Tyler, R. (1990). Us and them: Social categorization and the process of intergroup bias. *Journal of Personality and Social Psychology, 59*(3), 475–486.

Polzer, J. (2004). How subgroup interests and reputations moderate the effect of organizational identification on cooperation. *Journal of Management, 30*(1), 71–96.

Popham, A. (1998). Companies learn domestic violence is, in fact, their business. *The News Tribune,* April 5, p. G2.

Pruitt, D. (1981). *Negotiation behaviour.* New York: Academic Press.

Pye, L. (1982). *Chinese commercial negotiating style.* Cambridge, MA: Oelgeschlager, Gunn & Hain.

Rafaeli, A. (1997). What is an organization? Who are the members? In: C. Cooper, & S. Jackson (Eds), *Creating tomorrow's organizations* (pp. 122–155). New York, John Wiley & Sons.

Rodman, H. (1968). Family and social pathology in the ghetto. *Science, 161*(August), 756–762.

Rothbart, M., & Hallmark, W. (1988). In-group-out-group differences in the perceived efficacy of coercion and conciliation in resolving social conflict. *Journal of Personality and Social Psychology, 55,* 248–257.

Rousseau, D., & McLean Parks, J. (1993). The contracts of individuals and organizations. In: L.L. Cummings, & B. Staw (Eds), *Research in organizational behavior* (Vol. 15, pp. 1–43). Greenwich, CT: JAI Press.

Sahlins, M. (1972). *Stone Age Economics.* Chicago: Aldine Atherton.

Scaillet, N., & Leyens, P. (2000). From incorrect deductive reasoning to ingroup favouritism. In: D. Capossa, & R. Brown (Eds), *Social identity processes: Trends in theory and research.* London: Sage.

Scalora, M., Washington, D., O'Neil, D., Casady, T., & Newell, S. (2003). Nonfatal workplace violence risk factors: Data from a police contact sample. *Journal of Interpersonal Violence, 18,* 310–327.

Serwer, A. (2002). Martha's survival is on the chopping block. *Fortune,* June 25.

Sheppard, B., Lewicki, R., & Minton, J. (1992). *Organizational justice: The search for fairness in the workplace.* New York: Lexington Books.

Shore, L., Tetrick, L., Taylor, S., Shapiro, J., Liden, R., McLean Parks, J., Morrison, E., Porter, L., Roehling, M., Rousseau, D., Schalk, R., Tsui, A., & Van Dyne, L. (2004).

The employee–organization relationship: A timely concept in a period of transition. *Research in personnel and human resources management* (Vol. 23, pp. 291–370). Elsevier. Greenwich, CT.

Simon, H. (1976). *Administrative behaviour*. New York: Free press.

Smith, W. (1913). *Sabotage: Its history, philosophy and function*. Chicago: Black Swan Press.

Sparrowe, R., Dirks, K., Bunderson, S., & McLean Parks, J. (2004). Reinventing the wheel and spinning our wheels: Social exchange and discretionary attitudes and outcomes in organizations. Unpublished paper, Washington University at St. Louis.

Stuart, P. (1992). Murder on the job. *Personnel Journal, 71*(2), 72–84.

Tajfel, H. (1981). *Human groups and social categories*. New York: Cambridge University Press.

Tajfel, H., & Turner, J. (1986). The social identity theory of intergroup relations. In: S. Worchel, & W. Austin (Eds), *Psychology of intergroup relations* (2nd ed., pp. 7–24). Chicago, IL: Nelson-Hall.

Tangney, J., & Dearing, R. (2002). *Shame and guilt*. New York: Guilford Press.

Thompson, W. (1983). Hanging tongues: A sociological encounter with the assembly line. *Qualitative Sociology, 6*, 215–237.

Thompson, J., & Bunderson, S. (2003). Violations of principle: Ideological currency in the psychological contact. *Academy of Management Reveiw, 28*(4), 577–586.

Tompkins, P., & Cheney, G. (1985). Communication and unobtrusive control in contemporary organizations. In: R. McPhee, & P. Tompkins (Eds), *Organizational communication: Traditional themes and new directions* (pp. 179–211). Beverly Hills, CA: Sage.

Treanor, J. (2004). Barclays buys into Mumbai's booming offshore market. *The Guardian* (London ed.), August 17, p. 18.

Turnley, W., & Feldman, D. (1988). Psychological contract violations during organizational restructuring. *Human Resource Management, 37*, 71–83.

Tushman, M. (1977). Special boundary roles in the innovation process. *Administrative Science Quarterly, 22*, 587–605.

Van Dick, R., Christ, O., Stellmacher, J., Wagner, U., Ahlswede, O., Grubba, C., Hauptmeier, M., Höhfeld, C., & Moltzen, K. (2004). Should I stay or should I go? Explaining turnover intentions with organizational identification and job satisfaction. *British Journal of Management, 15*(4), 351–360.

Van Dyne, L., Cummings, L., & McLean Parks, J. (1995). Extra-role behaviours: A critical analysis and theoretical interpretation (A bridge over muddied waters). In: B. Staw & L.L. Cummings (Eds), *Research in organizational behaviour* (Vol. 17, pp. 215–285). Greenwich, CT: JAI Press.

Van Dyne, L., Graham, J., & Dienesch, R. (1994). Organizational citizenship behaviour: Construct redefinition, measurement and validation. *Academy of Management Journal, 37*, 765–802.

Van Vugt, M., & Hart, C. (2004). Social identity as social glue: The origins of group loyalty. *Journal of Personality and Social Psychology, 86*(4), 585–598.

Weber, M. (1947). *The theory of economic and social organizations*. New York: Free Press.

White, W. (1956). *The organization man*. Simon & Schuster, New York: Simon & Schuster.

Chapter 6

Complexity Theory and the Management of Change

Pamela M. Yeow and Paul R. Jackson

We start by outlining the 21st century organisation, discuss a variety of definitions of complexity, and then look into the importance and relevance of such theories to organisational change in the 21st century. By doing so, the relevance of complexity theory will be clear in understanding complex organisations in the present turbulent economic environment that most organisations find themselves in. The study of complex systems dynamics has mostly been in the natural sciences but it is increasingly showing its applicability in the field of the social sciences, and more specifically in the study of organisations. We apply complexity thinking to the management of change within organisations.

The New Competitive Environment

Organisations at the start of the 21st century are living in the age of complexity, and have to deal with issues of uncertainty, insecurity and increased amounts of competition (Beer & Nohria, 2000). In the same way, they have also had to deal with these issues at a much faster pace than organisations of the old (Ilinich, Lewin, & D'Aveni, 1998). This has to do partly with the proliferation and increased use of computers, technology and the Internet, which helped evolve and change the way people went about their life. Consequently, as Black and Edwards (2000) write, there has been a shift in how organisations operate that goes beyond the obvious convenience of advanced communications equipment and other high technology-based tools. The information revolution has enabled the knowledge economy and the knowledge society. With the ever-changing technology in

Developments in Work Organizational Psychology
Copyright © 2006 by Elsevier Ltd.
All rights of reproduction in any form reserved
ISBN: 0-08-044467-9

computers and microchips, the creation of the Internet, electronic mail and so on, has reduced the transmission of information and knowledge to mere seconds. Even time in the IT industry has been given the new name of 'web-time' where a web-year is a quarter of a normal calendar year. With these advances in technology, it is possible to increase the responsiveness of one process to another, making the exchange and creation of knowledge and information a much quicker process and an ever-changing one. With more knowledge, and acquired at such speed, it rather automatically creates a complex revolution. Related to this is that, with all this information, business systems that originally were only partially open have to be more open to information. To compete effectively, businesses have to see the changing nature of their customers, competition and the economic markets in ways that enable them to produce goods and services of genuine value (Kelly & Allison, 1998, p. 13).

Organisations are being created, transformed and disbanded quicker. Mergers and alliances are getting increasingly popular (see Jackson & Dackert, this book); and virtual organisations are created on short notice for specific purposes using outsourcing, project consultants, temporary workers and so forth (creating powerful challenges to those who are part of them, see McLean Parks & smith, this book). Cohen (1999) brings our attention to the 'formation and dissolution of an organisation's boundaries and to the forces that allow an organisation to have value "greater than the sum of its parts" ' (p. 374). New ways of working such as working from home (using the Internet and Intranet to be connected to the office), teleconferencing (so that people no longer have to travel to meet up with other parties) and the creation of virtual or network organisations (Black & Edwards, 2000) are all part of the information revolution. As a consequence, the manner in which organisational research is conducted and the way organisations are organised 'may need to re-gear to be able to manage change in organisations of the twenty-first century' (Black & Edwards, 2000, p. 567). A consequence of change, uncertainty and subsequent increased competition within industries is that not only the employees who are insecure and have to change to keep up with others, but companies too have had to be constantly vigilant. In the new competitive landscape, businesses can no longer expect to be stable and long-lived (Hitt, Ireland, & Koskisson, 1999).

The New Knowledge Landscape

It was Drucker who first coined the terms 'knowledge work' and 'knowledge worker' in order to capture the idea that the basic economic resource is no longer capital, natural resources or labour but rather knowledge (Drucker, 1993). Value is created through the application of knowledge to work. 'Knowledge workers' are then the people who know how to allocate knowledge to productive use. Tucker, Meyer, and Westerman (1996) have expanded on this theme in arguing that communicated knowledge is what brings enduring competitive advantage. This is not to say that land, labour and capital, previously understood economic resources, have disappeared. According to Drucker (1993), these have become secondary and can be obtained easily with knowledge. It is proposed that because the function of the organisation of the post-capitalist society (that is, the knowledge-based society) is to put knowledge to work — on processes, on work and on knowledge itself — the organisation must be organised for constant change (Drucker, 1993). Owing to the nature of knowledge that changes fast, today's innovation can become tomorrow's obsolete product. In the old economy, the challenge inside the firm was to coordinate the physical items produced by different employees. This was mainly an issue of managing the production and physical flow of (intermediate) products. In the knowledge economy, however, the challenge is to build, combine and integrate the knowledge assets of many thousands of individuals — a much more formidable task. Further, the new Internet-enabled economy is leading to the proliferation of new electronic marketplaces, making transactions in standardised and quasi-standardised products even more efficient. Hence, these integrated firms of the early 21st century need to be well equipped in knowledge creation, accumulation, protection and deployment capabilities, as compared to previously pure market-instigated arrangements (Nonaka & Teece, 2001).

Modern organisations have to build into their very structure the idea and practice of management of change; and the focus of this chapter is on how ideas from complexity theory can inform that process. The need to improve and constantly create the new has to be implicit within the organisation to ensure its survival and expansion. It has to not only adopt kaizen (the Japanese term for continuous improvement) but also learn to exploit so as to benefit from their successes. Finally, the organisation has to learn to innovate and innovate systematically. Without continuous improvement, creative exploitation and innovation, these organisations might eventually lose its ability to attract and keep the knowledge employees, on whom they depend on, for survival. Knowledge employees own their knowledge and can take it with them wherever they go. As Mirvis and Hall (1994) write, 'the future is projected to have large firms, through multiple divisions as well as joint ventures, regional alliances and private–public partnerships dominate major markets while entrepreneurs, franchisers and small businesses provide raw materials and technologies, handle support services, distribute goods and at the same time reach niche markets with their own products and services. These flexible firms are coming to be called boundaryless organisations' (p. 366).

It was suggested that the reason why there has not been great acceptance of such organisations, and why there has not been a smooth transition from the traditional organisation type to the boundaryless one is because the much needed transitional structures and mechanisms, such as flexible work options, retraining and redeployment programmes, family support services, career planning and placement assistance are not yet in place in large quantities to sustain such a career style (Mirvis, 1993; see also McLean Parks & smith, this book).

The Need for New Ways of Thinking about Organisations

Black (2000) writes that 'the lack of long-term predictability and the guarantee of change highlights the ineffectiveness of some of the organizing principles that we have been using for the past hundred or so years' (p. 522). As a result of this growing recognition that change is normal, Anderson et al. (1999) describes how there has been a shift in how researchers and academics view change in individuals, groups and organisations away from traditional, mechanistic models towards dynamic models. The *mechanistic* model can be seen to model the old order of the business system. By that, we mean that there is an assumption that the system structure was going to be in a stable form for an indefinite time into the future. The organisation is seen to be a stable entity, where boundaries can be defined, determined and identified. Hence, rules can be applied, as situations are predictable over time. Miles and Snow (1992) summarised a history of organisational forms, and in their summary noted that the matrix form (developed in the 1960s and 1970s) was focused on the primary aim to have the efficient production of standardised goods and services through the appropriate allocations of resources.

By contrast, *dynamic* models (Prigogine & Glansdorff, 1971; Prigogine & Stengers, 1984) recognise that complex organisation systems have great flows of energy, information and resources that generate a flux and a constant pressure to change and adapt to external environmental changes. Dynamic models have been shown to be comprehensive and more accurate for modelling what actually occurs in complex rapidly changing organisations (Lichtenstein, 2000). West (1985) describes four basic assumptions that underlie the dynamics of complex systems, contrasting them with the assumptions from mechanistic science. The four assumptions are that: change is constant; emergent systems are not reducible to their parts; there is mutual dependence within the complex organisation; and complex systems behave in non-proportional ways.

From the work of biologists writing about evolutionary processes, at least two schools of thoughts have emerged. Gell-Mann (1995) was of the opinion that although in principle the complex can be reduced to the simple, in reality this is not practicable and hence it is pointless to attempt reductionist explanations when they are not necessary or needed. On the other hand, Kauffman (1993, 1995) accepted the holistic notion that the complex is not inherently analysable into its simple components and although his ideas of complex and contingent causation are not explicit, his three-level framework of evolution of species, co-evolution of species in environments and the co-evolution of co-evolution itself through transformations of species and/in their environments is coherent.

Modern complexity theory has evolved from cybernetics (Ashby, 1956) which emphasised co-ordination, regulation and control using feedback loops; and general systems theory (Forrester, 1961; von Bertalanffy, 1968) which tried to explain the principles that underlie all types of systems whose components are linked by feedback loops (Anderson, 1999), to view organisations as open systems (Katz & Kahn, 1978) and the idea that organisations are loosely coupled, more so than physical systems (Weick, 1979). This has led to researchers embracing the understanding of equilibrium, with catastrophe theory (Thom, 1975) explaining how in some deterministic systems, a small shift in a parameter can send the system to a different equilibrium, and chaos theory exploring how apparently random and dynamic systems are in fact deterministic, demonstrating that simple laws can have complicated, unpredictable consequences (Thietart & Forgues, 1995). Complexity thinking has been applied to a variety or organisational forms (see Table 6.1).

Several theoretical perspectives have contributed to the increase in understanding of organisations as complex systems (cf. Maguire & McKelvey, 1999; Senge, 1990; Stacey, 1995; Holland, 1995; Gell-Mann, 1995). These have been

Table 6.1: Organisational applications of complexity thinking.

Economic and social systems: Anderson et al. (1989), Lewin (1992), Nicolis and Prigogine (1989)
Group transformation: Connie J. G. Gersick (1988), Smith and Comer (1994)
Entrepreneurial ventures: Cheng and Van de Ven (1996)
Innovation projects: Brown and Eisenhardt (1997), Brown and Eisenhardt (1998)
Large organisations: Stacey (1992), Kiel (1994)
Virtual/network organisations: Black and Edwards (2000)
Civil service organisations: Beeson and Davis (2000)
Academic disciplines: Jackson (2005)
Societies: Artigiani (1987), Adams (1988), Urry (2002)

variously applied and referred to as organisational learning systems, learning organisations, knowledge economies, transformed organisations and so on. In the past decade, the study of the 'science of complexity' has progressed, with the fastest penetration in the study of the natural sciences. However, recent tracks have been made in the study of organisational behaviour with the special issue of *Organization Science* (May–June 1999), *Strategic Management Journal*, along with many popular press books, on the applications of complexity theory to research in organisations. MacIntosh and MacLean (1999) write that in reconciling the split between the content and process approaches in strategy and the management of organisational transformations, complexity theory can be used effectively to develop and explain specific sequences of activities that underpin effective transformation (p. 297). According to them, complexity theory 'provides some justification for integrating specific elements of existing theories into a dynamic whole and thus provides a template for the management of transformation' (p. 300).

Organisations as Complex Social Systems

Closed systems such as a pendulum clock do not interact with their external environment, and they run down over time as they lose energy. This dissipation of energy is termed entropy, and such closed systems follow the second law of thermodynamics: eventually they cease to function and lose their structure. By contrast, almost all social systems are open to their environment, and through interactions with it they import energy. As a result, cultures, communities, organisations, groups and individuals are all systems with internal structure, and which interact with their environment. In the jargon of systems theory, they import energy from their environment. While all social systems are open to their environment, not all social systems are complex in their structure. Social groups vary in how they are organised, and the richness of connections with other communities also varies. The literature distinguishes between two kinds of complexity: organisational complexity and technological complexity.

Organisational complexity reflects the relationships among network members. Complexity increases with greater vertical or horizontal differentiation among network members (Simon, 1996). In general, complex social systems are hierarchical, with levels nested within levels. We can see that individuals form parts of work groups, which in turn are part of organisations based within communities and societies. The greater the number of levels in the hierarchy, the higher the complexity of the system and the problems of coordination of activities. Complexity also increases as a function of the number of interdependencies among network members. A more sophisticated analysis is offered by, for example, Thompson (1967) distinguishing between pooled, sequential and reciprocal interdependence. *Pooled* interdependence reflects the situation where each network member contributes partial knowledge, which is pooled to give a complete picture. *Sequential* interdependence occurs where the output from one network member becomes the input for another in sequence (as in a just-in-time production system — Jackson & Martin, 1996). *Reciprocal* interdependence reflects mutual dependencies among network members, where neither can act without input from the other. The second kind of complexity, *technology complexity*, reflect the character of the transformation of inputs into outputs. Complexity increases with greater variety of aspects of tasks: the number of inputs/outputs, the extent of diversity in the tasks needed to complete a product, and the level of diversity of specialists involved in a project. Complexity also increases with interdependency between tasks (or groups of tasks), teams, technologies and inputs (Jackson, Sprigg, & Parker, 2000; Sprigg, Jackson, & Parker, 2000).

Simple models incorporating varying numbers of network links have been explored by Kauffman (1995, 2000). In general, complexity increases with the density of networks, and the number of links among network members. Key defining characteristics of the degree of complexity in a system then are the size of the system (how many members it has) and the extent of interdependencies among them. These two features are captured by Kauffman's NK model, where N is the size of the network and K the number of linkages between one member and another. For a system of a given size, complexity increases as the number of linkages among system members increases. Three states of systems have been distinguished, depending on the degree of interdependence. Where linkages are few, the system is described as 'frozen', such that changes in one part of a system have few impacts elsewhere. At the other extreme, a high density of linkages among system members is described as 'hot' since changes that occur locally in one part of a system reverberate across the linkages between system members. Systems in a state of frozen rigidity will tend to maintain their state for long periods of time, while hot systems are randomly chaotic and constantly changing. Between these two extremes, Kauffman describes a position called the *edge of chaos*, which is characterised by intermediate levels of linkage among system members (Cramer, 1993; Brown & Eisenhardt, 1998). In this state, the system is open to change and also can maintain its state over time, such that individuals and organisations can learn from their past and also respond in positive ways to change (Bak, 1996; Cohen, 1999; Lewin, 1999). This position at the edge of chaos is characterised by rich connections with others inside and outside the organisation, continuous learning and flexibility in order to take advantage of unexpected and unpredictable opportunities.

The idea of edge of chaos position has proved an attractive one to a number of authors in the management literature in exploring how organisations can compete effectively in a rapidly changing world (Kelly & Allison, 1998; Marion, 1999). Brown and Eisenhardt (1998) argued that companies such as IBM, Intel and HP-Singapore were able to turn themselves round and became successful in their industry by positioning themselves on the 'edge of chaos'. The implications of this view for the management of organisations are explored in more detail in Chapter 9 (Jackson, this book), and here we confine our attention to a consideration of the management of change within complex social systems.

Managing Change in Complex Social Systems

The implications of the notion of planning are obvious, seeing that plans cannot be set out and expected to come true, except in some very specific cases. This is especially the case when it comes to systems that involve people. We are not advocating that organisations should cease to plan. The key would be to have a plan that is adaptable to nonlinear changes such that one does not end up rooted to a specific plan and yet have some form of structure. What is important is that the focus should be on 'planning as learning' (Brews & Hunt, 1999). Brews and Hunt (1999) found that in unstable environments such as in times of market and technological volatility, formal plans are more amenable to change. It was proposed that approaches such as environmental scanning and scenario planning should be used to help the organisation raise awareness and increase connectivity with the outside world.

Punctuated Equilibrium Models

Traditional change models (Burnes, 2004) assume a process, which involves change from one stable state to another. The best known example of such models is that of Lewin who proposed three steps: unfreezing the current state of a system, transition to a new state and re-freezing that state. A refinement of this model is the punctuated equilibrium model of change within work teams proposed by Gersick (1991) within which project teams experience long periods of broad stability punctuated by brief periods of revolutionary upheaval. Tushman and Romanelli (1985) applied the same idea to organisation change: 'organisations evolve through convergent periods punctuated by reorientations … which demark and set bearings for the next emergent period' (p. 171).

There are three key components of the punctuated equilibrium model: deep structure, equilibrium periods and revolutionary periods. The first of these, *deep structure*, refers to the paradigms that are the basis for organising actions within the system. These have been studied within the management in a variety of ways, including personal constructs, cognitive maps, mental models, schemas and world views (see Jackson & Dackert, this book; Hodgkinson, Maule, & Bown, 2004). They provide a basis for explaining and justifying the actions of agents within an organisational system; they define the criteria for evaluating alternative decision choices; they set out the rules of the organisational game, and the structure of the field on which that game is played out; and they give the basis for sense making within organisations (Weick, 1979). The actions of individuals, groups or departments are shaped by schemas, cognitive structures for understanding the meaning of alternative actions (indeed we would also argue that organisational actions are shaped by their culture). Where organisational actors deploy different schemas, there is clearly potential for conflict and misunderstanding. For example, Jackson, Sprigg, and Parker (2000) showed how differences across departments in understanding the meaning of the concept of teamworking led to resistance to planned changes in one site of a company, which greatly reduced the effectiveness of a planned organisational change initiative. On the other hand, bringing together people whose cognitive schemas differ (for instance in cross-functional project teams, or global work teams — see Turner, Parker, & Williams, this book) can encourage new integration of information and ideas to take place, resulting in creative synergies and renewal (Drazin, Glynn, & Kazanjian, 1999).

The second element of the model, *equilibrium*, describes periods of 'normal' working within organisations where changes occur within the framework of existing deep structure. Homeostatic mechanisms operate to preserve the deep structure and keep the system within a narrowly defined zone of equilibrium. The key feature of equilibrium periods is inertia or resistance, which serves to prevent the system from generating alternatives outside its own boundaries and pulling deviations back into line. Change within equilibrium periods has been described by Golembiewski, Billingsley, and Yeager (1976) as alpha and beta change (see Table 6.2).

The third element of the model encapsulates periods of *revolutionary* change, which involve fundamental alterations to an organisation's structure and systems, through changes in deep structure. Revolutionary change involves a process within which a system's deep structure comes apart, leaving it in disarray, until a new deep structure forms. Such change is deeply disturbing to organisational members, since the customary structures for guiding actions and decision-making no longer apply. For example, Nelson, Cooper, and Jackson (1995) studied a

Table 6.2: Forms of change.

Incremental change

   Alpha change: 'a variation in the level of some existential state, given a constantly calibrated measuring instrument related to a constant conceptual domain.'

   Beta change: 'a variation in some existential state, complicated by the fact that some intervals of the measurement continuum associated with a constant conceptual domain have been recalibrated.'

Revolutionary change

   Gamma change: 'a redefinition or reconceptualisation of some domain, a major change in the perspective or frame of reference within which phenomena are perceived and classified, in what is taken to be relevant in some slice of reality.'

water utility within the UK, and describe the impact of privatisation and subsequent restructuring on employees. Weick (1993) gives a graphic description of how dangerous such changes can be in a study of the consequences of the collapse of sense-making during a fire disaster, where a number of fire-fighters died when their established ways of making sense of the world fell apart.

Gersick (1991) asked the question, why should revolutions of change occur at all? The answers pointed to the fact that within deep-structured systems, inertia sets in, with a mutual interdependence of their parts and action patterns, and the fact that deep structures determine how systems obtain resources from the environment. According to her, these features expose the deep structures to two basic sources of disruption:

(1) That of internal changes that pull parts and actions out of alignment with each other or the environment. In the internal environment of the organisation, an organisation's growth or decline strains its existing structures and practices (Romanelli & Tushman, 1994) or reduces the need for unnecessary practices. It makes it difficult for organisations to expand based on its existing infrastructure. It also makes it difficult to run an organisation with redundant and cluttered infrastructure.

(2) That of environmental changes, which threaten the system's abilities to obtain resources (Gersick, 1991, p. 21). In the external environment, there is a less orderly source of change as there are both foreseeable changes such as the maturation of a market or product, or unforeseeable changes such as economic, social or political climate.

All these changes demonstrate that there is a need to change, but do not in themselves cause the changes. 'Punctuated equilibrium models suggest that failures may be extremely important in setting the stage for revolutionary change. But as long as events occur against the backdrop of the same deep structure, they are treated or interpreted in ways that preserve the system's inertia and therefore incremental solutions are sought.' (Gersick, 1991, p. 22) The point here is that there is a need to acknowledge that there is a necessity to change from deep structural levels in order to gain synergy for innovative and significant changes to aid the survival of the organisation.

Classical models of managerial behaviour state that the long-term outcomes of management actions are generally assumed to be predictable. This means that a successful organisation was viewed to be one where management stayed in control and long-term intentions and plans were fulfilled. However, the study of management from the complex systems perspective suggests 'organisations are changeable only when they are sustained far from an equilibrium fit with their environment and consequently are unstable in a certain sense' (Stacey, 1991, 1992). As long-term outcomes are unpredictable, it is not necessarily possible for management to fulfil long-term plans. Hence, when organisations that have been successful before operating on traditional methods start to fail, it is probably due to traditional organisational systems, rather than management incompetence. According to Parker and Stacey (1994), 'the survivors are systems that are sustained far from equilibrium, in bounded instability' (p. 49). In the paradoxical state known as the edge of chaos, these systems and agents are inherently changeable, thus capable of continuing innovation and variety. The dynamics of organisational life is turbulent, where everything keeps changing — peoples attitudes, fashion trends, consumers' needs and wants change all the time. Therefore, decision-makers in organisations have to react now and make decisions that will have uncertain consequences (Stacey, 1996).

Change within Complex Social Systems

Variables with simple cause–effect relationships among them are termed *recursive*, in that the state of a variable can be written in terms of the states of variables which are earlier in a causal sequence. In complex systems, feedback relationships among system elements mean that it is no longer possible to predict the impact of change in one part of the system based solely on the state of other parts of the system. Instead, the state of a one part of a system depends not just on the state of other parts but upon its own earlier states; and feedback loops can amplify changes through a system leading to massive instability. Change within such complex systems is called *non-recursive*, and the proportional (linear) link between causes and effects that we see in recursive systems is lost. Instead, interactions in complex social systems are all nonlinear, such that effects may not be proportional to causes. Within an interdependent system, changes in one part reverberate through the system (the degree of reverberation will depend on the precise patterning of interdependencies), with feedback effects that can either dampen or amplify the initial input. In this way, the same causal event can have either large or small effects, depending on the dynamics of the whole system.

Another less obvious feature of nonlinearity is that complex social systems display what is known as *path dependence*. The later states of complex systems can be extremely sensitive to small differences in initial conditions, such that systems with very similar initial states can end up having divergent paths over time. Business economists, for example, Garud and Karnøe (2001) have long studied how organisations in the same industry sector can evolve in radically different ways as a result of apparently small differences in their initial history. A well-known example is the contrast between Apple and IBM.

An important consequence of this characteristic of nonlinearity of change in complex social systems is that nonlinearity places severe constraints on our ability to make precise predictions (Bak, 1996; Cohen, 1999; Dooley & Van de Ven, 1999; Stacey, 1996). Indeed, Bak has argued (in discussing complex physical systems) that prediction in complex systems is unachievable, and therefore should not be used as a criterion for assessing the quality of theoretical models. While we would not go that far, we do agree with him that the pursuit of 'variance accounted for' in much social science research can lead us down scholarly cul-de-sacs.

Emergence

Following Simon (1996), we can see that complex social systems are intrinsically hierarchical: firms are nested within economies, departments are nested within firms, teams are nested within departments, and individuals are nested within teams. Much research effort tends to focus its attention on one level of analysis. Thus, the dominant paradigm of International Business research has been described as concerned predominantly with firm-level business activity (Toyne & Nigh, 1997). Similarly, psychologists (the authors of the chapters in this book) concern themselves predominantly with the individual level of analysis. There is, however, an emerging awareness of the importance of developing multilevel models that recognise the hierarchical nature of complex social systems and seek to understand the multiple-level influences on that complexity (Klein, Tosi, & Cannella, 1999). Many theoretical models (particularly in management and psychology) are contextual, in that they account for behaviour at one level on the basis of structural characteristics at a higher hierarchical level. For example, Sprigg, Jackson, and Parker (2000) examined how the performance and stress levels of employees (the individual level of analysis) varied depending on the degree of interdependence of the production process (the departmental level). Such contingency models focus our attention on how higher level characteristics are expressed at lower levels.

Adopting a complexity theory way of thinking switches our attention to ways in which actions at a lower level can serve to shape and influence higher level structure. This process is termed *emergence* (Kauffman, 1995, 2000). Structure in complex social systems emerges out of the adaptive actions of locally autonomous actors within richly connected networks; where the term adaptive means that the choices made by individual members of a social system reflect their best options based on what they know of their proximal environment (Black and Farias, 2000). When the macrosystem is composed of levels of complex systems, it is common to refer to the parts as 'adaptive agents' (Holland, 1995). The term *agent* is used to refer to elements in a system, and for social systems, agents would be individuals, groups or departments. The term *adaptive* captures the characteristic of agents that their actions are oriented.

One of the most provocative assertions of complexity theory is *emergence* of structure in social systems: that ordered patterns can emerge as a result of the relationships among system members without those patterns being imposed through any external design. A commonly used example is the flocking behaviour of birds. Flocks of birds act in a coordinated way, and it is difficult to avoid the view that there is a leader of a flock from which other birds take their lead. Computation modelling (through, for example, NetLogo, Wilensky, 1999) shows that what we see as structured behaviour of a flock can actually be reproduced on the basis of a few simple rules guiding the behaviour of each individual bird, each acting in ignorance of all but a few neighbouring birds.

Emergent order depends on the level of interdependence within a system. Weick (1979) writes that when there are too few agents or components or not enough interactions among them, patterns tend not to emerge. Conversely, systems in which every element is connected to each other in a feedback loop are unstable (Simon, 1996). Order arises then in complex systems when components are partially connected to each other. This allows room for change and yet a chance to maintain the previous stable form. In complex adaptive systems, agents only act on information available in their immediate environments, from those few agents connected to them in a feedback loop.

A key assumption of this view of organisations as complex social systems is that emergent structure has an internal integrity that cannot be understood either by looking at one level of analysis alone or by a reductionist approach of analysing its elemental components (West, 1985; Thelan & Smith, 1994).

Neither can organisations be examined in isolation, since each is part of the context for the actions of others (that is, they are the elements in a network of organisations within an industry or society). As a result, organisations are subject to evolutionary pressures because their fitness (competitive advantage in their market place) depends not just on their own actions but also on the actions of others. With the continual interaction among departments and groups of organisations, the actions of one trigger actions and reactions in other companies, whose actions trigger responsive actions in the first. Within industries, technological convergence can lead to the formation of new organisational communities that recombine elements of what were previously distinct and different populations. Nonaka and Takeuchi (1995) described the formation and re-formation of groups of employees in the Japanese electronics company Matsushita as they tried to come up with a fully automated home-bakery machine. Other examples of emergence of new levels of organisational order have been described in Lichtenstein (2000), including Cheng and Van de Ven's (1996) creation of innovation projects, Gartner et al's (1992) new venture emergence, and organisational change and development (Dooley, 1997; Poole et al., 2000). Similar forces operate at all levels. Within organisations themselves, groups, teams or task forces integrate the ideas and attitudes of their members and become arenas within which creative new ideas emerge from the interaction of their members (Arrow, McGrath, & Berdahl, 2000).

Perhaps one of the more interesting aspects of complex social systems is their ability to self-organise; for ordered patterns to emerge simply as a result of the relationships and interactions of the constituent agents, without any external control or design. When a complex system is at the edge of chaos it is in a state where change may occur easily and spontaneously. Kauffman (1995) refers to this as '*order for free.*' It does not arise through conscious design but is something immanent within the system — a property of the relationships between the elements rather than the elements themselves.

Because energy is used up — or dissipated — in the course of the organisation, self-organising systems are also called '*dissipative systems*' (Kelly & Allison, 1998, p. 4). Hence, dissipative systems can only be maintained when its members or agents are induced to contribute energy to them. Parker and Stacey (1994) argue that organisations are fundamentally dissipative structures. Dissipative structures are defined as systems that consist of forces that, due to aggravation, dissipate energy and yet still retain a structure. They are of the opinion that these organisations demonstrate both stability and instability *at the same time.* Previously, the world was seen to be in order, and things happened in a predictable, pre-ordained manner, where 'according to deterministic natural laws, orderly causes lead to orderly effects' (Parker & Stacey, 1994, p. 11). Nowadays, things are viewed differently, with happenings occurring in an essentially complex and paradoxical manner. It is suggested by Anderson (1999) that the more turbulent an organisation's environment is, the more energy must be generated to keep the system above the threshold beyond which self-organisation is sustained (p. 222).

An example of self-organisation would be that of Darwin's theory of evolution where through natural selection, some species continue to live and others fail, ending up becoming extinct. In this theory, the characteristics that assist individuals in surviving end up becoming more common within the species, as these individuals who possess these characteristics end up living longer and mating more successfully, thus passing on these characteristics to their offspring. Hence the edge of chaos captures the self-organised behaviour that occurs when there is some structure but not very much.

Managing Emergent Change

A traditional approach to designing organisations is through command and control to specify the form of structure which is appropriate for the environment within which the organisation operates. Complexity theory offers a radically different perspective: that organisational structure is an emergent property of the local actions of adaptive agents working at a lower level. From the perspective of emergence, the role of management is not to specify structure, but rather to change the favourability of the adaptive options. This is what Levinthal and Warglien (1999) called tuning the fitness landscape on which organisational members operate. In order to understand this idea, we need first to explain the concept of a fitness landscape.

The term *fitness landscape* was introduced to evolutionary biology by Wright (1932) in order to describe the survival of species. Fitness in this context refers to the survival value of an organisation, and landscape is the term for the array of all possible alternatives open to an organisation seeking to adapt to its environment. The height of the landscape at a specific point reflects the survival value (or fitness) of that adaptive action. It is reasonable to expect that an organism will choose the alternative actions that maximise its survival value. In so doing, it is said to move upwards on its fitness landscape — a process called hill-climbing. Fitness landscapes differ in shape (in just the way that physical landscapes do). Where there is only one alternative action which maximises fitness and all other alternatives are lower, then the landscape is referred to as *single-peaked*. In such a case, choosing is easy — evaluate all local options, and then walk uphill. Not all landscapes are like this, however, since it is possible that a number of alternatives might offer roughly equal survival value. This type of landscape is called *rugged*, rather like a mountain range with many peaks, some higher than others. There may well be one peak higher than all others (called a global maximum), but unlike the single-peaked landscape the simple rule of 'evaluate all local options and then walk uphill' does not guarantee reaching the global maximum. Much depends on the starting point (this is precisely the idea of path dependence, introduced earlier), and the hill-climbing rule guarantees reaching a local maximum, but not that this will be the highest possible.

What factors influence the shape of a fitness landscape, determining whether it is single-peaked or rugged? It turns out that the degree of peakedness is directly related to interdependence. Social systems differ in the degree of interdependency among their constituent elements, and we can distinguish between two types of interdependence:

(1) Linkages between attributes of a system, such that each attribute cannot be dealt with alone. For example, change management consultants are well aware that it is impossible to consider sub-systems of organisations in isolation. Efforts to change accounting systems also have to consider HR practices, performance management, IT systems and so on.

(2) Linkages between individuals who work together as part of teams or groups, such that organisational goals cannot be achieved except by individuals working together (e.g. Sprigg, Jackson & Parker, 2000; Turner, Parker, & Williams, this book).

Consider a member of an organisation who has no dependency relationships with any other organisational member (unlikely in reality, but possible in theory). Such a person's adaptive options are not influenced by others, and it is a simple matter to select the option that gives maximum benefit. The fitness of an organisation consisting entirely of independent members would thus be calculated by adding up all the individual fitnesses. By contrast (and more realistically) organisational members who work interdependently will find that the adaptive value of their individual alternative actions will be heavily influenced by their dependent others.

Where there is zero interdependence, the effectiveness (adaptive fitness) of a system is the sum of the effectiveness of its constituent elements. The consequence of high interdependence is that the combined effectiveness (fitness) of a system is not simply the aggregate of the effectiveness of individual elements. When the adaptive choices of organisational actors depend on the choices of other actors (because of the interdependencies among them), there are inevitably trade-offs, compromises and contradictions between system components, such that the likelihood of a single peak of maximum fitness is much lower (for a more detailed exposition of this idea, see Kauffman, 2000). In this way, the ruggedness of the fitness landscape is a reflection of the complexity of the social system. These are what create the ruggedness of the fitness landscape.

An example of a single-peaked organisational process is lean production (for example the Toyota Production System, Monden, 1994), where processes are organised on the basis of pull relationships between successive parts of the production process (Jackson & Martin, 1996; Jackson & Mullarkey, 2000). Here, each step in the production process depends only on the immediately prior step; and the limited interdependency within lean production systems, which this implies creates a single-peaked knowledge landscape on which employees can engage in kaizen, identifying incremental improvements in production processes. The single peak guarantees that each such change moves the system towards its peak, thus increasing effectiveness for the process as a whole. By contrast, cross-functional work teams (see e.g. Turner, Parker, & Williams, this book) are examples of locally dense networks of people operating on rugged fitness landscapes. The ruggedness arises from the density of the relationships among people and the variability across functional specialisms in the schemas that team members use to inform their work. For an example of applying the same ideas to the development of an academic discipline (indigenous psychology) see Jackson (2005).

Tuning fitness landscapes. We have seen how the fitness landscape reflects the shape of the payoffs for alternative actions open to individuals, groups or organisations. The concept of tuning of the fitness landscape was introduced by Levinthal and Warglien (1999) as a means of describing a form of managing change which influences the relationships between individual action and payoffs, rather than directing individual's actions themselves. 'The underlying idea is that by designing the surface on which adaptation processes take place, one may affect the quality of the adaptive process without the need to specify directly individual behaviour. The approach is inherently dynamic, focusing on designs for local adaptation — the behaviour of individuals that is guided by feedback from their particular task environment' (Levinthal & Warglien, 1999, p. 342).

The responsibility of senior management remains that of defining a vision for the organisation, but does not consist of specifying precise behaviours for employees. Therein lies command-and-control, appropriate and effective for bureaucratic organisations in predictable environments. We started this chapter by describing the modern world of increasing turbulence, where information and communication technologies exert dramatic influences on the very fabric of business life. In such a world, the only way for organisations to survive is to unlock the creativity which lies in the wisdom of all of their members through principled autonomy. Organisations will survive when their members are empowered to act in ways that are adaptive to their local context but the shape of the landscape for such adaptive actions is tuned by management to be consistent with their vision for the organisation. Instead of seeking to predict the future, we argue that those in managerial positions will have to look towards 'a self-organising process of organisational learning from which futures emerge unpredictably without prior shared intention'(Parker & Stacey, 1994, pp. 14–15). Wisdom lies in accepting the futility of discerning what will be *the* successful strategy for the long term, and instead create the conditions for organisations to invent and re-invent. ...

References

Adams, R. N. (1988). *The Eighth Day: Social Evolution as the Self-Organization of Energy*. Austin, TX: University of Texas.

Anderson, P. (1999). Complexity theory and organization science. *Organization Science, 10*(3), 216–232.

Anderson, P., Meyer, A., Eisenhardt, K., Carley, K., & Pettigrew, A. (1999). Introduction to the special issue: Application of complexity theory to organization science. *Organization Science, 10*(3), 233–236.

Arrow, H., McGrath, J. E., & Berdahl, J. L. (2000). *Small groups as complex systems: Formation, coordination, development, and adaptation*. Thousand Oaks: Sage.

Artigiani, R. (1987). Revolution and Evolution: Applying Prigogine's Dissipative Structure Model. *Journal of Social and Biological Structures, 10*, 249–264.

Ashby, R. (1956). *An introduction to cybernetics*. London: Chapman & Hall.

Bak, P. (1996). *How nature works*. New York: Springer.

Beer, M., & Nohria, N. (Eds). (2000). *Breaking the code of change*. Boston, MA: Harvard Business School Press.

Beeson, I., & Davis, C. (2000). Emergence and accomplishment in organizational change. *Journal of Organizational Change Management, 13*(2), 178–189.

Black, J.A. (2000). Fermenting change: Capitalizing on the inherent change found in dynamic non-linear (or complex) systems. *Journal of Organizational Change Management, 13*(6), 520–525.

Black, J. A., & Edwards, S. (2000). Emergence of virtual or network organizations: Fad or feature? *Journal of Organizational Change Management, 13*(6), 567–576.

Black, J. A., & Farias, G. (2000). Dynamic strategies: Emergent journeys. *Emergence, 2*(1), 101–113.

Brews, P. J., & Hunt, M. R. (1999). Learning to plan and planning to learn: Resolving the planning school/learning school debate. *Strategic Management Journal, 20*, 889–913.

Brown, S., & Eisenhardt, K. (1997). The art of continuous change: Linking complexity theory and time-based evolution in relentlessly shifting organizations. *Administrative Science Quarterly, 42*, 1–34.

Brown, S. L., & Eisenhardt, K. M. (1998). *Competing on the edge: Strategy as structured chaos*. Boston: Harvard University Press.

Burnes, B. (2004). Managing change: A strategic approach to organisational dynamics (4th ed.). Harlow, Essex: Pearson Education Limited.

Cheng, Y., & Van de Ven, A. (1996). The innovation journey: Order out of chaos? *Organization Science, 6*, 593–614.

Cohen, M. (1999). Commentary on the *Organization Science* special issue on complexity. *Organization Science, 10*(3), 373–376.

Cramer, F. (1993). In: D.L. Loewus (Trans), *Chaos and order: The complex structure of living things*. New York: VCH.

Dooley, K. (1997). A complex adaptive systems model of organization change. *Nonlinear Dynamics, Psychology and the Life Sciences, 1*, 69–97.

Dooley, K. J., & Van de Ven, A. H. (1999). Explaining complex organizational dynamics. *Organization Science, 10*(3), 358–372.

Drazin, R., Glynn, M. A., & Kazanjian, R. K. (1999). Multilevel theorizing about creativity in organizations: A sensemaking perspective. *Academy of Management Review, 24*(2), 286–307.

Drucker, P. F. (1993). *Post-capitalist society.* Oxford: Butterworth-Heinemann Ltd.

Forrester, J. (1961). *Industrial dynamics.* Cambridge, MA: MIT Press.

Gartner, W. B., Bird, B. J., & Starr, J. A. (1992). Acting as if: Differentiating entrepreneurial from organizational behavior. *Entrepreneurship Theory and Practice, 16,* 13–30.

Garud, R., & Karnøe, P. (Eds). (2001). *Path dependence and creation.* Mahwah, NJ: Lawrence Erlbaum Associates.

Gell-Mann, M. (1995). What is complexity? *Complexity, 1,* 16–19.

Gersick, C. J. G. (1988). Time and transition in work teams: Toward a new model of group development. *Academy of Management Journal, 31,* 9–41.

Gersick, C. J. G. (1991). Revolutionary change theories: A multilevel exploration of the punctuated equilibrium paradigm. *Academy of Management Review, 16*(1), 10–36.

Golembiewski, R., Billingsley, K., & Yeager, S. (1976). Measuring change and persistence in human affairs: Types of change generated by OD designs. *Journal of Applied Behavioral Science, 12,* 133–157.

Hodgkinson, G. P., Maule, A. J., & Bown, N. J. (2004). Charting the mind of the strategic decision maker: A comparative analysis of two methodological alternatives involving causal mapping. *Organizational Research Methods, 7,* 3–21.

Holland, J. H. (1995). *Hidden order,* Reading, MA: Addison-Wesley.

Ilinich, A. Y., Lewin, A. Y., & D'Aveni, R. (Eds). (1998). *Managing in times of disorder: Hypercompetitive organisational responses.* Thousand Oaks: Sage.

Jackson, P. R. (2005). Indigenous theorising in a complex world. *Asian Journal of Social Psychology, 8,* 51–64.

Jackson, P. R., & Martin, R. (1996). The impact of just-in-time on job content, employee attitudes and well-being: A longitudinal study. *Ergonomics, 39*(1), 1–16.

Jackson, P. R., & Mullarkey, S. (2000). Lean production teams and health in garment manufacture. *Journal of Occupational Health Psychology, 5,* 231–245.

Jackson, P. R., Sprigg, C. A., & Parker, S. K. (2000). Interdependence as a key requirement for the successful introduction of teamworking: A case study. In: S. Procter, & F. Mueller (Eds), *Teamworking: Issues, concepts and problems* (pp. 83–102). London: Macmillan.

Katz, D., & Kahn, R. L. (1978). *The social psychology of organizations* (2nd ed.). New York: Wiley.

Kauffman, S. A. (1993). *The origins of order: Self-organization and selection in evolution.* New York: Oxford University Press.

Kauffman, S. A. (1995). *At home in the universe: The search for laws of self-organisation and complexity.* New York: Oxford University Press.

Kauffman, S. A. (2000). *Investigations.* Oxford: Oxford University Press.

Kelly, S., & Allison, M. A. (1998). *The complexity advantage: How the science of complexity can help your business achieve peak performance.* New York: McGraw-Hill.

Kiel, D. (1994). *Managing chaos and complexity in government.* San Francisco, CA: Jossey-Bass.

Klein, K. J., Tosi, H., & Cannella, A. A. J. (1999). Multilevel theory building: Benefits, barriers, and new developments. (Special Topic Forum on Multilevel Theory Building.) *Academy of Management Review, 24*(2), 243–148.

Levinthal, D. A., & Warglien, M. (1999). Landscape design: Designing for local action in complex worlds. *Organization Science, 10*(3), 342–357.

Lewin, A. Y. (1999). Application of complexity theory to organization science. *Organization Science, 10*(3), 215.

Lewin, R. (1992). Complexity: Life at the edge of chaos. New York: Macmillan.

Lichtenstein, B. M. B. (2000). Emergence as a process of self-organizing: New assumptions and insights from the study of nonlinear dynamic systems. *Journal of Organizational Change Management, 13*(6), 526–544.

MacIntosh, R., & MacLean, D. (1999). Conditioned emergence: A dissipative structures approach to transformation. *Strategic Management Journal, 20*(4), 297–316.

Maguire, S., & McKelvey, B. (1999). Complexity and management: Moving from fad to firm foundations. *Emergence, 1*(2), 19–61.

Marion, R. (1999). *The edge of organisation: Chaos and complexity theories of formal social systems.* Thousand Oaks: Sage

Miles R. E., & Snow, C. C. (1992). Causes of failure in network organisations. *California Management Review, 34*(4), 53–72.

Mirvis, P. (Ed.) (1993). Building a competitive workforce: Investing in human capital for corporate success. New York: John Wiley & Sons.

Mirvis, P. H., & Hall, D. T. (1994). Psychological success and the boundaryless career. *Journal of Organisational Behaviour, 15*, 365–380.

Monden, Y. (1994). *Toyota production system.* London: Chapman & Hall.

Nelson, A., Cooper, C. L., & Jackson, P. R. (1995). Uncertainty amidst change: The impact of privatisation on employee job satisfaction and well-being. *Journal of Occupational and Organisational Psychology, 68*, 57–71.

Nicolis, G., & Prigogine, I. (1989). *Exploring complexity: An introduction.* New York: Freeman.

Nonaka, I., & Takeuchi, H. (1995). *The Knowledge-creating company: How Japanese companies create the dynamics of innovation.* Oxford: Oxford University Press.

Nonaka, I., & Teece, D. (Eds). (2001). *Managing industrial knowledge: Creation, transfer and utilization.* London: Sage.

Parker, D., & Stacey, R. (1994). *Chaos, management and economics: The implications of nonlinear thinking.* Hobart Paper 125. London: Institute of Economic Affairs.

Poole, M., Van de Ven, A. H., Dooley, K., & Holmes, M. E. (2000). *Organizational Change and Innovation Processes.* Oxford: Oxford University Press.

Romanelli, E., & Tushman, M. L. (1994). Organizational transformation as punctuated equilibrium: An empirical test. *Academy of Management Journal, 37*(5), 1141–1166.

Senge, P. M. (1990). *The fifth discipline: The art and practice of the learning organisation.* New York: Doubleday.

Simon, H. A. (1996). *The sciences of the artificial* (3rd ed.). Cambridge, MA: MIT Press.

Smith, C., & Comer, D. (1994). Change in the same group: A dissipative structure perspective. *Human Relations, 47*, 553–581.

Sprigg, C. A., Jackson, P. R., & Parker, S. K. (2000). Production teamworking: The importance of interdependence and autonomy for employee strain and satisfaction. *Human Relations, 53*(11), 1519–1543.

Stacey, R. (1992). *Managing the Unknowable.* San Francisco, CA: Jossey-Bass.

Stacey, R. (1995). The science of complexity: An alternative perspective for strategic change processes. *Strategic Management Journal, 16*(6), 477–495.

Stacey, R. D. (1991). The chaos frontier: Creative strategic control for businesses. London: Butterworth-Heinmann.

Stacey, R. D. (1996). Complexity and creativity in organisations. San Francisco: Berrett-Koehler Publishers.

Thelan, J., & Smith, L. (1994). *A dynamic systems approach to the development of cognition and action.* Cambridge, MA: Bradford/MIT Press.

Thietart, R. A., & Forgues, B. (1995). Chaos theory and organization. *Organization Science, 6*(1 Jan–Feb), 19–31.

Thom, R. (1975). Structural stability and morphogenesis. New York: Benjamin Addison Wesley.

Thompson, J. (1967). *Organisations in action: Social science bases of administrative theory.* New York: McGraw-Hill.

Toyne, B., & Nigh, D. (Eds). (1997). *International business: An emerging vision.* Columbia, SC: University of South Carolina Press.

Tucker, M. L., Meyer, G. D., & Westerman, J. W. (1996). Organisational communication: Development of internal strategic competitive advantage. *Journal of Business Communication, 33*(1), 51–69.

Tushman, M. L., & Romanelli, E. (1985). Organisational evolution: A metamorphosis model of convergence and reorientation. In: B. Staw, & L. Cummings (Eds), *Research in Organisational Behaviour* (Vol. 7). Greenwich, CT: JAI Press.

Urry J. (2000). Sociology Beyond Societies. London: Routledge.

Urry, J. (2002). Global complexity. London: Polity Press.

Von Bertalanffy, L. (1968). *General system theory: Foundations, development, applications.* New York: G. Braziller.

Weick, K. E. (1979). *The social psychology of organizing* (2nd ed.). New York: Random House.

Weick, K. E. (1993). The collapse of sensemaking in organisations: The Mann Gulch disaster. *Administrative Science Quarterly, 38*(4), 628.

West, B. (1985). *On the importance of being nonlinear.* Berlin: Springer.

Wilensky, U. (1999). NetLogo. Evanston, IL: Center for Connected Learning and Computer-Based Modeling, Northwestern University.

Wright, S. (1932). The role of mutation, inbreeding, crossbreeding and selection in evolution. In: W. B. Provine (ed.), *Evolution: Selected papers* (pp. 161–171). Chicago: University of Chicago Press.

Chapter 7

Emotion at Work

T. Kiefer and R. B. Briner

Introduction

The two aims of this chapter are first, to provide a non-specialist and hence fairly general overview of psychological research into emotions at work and, second, to consider the implications of this research for understanding behaviour at work. As we were asked to make this chapter accessible to students who have little or no experience of organizational psychology and organizational behaviour, we have kept the use of technical terms to a minimum and provided explanations of psychological ideas and concepts. Should the reader wish to explore the psychology of emotion at work further, more specialist reviews (e.g. Brief & Weiss, 2002; Briner & Totterdell, 2002; Weiss, 2001), collections of papers (e.g. Ashkanasy, Härtel, & Zerbe, 2005; Fineman, 2000; Lord, Klimoski, & Kanfer, 2002) and critiques (e.g. Briner & Kiefer, 2005; Weiss, 2002).

Although research into emotion at work is relatively new, and still very much an emerging field, it is possible to provide such an overview even though many key issues remain somewhat under-explored. First, a general introduction to emotion at work is provided. This considers the relevance and importance of emotion, some popular myths about emotion at work, the history of the field and where we are today. The final part of the introduction highlights some of the ways in which emotion at work has great practical relevance. The second section reviews some basic psychological theory and research about emotion at work focusing, in particular, on definitions and theories and the links between emotion and behaviour, and between emotion and thinking. In the third section, several examples of how emotion plays a role in behaviour at work are considered including emotion during change, emotions and leadership and jobs that require employees to display emotion as part of the job role. Last, we draw out some general conclusions and implications for understanding and dealing with emotion at work.

Emotions at Work: Relevance, Myths and Historical Background

In this section, we first consider the relevance and importance of emotions at work, then discuss some common myths about emotion, and finish by outlining a brief history of the field.

Who Cares About Emotion at Work?

There are lots of reasons why individuals, managers and organizations care about emotions at work. At the personal level, we all care about how we feel. Generally, we prefer to experience positive emotions, such as joy and excitement, and to avoid negative emotions, such as shame or anger, though, as we shall go on to discuss, the picture is rather more complicated and subtle. In some situations, negative emotions can be helpful and positive emotions can lead to undesirable outcomes.

Moving beyond personal concerns, why else might we care about emotions at work? There are many reasons but some of the main ones are listed in Box 1.

It is important to note here that emotions are just a normal feature of daily life and daily working life. We wake up in the morning and may feel, for example, excited or anxious about the day ahead. Later that day, in a meeting, we start to feel a bit embarrassed because everyone else seems to know a lot more about

Box 1: Some reasons to care about emotion at work.

- Emotions are part of everyday working life and therefore deserve attention
- Emotions have, in the past, been ignored and to some extent continue to be ignored both by organizations and researchers
- Emotions help define our experience of work: What it feels like to work and to be at work
- Emotions strongly shape the way we behave and the way we think
- Focusing on emotions can be a more useful way of understanding feelings at work than the ideas job stress and job satisfaction

what is going on than we do. On checking our email, we feel very relieved to see that an impossible deadline for an important and difficult project has been extended by a few months. Emotions are, therefore, not something exceptional or extraordinary. Rather they are a core feature of much of our behaviour, thinking and experience.

Some Common Myths About Emotion and Emotion at Work

Emotions do not just happen to people: Rather we are active in this process. We all have beliefs about emotions that shape our experience of emotion, and many of these beliefs are culturally and socially determined. In different cultures and social contexts, experiencing and displaying some types of emotions, such as anger or embarrassment, may be thought of as more or less acceptable. While some of these beliefs simply reflect preferences or dislikes, others reflect core beliefs about the nature of emotion. On closer inspection, it seems that many of these beliefs are best viewed as myths or taken-for-granted assumptions that bear little relation to the evidence. We listed some common beliefs in Box 2.

Why, then, are these myths important? One reason is that they partly help to explain why researchers and organizations have been a bit slow to recognize the relevance of emotion at work. They are also important because they influence the way we actually experience and react to emotion.

As discussed above, emotions play a key role in much of our behaviour and thinking. This is why we describe the sorts of ideas mentioned here as myths: Because they try to deny that emotions do affect our thinking and our behaviour — and do so at work as much as they do in any other aspect of our lives.

When the first author was conducting research in a bank, she asked a senior manager about his everyday emotions at work. He replied, "I don't have any emotions at work, neither positive nor negative ones, I am professional.... Maybe ... except surprise. It is unclear if surprise is positive or negative". He was then asked

Box 2: Some myths about emotion.

> - Thinking and feeling are opposites
>   - ○ We make decisions with our head or our hearts — and 'head' decisions are more rational than 'heart' decisions
> - Feelings should not play a role in important decisions
> - Emotions get in the way of doing things
> - The workplace is about working and emotions should be kept out of work
> - Behaving professionally means not getting emotional

about the emotional situations and experiences he observed in his team. His reply was that "they do not have any emotions either, I am leading with a positive example". Ironically, this reply was laden with emotion as he seemed very proud of the fact neither he nor his team had emotions. It is unclear whether he really meant that neither he nor his team had any emotions or whether he thought it was inappropriate to admit to such emotions. Whatever is the case, this example illustrates some of the common myths about emotion.

Historical Background

As mentioned earlier, research into emotion at work has only become a recognisable area of research fairly recently. Although one of the earliest examples of a study specifically asking people at work about their emotions appeared in the 1930s (Weiss & Brief, 2001), there was almost no other research into the topic until the mid- to late-1980s. While there was very little interest in emotions at work during this period, there was plenty of research on job satisfaction and job stress, which, though they are linked to feelings are not specific emotions as such. There was strong focus on examining the relationship between satisfaction and performance and, later, on examining the relationship between stress and performance.

The relatively recent surge of research activity around emotion at work can probably be traced to the publication of a book written by a sociologist, Arlie Hochschild (1983). She observed that, in some jobs, employees are required to display emotion as part of their job role — in order to get the job done. This phenomenon, emotional labour, will be discussed later. It is worth noting that other early publications on emotions at work (e.g. Fineman, 1993a) were, again, not necessarily written by organizational psychologists. Though initially slow, organizational psychology and other related disciplines have been moving quickly to establish a basic understanding of the multiple roles of emotion at work.

Fast-growing and fashionable research fields seem, inevitably, to have a number of undesirable characteristics. For example, researchers, in their enthusiasm, may sometimes claim that more is known or understood than is actually the case. Also, researchers may start to see their previous work as relevant to the new field and thus describe their research in terms of the new field whether or not it is actually relevant. This latter characteristic certainly seems to be present in the field of emotion at work, with research about phenomena such as mood, stress and satisfaction sometimes being described as research about emotions. There are important differences between emotion and these other phenomena that will be discussed in the next section.

While current research is quite diverse, it can broadly be categorized into emotions as a consequence of work and as an influence on work. In addition, this is done on different levels: the individual, the team and the organization (see Table 7.1).

Table 7.1: Examples of research areas: emotions/affective phenomena.

	Emotions as a consequence of work and organization	**Emotions as an influence on work behaviour and organization**
Work/Individual	Emotional experiences, stress, burnout, psychological contract breaches	Emotion regulation Emotional intelligence Decision-making
Group/Team	Conflicts, mobbing, aggression, compassion	Emotion at work Group dynamic
Organization	Commitment, trust	Feeling rules, organizational virtues

Thus far, we have only discussed the history of research into emotion at work: But what about the history of emotions in organizational practice? It appears that organizations have been primarily interested in employee's feelings and emotions only when organizations believe they are relevant in some way to performance. While some organizations are, of course, concerned about the well-being of their employees, others are only likely to regard emotions as important if they help or hinder employee performance. There are at least three ways in which organizational practice has, in relatively recent times, paid attention to emotion. The first is through the concept of emotional labour mentioned above and discussed in more detail later. As the performance of certain employees, such as waiting staff in restaurants or staff in call centres, depends on their emotional displays, organizations have become interested in how staff with the right skills can be selected and how such skills can be trained. A second way in which emotions has started to play a part in organizational practice is through the concept of emotional intelligence popularised by Goleman (1995). While there is considerable debate about what emotional intelligence actually is and whether it relates to performance appears to have caught the imagination of many organizations, some of whom, for example, attempt to develop and increase levels of emotional intelligence in their managers. The third way in which organizations have become interested in emotion is in relation to performance more generally. While job satisfaction has shown some rather weak links with motivation and performance, it may be that more specific emotions are more strongly related to performance and particularly aspects of performance like loyalty and wanting to "go the extra mile". Rather than reducing stress or increasing satisfaction, some organizations are exploring ways of encouraging employees to experience positive emotions at work even though the extent to which emotions can be "managed" in this way remains unclear.

While both research and practice around emotions at work are relatively new, a number of issues and areas or interest have emerged. The remainder of the chapter discusses some of these.

Emotion as an Interplay Between Feeling, Thinking and Behaving

The main purpose of this section is to give an overview of how emotions are viewed within psychology and their main causes and consequences. (For a good overview of models and current thinking, see Scherer, 2000 or Cacioppo & Gardner, 1999.) We start with differentiating emotions from other common affective phenomena and discuss what emotion is not.

Distinguishing Emotion from other Affective Phenomena

Emotions such as anger, disgust, relief or joy, are generally viewed as short-term, quite intense feeling states that follow an event or experience. Thus, emotions are something rather specific. The term is, however, sometimes used to mean feelings in general, but can and should be differentiated from other affective constructs. Here, we briefly consider six related constructs that are *not* emotion as such:

- mood
- emotion-laden judgements
- affect
- affectivity
- job stress and strain and
- job satisfaction

First, in contrast to emotion, *mood* (e.g. tired, content, calm) is not seen necessarily as a reaction to a specific event, as its origin is rather diffuse. Moods operate more in the background, with lower intensity and are more pervasive. Second, there are a number of *emotion-laden constructs* such as fairness or injustice, commitment and trust, which, while they certainly relate to or contain emotion, are not in themselves emotion. Third, the term *affect* is typically used generally as an umbrella term for many affective phenomena though *positive affect* and *negative affect* usually refer specifically to mood. Fourth, the expression *affectivity* is used to refer to a personality trait, rather than an affective state (e.g. being the sort of person who is just quite often anxious). Fifth, while the idea of *job stress* and *job strain* is used to describe a state in which a person is experiencing any one or combination of a range of negative emotions, it is not in itself emotion but rather a somewhat imprecise term for a range of unspecified negative emotions. Last, *job satisfaction* is perhaps the best example of a construct that is not in itself emotion, but which is sometimes used in ways that suggest that it is almost interchangeable with emotion. While job satisfaction may partly be about emotions or at least some sort of feeling, it is diffuse rather than specific and is often the result of an overall evaluation or judgement rather than an event-induced-specific feeling.

Emotion does not, therefore, refer to any or every type of feeling. Rather it is a specific kind of feeling state and is different from the other feeling states discussed here. We now go on to discuss in more detail what emotion is, rather than what it is not.

Defining Emotion by its Components

As mentioned above, emotions are usually viewed as reactions to specific, individually meaningful events. Although, researchers still debate exactly how emotion should best be defined, there is some consensus that it involves a number of components: cognitive, motivational, communicative, neurophysiological and social (e.g. Parkinson, 1995; Scherer, 1984). Emotions are experienced in response to an individually significant event, which elicits interrelated changes in these components. These changes are accompanied by a subjective feeling (e.g. feeling angry). We will here briefly describe these five components and their significance to understanding emotions at work.

The Cognitive Component

While emotions have many causes, the most widespread view is that emotions are a result of the cognitive appraisals (evaluations) made following an event that is of major importance to an individual (e.g. Lazarus, 1999a; Lazarus & Folkman, 1984). In other words, events and situations provoke emotions because they are meaningful to us in some way. It is the process of cognitive appraisal that determines if and how events and situations are meaningful. Appraisals describe the cognitive evaluation of an event (or object or action). We evaluate an event in relation to, for example, our goals, coping abilities, personal values and norms. The theoretical description of these appraisals helps us understand the nature of discrete emotions, and differentiates fear from anger, for example, within a specific culture. An event that has no meaning to us will not elicit emotion. According to Ortony, Clore, and Collins (1988), anger in a Western culture indicates disapproving of somebody else's action or the related consequences, whereas fear is characterized as existential threat based on the appraisal of an event which has not yet happened but which is anticipated to occur in the future.

The Motivational Component

Motivation is a key part of emotion. From personal experience we know how anger and enthusiasm can fuel our attempts to achieve a goal, or how disappointment and frustration can leave us drained and unfocused. In emotion psychology, different emotions are viewed as linked to different behavioural or action tendencies (e.g. Frijda, 1986). Some emotions, such as fear, make it more likely that we will behave in ways that will allow us to withdraw, hide, or get away from the object or situation that we perceive is causing us to feel scared. These behavioural tendencies have a strong adaptive function, helping the individual to adjust to or shape the changing environment. However, it is not suggested that individuals always or necessarily act out emotion-specific action tendencies in everyday situations as these may be inhibited and there are many other factors influencing our situational behaviours. Thus, unlike our lay assumptions about emotions as being irrational and hindering efficient work, psychology views emotions (on the whole) as not only functional but essential for everyday behaviour.

The Neurophysiological Component

Emotions are usually accompanied by physiological changes (e.g. heart rate). As individuals, we may experience some of these bodily changes in a variety of ways, such as feeling hot or red-faced during extreme anger or feeling cold when experiencing fear. It is assumed that such physiological and neurological changes have a range of functions including providing the individual with resources necessary for appropriate behavioural reactions discussed immediately above and shaping the subjective feeling of emotion. At work, such physiological changes are important as they impact not only on our physical behaviour but also on many aspects of the way we think such as learning and memory, problem-solving, creativity and the way we think in general.

The Expressive or Communicative Component

Our emotions become visible to other people in many different ways, as emotions have a vital communicative component. In other words, one of the main purposes of emotion is to communicate to others how we feel. Emotions may be communicated in many ways including what we say, the way we say it, and our bodily posture and gestures. Of course, in some circumstances, we may not want to let others know how we are feeling and cultural, social and organizational norms and rules moderate the expression of emotion through display rules (e.g. Ekman & Friesen, 1971; Rafaeli & Sutton, 1989). So, for example, although a shop worker may feel angry towards a customer they may choose to try to suppress the anger and be polite to the customer. Some primary facial expressions of emotion, such as anger, appear to be understood universally throughout different cultures (e.g. Ekman, 1994) while at the same time they also contain a culture-based element (Russell, 1991). The communicative component is very relevant to work and organizations in a number of ways. First, it is an important feature in any communication or social interaction at work (including negotiations, client or leader — team member communications). For example, when a manager asks someone to undertake an assignment the manager will also be communicating some kind of emotion (e.g. anxiety or urgency, gratitude, anger or frustration). Further, as mentioned above, many jobs, especially those in the service industry (e.g. workers in call centres, nurses, flight attendants, management trainers, etc.), require employees to express specific emotional expressions when dealing with customers and clients (see also later section on emotional labour).

The Social Component

More recently, the *social component* has come to be considered as a key aspect of what emotions actually are (e.g. Harré, 1986; Parkinson, 1996). According to such perspectives, the major causes and functions of emotions can be thought of as relating largely to our social behaviour. For example, we learn to appraise and give meaning to events, in part, through observing the ways in which others do so. Also, for example, the function of the communicative component is to let those around us know how we are feeling and therefore how they should respond to us. This development in thinking about emotion, reflects a broader critique of earlier thinking that tends to view emotion more as private physiological responses rather than something which has clear social causes and consequence.

In summary, emotions such as enthusiasm, fear or pride are usually triggered by events that are personally relevant or important. We do not tend to react emotionally to events and situations, which have no meaning for us. Rather, emotional events are those we perceive to affect our well-being, goals, values and expectations. The experience of emotions is therefore neither random nor irrational, but follows certain kinds of social and personal rules. Fear or anxiety, for example, may be felt when there is some threat to goals that are important to us. Pride, for example, is likely to be felt as a consequence of overcoming difficult obstacles to achieve a goal.

Thus, different emotions have different causes. At the same time, different emotions tend to have different consequences. For example, anger causes us to behave in ways that are aimed at overcoming obstacles that are getting in our way. Paying attention to emotions at work may therefore teach us a lot about how people perceive and respond to work events and situations.

Having discussed emotions in general, we can now start to consider the role and relevance of emotion in the workplace.

How are Emotions Relevant to Work?

Given the five-component definition of emotion provided above, it should by now be clear that emotions are relevant to most, if not all, aspects of workplace behaviour. If we think about some common topics within organizational psychology and organizational behaviour such as motivation, thinking, teamwork, leadership and organizational culture, emotion will play and important role in each of these. While, as indicated earlier, emotions at work were largely ignored, their role is now beginning to be more appreciated and understood as shown by the rapidly increasing publication of research in the field (e.g. Ashkanasy, Härtel, & Zerbe, 2002, 2005; Brief & Weiss, 2002; Fineman, 1993b, 2000; Lord et al., 2002; Payne & Cooper, 2001; Weiss, 2001).

In this section, we provide a fairly general overview of the experience, causes and consequences of emotion at work. The section following this gives some more specific examples of the roles of emotion at work.

The Experience of Emotion at Work

So, which emotions do we experience how often at work and why? We know surprisingly little about how people actually feel at work and if there are differences between different groups at work (e.g. managers versus employees, women versus men, fire-fighters versus insurance brokers).

In order to provide some examples, we draw here on data collected by the first author in a number of countries. In one study, 470 employed individuals living in the US working for different companies were asked how frequently they had experienced a number of emotions in the previous two weeks at work. As you can see from Figure 7.1, frustration and annoyance were the most commonly reported everyday emotion at work. This finding suggests that these emotions are the most commonly actually experienced. However, it may also be the case that it is easier for people to admit to and remember the experience of these emotions rather than other emotions. In another study, conducted with employees of the chemical and pharmaceutical industry in Switzerland, over 50% of respondents reported frustration, anger, mistrust, disappointment, worry and fear in the previous two weeks. At the time of the study, this sector was undergoing radical organizational changes and we can only speculate

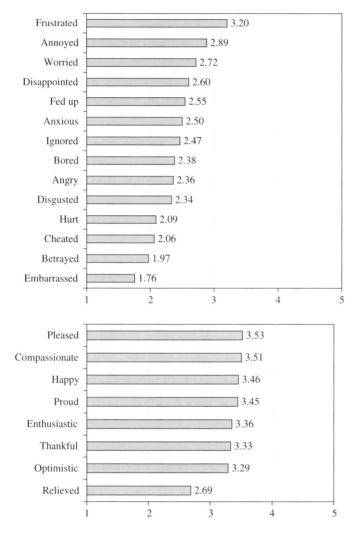

Figure 7.1: How frequently did you experience the following negative and positive emotions in the last two weeks at work? *Note.* 1=hardly ever, 5 =very often (*N*=470).

about how such changes may have affected the emotions experienced by these employees. The issue of emotions and change is discussed later in the chapter.

In all the studies by the first author, there were no differences found between men and women in the extent to which positive and negative emotions were reported. There were, however, some differences between employees and managers. In the US study, for example, employees report more negative emotions than middle and senior managers. In particular, employees reported that they experienced more of the emotions frustrated, disappointed, annoyed, disgusted and bored.

Looking at different levels of management, this study also found senior managers to be the least frustrated, disappointed, annoyed and disgusted, whereas junior managers reported the highest levels of these emotions, even more than employees. While the study cannot tell us exactly why these differences occur, it may be a consequence of the more difficult positions junior managers often find themselves in. When it comes to the experience of positive emotions, no differences between employees, junior, middle and senior managers were found. While this result is interesting in itself, it also shows that the experience of positive emotions at work and elsewhere is not simply the opposite of negative emotions. In other words, during a working day, individuals may report a high or low level of both positive *and* negative emotions. Just because a person reports high levels of positive emotions it does not mean they will also report low levels of negative emotions, as the two are relatively independent.

Typical Causes and Consequences of Emotion at Work

Although it is interesting to know how individuals feel at work and to compare different groups or organizations, it is more important to understand the causes and consequences of emotions at work. As emotions occur in nearly every working situation, it is helpful to have a broad way of thinking about emotional events and their consequences. First, we provide an overview of typical categories of causes and consequences of discrete emotions encountered at work, second we present a framework, Affective Events Theory (AET), for understanding the process of emotion and its causes and consequences at work.

Categories of Typical Causes and Consequences of Emotions at Work

In the previous section, we described the range of positive and negative emotions that may be experienced at work. Different emotions are likely to be about very different issues and have different causes, thus are also likely to have different consequences. One of the most common ways of thinking about the causes and consequences of emotion is in relation to the individual's goals. Table 7.2 shows how different emotions relate to goals.

Happiness, for example, is associated with the achieving goals and is likely to lead to a continuation of the activity or plan. The emotion of anxiety or fear, on

Table 7.2: Goals and plans, basic emotions and behaviours.

Goal/plan stage	Basic emotion	Next behaviours
Sub-goals being achieved	Happiness	Continue with plan modifying as necessary
Failure of major plan or loss of active goal	Sadness	Do nothing or search for new plan
Self-preservation goal threatened	Anxiety	Stop, attend vigilantly to environment and/or escape
Active plan frustrated	Anger	Try harder and/or aggression

Source: Based on Oatley and Johnson-Laird (1987).

the other hand, occurs when a goal related to self-preservation is in some way threatened. The behavioural consequence of anxiety is paying more attention to the environment, in order to find out more about the threat and how it can be dealt with, or escaping from the threatening situation. While emotions are clearly much more complex than this, thinking about emotions in relation to goals is a useful way of understanding both the causes of emotions and why specific emotions lead to particular kinds of behaviours.

There have been a few attempts to categorize different causes of emotions at work in particular (e.g. Basch & Fisher, 2000). It is of course impossible to list or categorize all possible causes and consequences of emotions at work. Nevertheless, such a broad categorization can, for example, help promote a better understanding of the diverse emotional processes at work or to more clearly identify the effects they may have on the individual and organization. Here a broad categorization of such emotion-specific causes and consequences is presented. Understanding this emotional landscape at work can potentially give us some insights into what is happening at work and in teams, which in turn is crucial for planning and implementing interventions and for effective leadership.

In order to categorize the main groups of causes and consequences of emotions at work, Kiefer and Müller (2003) asked 397 employees and managers to describe the most dominant emotional experience of the last two weeks at work and to describe the causes and consequences of this emotional event. Four basic categories of causes of positive and negative emotions at work were found: Those relating to the job and work task itself; one's personal situation and future; social relationships with co-workers and line-managers; and relationship with the organization as a whole. Table 7.3 shows examples of typical emotional events and issues at work and frequent types of causes.

Thus, specific emotions tend to have specific causes, which are likely to have different effects on their behaviour, attitudes and thinking. It appears that, in

Table 7.3: Examples of typical causes of emotions at work and its consequences.

	Positive emotional issues	**Negative emotional issues**
(a) The job itself		
Emotions	Enthusiasm, flow, joy	Anger, frustration
Common causes	Doing the job/work, contents of work and job	Work interruptions, ineffective processes, procedures, heavy workload
Consequences	Motivation for job/task	Inefficiency, withdrawal from organization
(b) Personal situation and future		
Emotions	Pride, joy	Anxiety, worry
Common causes	Personal successes, achievements, personal development	Job insecurity, fear of loss of status, control, competencies during change
Consequences	Motivation for job	Health issues, lack of concentration
(c) Social relationships with co-workers		
Emotions	Liking, sympathy, thankfulness, fun	Frustration, anger
Common causes	Sense of belonging to team, closeness to line-manager, enjoying company of co-workers	Perceived lack of social and professional competence in others, social conflicts, being bullied
Consequences	Provide strength and resources to deal with negative emotions and to remain in company	Inefficient working, health issues in case of bullying
(d) Relationship with management and the organization		
Emotions	Hope, relief	Mistrust, disappointment, anger, frustration
Common causes	Believing in organizational values, identification with organization	Lack of fairness in organization, lack of acknowledgment from management, lack of belief in management
Consequences	Providing hope to remain in company	Withdrawal from organization, cynicism

Source: Adapted from Kiefer and Müller (2003).

general, negative emotions are about not being able to work professionally (interruptions, ineffective procedures and processes) as well as not identifying with or trusting the organization. The effects of these emotional events were psychological withdrawal from the organization, but not necessarily from the job. Fear and anxiety, however, were not linked to withdrawal from the organization or to lack of commitment to the job. Positive emotions, especially enjoying the work task and succeeding in achieving goals, were generally associated with stronger engagement in the job and task, but not stronger engagement with the organization as whole. This suggests, again, that positive emotions are not just the absence of negative emotions and that separate processes drive positive and negative emotions. In both research and practice, there has been a tendency to focus on negative emotions at work, probably because these seem to be more difficult and more important to deal with.

Recently, however, organizational psychologists have begun to explore the role of positive experiences such as courage or compassion (e.g. Frost, 2000; Worline, Wrzesniewski, & Rafaeli, 2002), while others focus on causes and consequences of positive emotions. Fredrickson suggests that positive emotions at work may not only buffer negative experiences, but also broaden our thinking and strengthen our resources. In Box 3, we summarize some of the potential

Box 3: Some consequences of positive emotions at work.

- Positive emotions undo negative emotions: Feeling enthusiastic about the job may neutralize negative feelings, e.g. about the lack of fairness in the company
- Positive emotions build optimism and fuel resilience: More than just neutralizing, they help build strength to deal with difficulties
- Positive emotions broaden thinking and build resources: They build resources that may contribute to creativity and generating new ideas and also builds intellectual and social skills
- Positive emotions trigger upward spirals toward optimal functioning and increased well-being: Having positive emotions today means you are more likely to feel good at work in the future
- Positive emotions may produce optimal functioning in organizations: Doing good makes you feel good. Through compassionate acts and helping others the workplace can become more effective
- Positive emotions are contagious: The positive feelings of a leader or a colleague can infect the whole team

Source: Adapted from Fredrickson (see www.bus.umich.edu/Positive/Contributors/BarbaraFredrickson. htm).

consequences of positive emotions at work drawing on Fredrickson's broaden and build model (e.g. Fredrickson, 2001).

Understanding Links Between Antecedents and Consequences of Emotions at Work: Affective Events Theory

While we have described above some aspects of the experience, causes and consequences of emotion at work we have not thus far provided a way of thinking about the processes involved in emotions at work. A fairly recent and comprehensive attempt to provide a framework for thinking about the causes and consequences of moods and emotions and work, called Affective Events Theory (AET), was developed by Weiss and Cropanzano (1996). It should be noted here that while AET deals with both moods *and* emotions, and this chapter is about emotion at work, it still provides a potentially useful framework for thinking about emotions at work.

AET was developed by integrating existing theory and evidence about moods and emotions, and has been quite influential in shaping subsequent research into emotion at work. In particular, AET was developed as a reaction to the limitations of research on job satisfaction, which, as mentioned above, has dominated thinking, and research into feelings at work. More recently, Weiss and Beal (2005) have reflected on the nature and influence of AET. They identified six of the main assumptions and suggestions made by AET. These are listed and described in Box 4 along with some of their implications.

Perhaps the most generally important aspect of AET is its emphasis on the daily, hourly or even minute-to-minute fluctuations in emotions, thoughts and behaviours. While most research into emotion at work, even research that aims to explore AET, is still not conducted in ways that can assess these small but potentially important fluctuations over time (see also Briner & Kiefer, 2005), it is likely that such research will become more common.

While it is possible to make a fairly simple list of the causes and consequences of work, understanding the relationships between emotion, thought and behaviour requires a more sophisticated and process-oriented approach like AET.

Examples of Roles of Emotion at Work

In this section, we are going to present in more detail four areas where emotion is assumed to play an important role, the psychological contract and emotion, leadership and emotion, emotional labour and organizational change and emotion. We chose these examples to demonstrate how and why emotion is a crucial factor in four aspects of organizational life.

Box 4: Assumptions and research suggestions of AET.

Job satisfaction is not the same thing as emotion: Researchers often incorrectly believe that job satisfaction is about feelings whereas it is best thought of as an evaluation or calculation about how good one's job is which may, or may not, be related to feelings or emotions about the job.

Events are the most immediate causes of emotion: Traditional thinking emphasises the role of general work conditions or job characteristics as determinants of feelings. However, it is changing events that are the immediate causes of emotion.

Some behaviours are driven by feelings and some by evaluations: Not all behaviours are influenced equally by feelings as some are influenced more strongly by evaluations and judgements. For example, it is suggested that behaviours such as volunteering to help colleague are related to current feelings and emotions, whereas a behaviour such as quitting a job is more strongly related to evaluations or judgements.

Feelings ebb and flow and change over time: Though this seems obvious, most previous research into feelings and emotions at work has failed to take account of, study, or understand the ebb and flow of feelings and the implications of this for behaviour at work.

Specific and discrete emotions are important: As mentioned earlier, stress and satisfaction do not describe or relate to specific emotions and are very general and quite vague descriptions of feeling states. While positive and negative moods or affect is a little more specific, looking at very specific and discrete emotions such as anger or shame is more likely to tell us more about how emotions affect behaviour.

Emotional experiences occur as episodes: Rather than thinking of emotions as simple reactions to an event or stimulus, it is important to recognize that emotions are connected and occur in sequences or patterns over time that relate to a particular theme or situation or incident. For example, an employee may be worried about a deadline they are working towards, but then feel pleased they are making progress in the task, and then get angry because other colleagues are interrupting them.

The Psychological Contract and Emotion

In most paid jobs there is a formal, written employment contract which specifies, for example, the tasks and roles that an employee is expected to undertake and what the employer will provide in return in terms of pay and other benefits. At the same time, however, there is an informal and unwritten psychological contract between employee and employer that can be just as important or even more important than the formal employment contract. It is both the formal and informal aspects of the "deal" between employee and employer that lie at the heart of the employment relationship.

In this section, we consider the history and definition of this idea, how the psychological contract works, and the relationships between the psychological contract and emotion. (For a recent overview of psychological contract theory and research, see Conway & Briner, 2005.)

Defining the Psychological Contract

While the idea of the psychological contract has been around since the 1960s, it is only since a more recent publication, by Rousseau (1989), that researchers have begun to think about and research the psychological contract in a more systematic and serious way.

One way of getting at the thinking behind the psychological contract is to consider all the things employees give and contribute at work, all the things they receive from their organization and employer, and just *how few* of these are actually in any written contract. Employees may, for example, be prepared to be particularly conscientious in doing their job if, in return, the employer treats them with respect. However, this aspect of the "deal" would not appear in any written employment contract. So, what appears to be happening is that many of the contributions made and rewards received by employees are an essential part of the employment relationship and what happens at work yet none of this is formalized or explicitly agreed. It is the nature of this *psychological* contract that researchers in this field have sought to understand.

> One of the most widely used definitions of the psychological contract comes from Rousseau (1995, p. 9): "The psychological contract is individual beliefs, shaped by the organization, regarding terms of an exchange agreement between the individual and their organization."

There are three key aspects to this definition. The first is that the psychological contract involves *individual beliefs*. In other words, the psychological contract is about what the individual believes in the case. The second aspect is that these beliefs are in some way *shaped by the organization*. That means what the individual experiences in the organization will in some way affect or shape these beliefs. For example, an employee may change their beliefs about what they can expect to happen at work through observing what happens to other employees. The final key aspect of this definition is that these beliefs are about an *exchange agreement* between the individual and their employer. The psychological contract, like any contract, is about an exchange where a person gives something on the basis that they will receive something in return.

So what might these beliefs consist of? What are the beliefs that make up the psychological contract? First, we need to consider what is being exchanged. Table 7.4 shows just *some* of the things that an employer may offer the organization and the organization may offer the employer.

Second, we need to consider what the nature of the exchange might be: Exactly what is being exchanged for what? For example, the employer may believe the exchange agreement to be quite general in that they are prepared to do a very wide range of things in return for a wide range of rewards and contributions from the organizations. On the other hand, the perceived terms of the exchange may be quite specific: In return for high levels of effort and flexibility, the employee may expect opportunities for promotion in particular rather than, say, interesting tasks.

Table 7.4: Examples of what is exchanged between the employee and their organization.

What employees may offer	What organizations may offer
• High level of effort	• Pay commensurate with performance
• High levels of attendance and punctuality	• Opportunities for training and development
• Loyalty to the organization	• Opportunities for promotion
• Extra hours on occasions if required	• Feedback on performance
• Learning new skills and update old skills	• Interesting tasks
• Flexibility	• An attractive benefits package
• Courtesy towards clients and colleagues	• Respectful treatment
• Honesty	• A pleasant and safe working environment

While there have been several attempts to identify different types of contract (see Conway & Briner, 2005), the key point here is that employees hold beliefs about what they can expect to get back from the organization if they behave in particular ways. In other words, employees have a sense, which may be quite implicit of what the "deal" is between themselves and their employer — and the contents of this deal lie outside formal employment contracts.

How Does the Psychological Contract Work?

Like in any contract, if both parties to the contract are meeting the terms of the deal then both parties are likely to be satisfied and continue to want to remain in the contract and continue to meet the terms of the deal. Translating this general example to the psychological contract, if both parties are meeting the terms of the deal then employees are likely to feel more satisfied, work harder, feel more committed to the organization, and so on.

However, theorizing about the psychological contract has tended to focus not so much on when both parties to the psychological contract, the employer and employee, are each fulfilling their side of the deal but, rather, when one side, the employer, is failing to deliver on what the employee believes has been promised to them. This has been described as a violation of the psychological contract. As will be discussed in the next section, when employees experience a violation they are likely to feel upset and angry. In the longer-term, an employee who has experienced a violation may also begin to feel let down by the organization, less committed to it, decide to make less effort and even think of quitting. It seems likely that most violations do not result in the employee leaving the job but rather, as with any contract that goes wrong, each party may decide to explicitly or implicitly renegotiate the terms of that deal in various ways. For example, an employee may realise that "the deal" is perhaps not as good as they first thought it to be but they can still accept it as a fair one.

Where and How Does Emotion Fit in with the Psychological Contract?

As mentioned immediately above, the main way in which emotion fits in with the psychological contract is in employees' reactions to violation. One way of understanding the sorts of emotions that are involved in a violation is by thinking about the emotions we experience when we believe someone has broken a promise they made to us. If this promise was important to us and we also made a lot of effort to meet what we thought was our side of the deal and the other person completely fails to meet their side of the deal, then we are likely to get angry and disappointed.

The idea of psychological contract violation is very similar: An employee believes that a promise has been made to them that they will get something in return for certain contributions and the organization has broken that promise. Table 7.5 shows some of the possible emotional reactions along with the thoughts and feelings that may follow a violation of the psychological contract.

Emotional and behavioural reactions to violation can be in some circumstances very strong. Indeed, it may be the case that many of the strongest experiences of anger experienced at work are related to the psychological contract. One possible explanation for this is the implicit nature of the promises that are broken. If people are aware that a deal has been made and that the other party to that deal might somehow let them down, they can at least mentally prepare for what that will feel like. In the case of the more implicit promises that are part of the psychological contract, it may be that individuals are actually unaware that they hold certain beliefs about promises that have been made between themselves and their employer until those promises are broken.

Throughout this section, we have discussed some of the possible or likely emotional responses to psychological contract violation. This is because there are very few published studies of such immediate, short-term and intense emotional reactions to violation. Most studies tend to ask employees in general surveys if they feel their organization has met all the promises it has made to them and then relates the responses to this question to measures of attitudes such as commitment

Table 7.5: Examples of possible feelings, thoughts and actions following psychological contract violation.

Feelings	Thoughts	Actions
• Anger • Annoyance • Upset • Rage • Dissatisfied • Betrayal • Sadness	• "How can I can trust this organization anymore" • "I not going to put myself out again for this organization" • "What's the point in being loyal to this organization when they behave in this way?" • "How dare they treat me like this?"	• Put in less effort • Refuse to work beyond their contract • Retaliate — through turning up late, leaving early, taking days off, using company equipment for purposes unrelated to work • Look for other jobs

Source: Adapted from Conway and Briner (2005).

or satisfaction rather than emotion. One exception to this approach was a diary study undertaken by Conway and Briner (2002) in which they asked employees on a daily basis whether they felt the organization had broken any promises that day and also asked them about their emotional experiences that day. This study showed that those employees who reported a broken promise were also more likely to report feeling betrayed and hurt.

Implications for Management

The nature of the employment relationship between employee and employer can potentially be a useful way of understanding the causes and consequences of emotion at work. The main implications for management are therefore as follows. First, as the written and explicit employment contract may exert far less influence over behaviour than the psychological contract, it is important to try to be aware of what this contract may contain for both management and employees. Second, having some understanding of the psychological contract may also help avoid making changes that may violate the psychological contract therefore elicit strong emotional responses. Finally, if employees are experiencing strong negative emotions in relation to a psychological contract violation, then dealing effectively with those negative emotions is likely to require an appreciation of what aspect of the psychological contract has, from the employees' point of view, been violated.

Emotional Labour

When we engage in a work activity we use various resources. Physical strength and energy is required for manual labour and a job that requires a lot of thinking or problem-solving will involve mental energy. However, a third type of work is work that requires us to use emotional resources. This, broadly speaking, is what is referred to as emotional labour.

What is Emotional Labour and Who Does It?

Hochschild (1983) not only made one of the first contributions to the field of emotion at work, as mentioned earlier when discussing the history of the field, she also first identified and described the phenomenon of emotional labour. She defined it as: "… the management of feeling to create a publicly observable facial and bodily display; emotional labour is sold for a wage and therefore has exchange value". (Hochschild, 1983, p. 7)

In other words, in emotional labour, feelings are somehow managed to create a display for which an employee is then rewarded through pay. While this idea may sound at first quite strange, it is clear that many jobs require employees to display and indeed suppress certain emotions. Some jobs seem to require a high level or high intensity of emotional labour such as flight attendant, salesperson, hotel receptionist, teacher, nurse, criminal interrogator, debt collector and so on. In these jobs, displaying appropriate emotions is an essential part of getting the job done.

Other jobs, such as general manager, factory worker, or craftsperson may involve less emotional labour but still involve some. Indeed, it could be suggested that any job requiring some interaction with other people will also require emotions to be managed in some way.

How Do Employees Do Emotional Labour?

The main way in which employees do emotional labour is through following display rules that state what rules ought to be displayed. There is nothing unusual about display rules. Many social situations and roles also have display rules. Consider the feelings that one is supposed to display in these different situations: At your birthday party; at a funeral; during a job interview; and, when listening to a friend who is upset. In each of these situations we are aware of and are likely to follow the somewhat different display rules the situation requires.

While emotional labour is only done in situations where there are some sort of display rules, these rules can vary in a number of ways. First, they can be relatively implicit or explicit. In some cases, display rules are very explicit and may actually be written out as instructions and form part of training whereas in others employees may pick up — through observing co-workers — which emotions it is appropriate to express. Second, they can be relatively simple or complex. Fairly simple display rules may instruct employees to smile at all customers. More complex rules may require employees to mirror customer emotions or to deploy displays of particular emotions in order to influence a customer. For example, salespeople may mirror the emotions of a customer in order to show they understand the customer and are being genuine. Third, display rules may be strongly enforced or just encouraged. Even where display rules exist, there appears to be large differences in the extent to which they are enforced. In some contexts, employees can choose when to follow rules but in others their behaviour may be closely monitored and any deviations identified and corrected.

While the explicitness, complexity and level of discretion involved in display rules may vary, display rules are the main way in which emotional labour is regulated. Employees may also display emotions appropriate to the display rules even if they are not aware of the display rules. For example, a nurse may "naturally" or automatically display concern for a patient who is in distress whether or not they are aware of the display rules of the job. In other words, some employees may already have internalised relevant display rules, and do not follow these rules as such, when displaying emotion.

What are the Emotional Consequences of Emotional Labour?

Displaying an emotion is not necessarily the same thing as actually feeling an emotion. However, there are several ways in which displaying an emotion may affect the emotions of the person displaying that emotion. First, Hochschild (1983) argues that in order to display emotions we do not really feel we do so in two main ways — through surface acting and deep acting. While surface acting does not involve feeling the emotion, deep acting does, because it involves the active invocation of thoughts, memories and images that will produce the relevant emotion. In other words, when employees engage in deep acting in order to display emotion they also try to make themselves feel the emotion.

A second way that the display of emotion may affect how the person displaying the emotion actually feels is that sometimes displaying an emotion can start to cause that emotion to be felt. There are a number of explanations for this process. One is the idea that displaying an emotion, such as happiness through smiling, changes the way we hold our facial and other muscles. This in turn acts as feedback and can start to make us experience the emotion we started out just displaying. Another way of explaining how displaying an emotion may make us feel an emotion is that when we display an emotion, it influences how those around us behave which in turn affects our feelings. For example, if we display friendliness and happiness, people are likely to behave in a more pleasant way and actually make us feel happier.

Display of emotion also affect the feelings of those who witness such displays: this is, after all, the whole purpose of emotional labour. For example, a customer or client who is upset about some aspect of the service they receive is likely to feel better if the employee who is dealing with them displays concern about their problem. Likewise, a debt collector who displays annoyance and urgency with a debtor is more likely to make the debtor feel concerned and anxious about paying back their debt.

Display of emotion by employees can also have unintended consequences, particularly when the customer or client does not perceive the employee's display of emotion to be genuine. For example, employees who repeatedly say "have a nice day!" and clearly do not mean it, are more likely to irritate than please customers.

Emotional labour has a wide range of emotional consequences for both co-workers and customers or clients. It is important to re-state, as mentioned above, that emotional labour is important in almost any job which requires inter-action with other people as the emotions of one person are likely to always affect the emotions of others.

Leadership and Emotion

Many individuals within organizations engage in some form of leadership — not only senior managers or directors. For example, line managers, supervisors and team leaders all have a leadership role. It can be argued that, as leadership is fundamentally a social process, it is also inherently an emotional process as all social processes are infused with emotion. Almost all aspects of leadership involve the use of emotion. Leaders display emotion and use emotion to create influence on their followers or fellow leaders (e.g. in communication or negotiation). They utilize their emotions in their own decision-making and problem-solving. They create emotion in others and deal with emotions of others. Box 5 gives an overview of ways in which leadership and emotion are linked.

Box 5: Examples of links between emotion and leadership.

Effects of leaders' emotions on themselves (particularly cognitive processes)

- Decision-making
- Information processing
- Creativity

Effects of leaders' emotions on others

- Relationships with others
- Creating or preventing emotions in others (e.g. create enthusiasm or fear)
- Affecting behaviours in others (e.g. pro-social behaviours)
- Impression of leader held by followers

Effects of others' emotions on leaders
- re-directing attention to the source of the emotion
- affecting leader's mood
- relationship with leader

Note: "Others" can include subordinates, clients, colleagues, team members or superiors.

Although leadership has always been viewed, at least in part, as an emotional process, it is only recently that researchers have started to investigate more systematically the links and processes involved, empirical evidence remains scarce. The material in this section is drawn mainly from George (2000) and Humphrey (2002; and the other articles in this special edition in *Leadership Quarterly*, Vol. 13). When it comes to leadership processes, both moods and emotions play a vital role and in this section, unlike others in the chapter, we make no distinction between mood and emotion. This is not because such distinctions are not important but, rather, because there is very little research around leadership which makes this distinction and because mood and emotions interact in complex ways.

First, we discuss the effects of leaders' emotions on the leader and others. Second, we describe *how* leaders affect the emotions of others by drawing on the notion of emotional intelligence. While leadership research tends to focuses on positive links between emotion and leadership, we know too well from everyday experience that leaders can also cause negative emotions at work.

Effects of Leaders' Emotion on Self and Others

The main focus of leadership research has been on understanding the social effects of leaders' emotion — in other words the effects leaders have on others through expressing and using emotions. However, other areas of research can inform us about how emotions affect one's own cognitive processes and behaviours that in turn affect leadership (see Box 5).

Effects of leaders' emotion on the leader   Emotions are known to interrupt our current flow of thoughts and activities in order to inform us of something relevant to us (Lazarus, 1999b; Simon, 1982). A supervisor's anger about a senior management's decision or frustration about a quarrel amongst his/her subordinates may lead the supervisor to re-direct his/her attention to the underlying cause of the problem in order to solve the problem or improve the situation. Of course, these events influence his/her mood. Moods have been shown to influence evaluations and judgements, memory and also attributions about failure and success as well as attributions about other people. For example, being in a positive mood leads to more favourable evaluations of others and of personal successes, makes people more self-assured and more helpful (increases pro-social behaviours) and decreases the likelihood of accepting blame for failures. Further, it is believed that positive emotions and mood facilitate creativity and inductive reasoning, whereas negative mood may influence deductive reasoning. Thus, this supervisor's mood and emotions are inextricably bound to how he/she thinks and behaves as well as the decisions he/she makes.

Effects of leaders' emotion on others   Owing to the inherently social nature of emotions, the emotions we experience and express at work have a strong impact on others, including clients, fellow team members, subordinates and superiors. Leaders' emotions can, for example, "infect" the feelings of other individuals and even teams.

The leadership literature distinguishes between transformational and transactional leadership. Transformational leadership suggests that the emotional bond between leader and followers creates identification with the leader, which is necessary for commitment to the leader and common goals (as opposed to transactional leadership, which focuses on reciprocal exchanges or transactions between leaders and followers). Leaders who are able to create emotional bonds with subordinates are often described as "charismatic" and are seen to create a positive relationship between themselves and others, to have an effective and appropriate emotional communication style — which strongly relies on emotional messages — and which instils positive emotions in their followers. On the basis of such emotional communications, followers tend to make judgements about a leader's authenticity (Dasborough & Ashkanasy, 2002).

Research on transformational leadership tends to focus on the individual characteristics of leaders to explain the success of leaders. From this perspective, therefore, little is known about how the situation or the relationship between leaders and followers impact on successful leadership. Charismatic leaders have been found to express and communicate more positive emotions. Some research suggests that these positive emotions can be "contagious" and are "caught" by team members (Cherulnik, Donley, Wiewel, & Miller, 2001), which may then have a positive impact on team performance and climate. Display of negative emotions by leaders, such as anger, have also been found to influence followers making them feel more nervous and less enthusiastic (Lewis, 2000). While there clearly are differences in how specific leader' emotions affect team members where this topic has rarely been addressed.

By expressing emotions, leaders also impact on their relationships at work. George (2000) suggests that leaders who frequently express anger may have difficulties building a sound and trusting relationships with their followers. Relationship quality between leader and followers is viewed as vital for team members' commitment and performance.

How Leaders Manage Others' Emotion

In the above section, we discussed effects of leaders' emotion on their own and on others' thoughts, judgements and behaviours. In this section, we discuss in more detail how leaders manage the emotions of others. We focus in particular on how leaders manage and deal with team members, followers, or subordinates — though these same ways of managing emotion are also likely to have similar effects on others with whom the leader interacts such as clients, superiors or members of other teams.

First, the notion of emotional intelligence is briefly described as a guiding framework for understanding how leaders manage emotion. Second, some examples of emotion management are provided. Third, we discuss one example of emotion management in more detail; namely, dealing with the negative emotions of team members.

The role of emotional intelligence in managing others' emotion   There are many ways in which we can explain why the leadership process is inherently emotional and how leaders have an impact on others' emotions. George (2000) draws on the concept of emotional intelligence to show how emotion is used in leadership. Emotional intelligence has been conceptualised in different ways. Salovey and Mayer and colleagues were the first to define the concept (Salovey, Hsee, & Mayer, 1993; Salovey & Mayer, 1998; Salovey, Mayer, Goldman, Turvey, & Palfai, 1995) and, according to these authors, emotional intelligence is the ability to perceive and understand emotions in self and others, to generate emotions in self and others and to manage emotions in self and others (Box 6). While there is considerable debate about what emotional intelligence is and what it can or cannot explain we will not enter into this debate here. Rather we will simply make use of this conceptual framework to understand some of the links between leadership and emotion.

Being able to appropriately express and recognize emotions in self and others is a basic requirement for many aspects of leadership. For example, if a leader cannot tell the difference between anger and fear in their followers they will be unable to assess the situation properly, make adequate judgements or appropriate decisions about how they should respond. Understanding one's own and others' emotions is important because, as discussed elsewhere, emotions contain valuable information. Anger, for example, reflects a strong disapproval of someone else's action against us or our norms and standards while fear is viewed as the anticipation of an event that carries a threat to the self (Lazarus, 1991; Ortony et al., 1988). Although these are somewhat abstract ways of describing the causes or meanings of emotions behind every emotional experience at work is a concrete, specific and highly meaningful event. Knowing the general causes and consequences of emotions such as anger or fear is, therefore, a crucial feature for emotion management. In the section on emotion and change, we will discuss how understanding causes and consequences of emotions can help leaders during organizational change.

Box 6: Leaders impact on emotion in self and others.

Appraisal and expression of emotion

- Awareness of own emotions
- Accurate expression of own emotion
- Aware of others' emotions
- Showing empathy for others' emotions

Knowledge about emotion

- Knowing causes of emotions
- Knowing consequences of emotion
- Knowing how emotion can progress over time

Use of emotion to enhance cognitive processes and decision-making

- Directing attention to the source of the emotion (own and others')
- Using emotion to facilitate making choices
- Using specific emotions to enhance certain cognitive processes

Management of emotions

- Meta-regulation of mood to achieve goals
- Inducing emotions in others to achieve goals
- Positive mood maintenance (in self)
- Negative mood repair or improvement (in self)
- Management of others' emotions (e.g. optimism and frustration)

Note: Adapted from George (2000).

Emotion Management

One means of achieving important goals is to regulate our own or other people's emotions. Examples are listed in Box 6 under the third and fourth heading. If a leader understands the potential influence of emotion on behaviour, he or she may consciously or unconsciously try and manage the emotions of team members in order to achieve organizational goals. The leader may try to instil or maintain positive or negative emotion and mood, depending on the goal, and to achieve or to prevent negative emotions such as frustration. The term emotion management may sound dangerous or sinister as it implies some kind of manipulation or attempt at mind control by leaders. Such manipulation can be regarded as unethical as it interferes with employees' inner or real feelings. While this may be the case, it is also potentially the case for leadership in general. However, from a psychological point of view regulating or managing emotions is not necessarily unethical and is a normal and quite often necessary aspect of daily life. There are many examples of this. In an important meeting, we try to hide the fact that we are very worried about our sick child. We may want to reassure someone who is very anxious about making a presentation — to make them feel less scared. Also, we manipulate our own emotions in order to get ourselves "in the right mood" to do a task we find difficult or boring. Likewise, a leader convinced of the benefits of a new and unpopular business plan will try to be as optimistic, serious and enthusiastic as he can. Hence, emotion management is not inherently unethical though of course it could be used in unethical ways.

Humphrey (2002) suggests that managing the emotions of team members is a key duty or responsibility of a leader as it is one of the main ways in which leaders influence performance and commitment. As mentioned earlier, frustration is a very commonly experienced emotion that arises during many work tasks. A study by McColl-Kennedy and Anderson (2002) showed that transformational leadership has an impact on team members' frustration and optimism and that the role of the leader in maintaining an optimistic mood, especially in times of ongoing change, is crucial for success. It has further been argued that leaders function as managers of group emotions. Leaders can help team members cope with frustration and thereby can have a significant effect on overall team mood and climate helping team members to cope with negative events at work (e.g. Pirola-Merlo, Hartel, Mann, & Hirst, 2002). While these researchers showed that leaders manage to suppress negative effects of frustrating obstacles on team climate, other authors suggest that negative emotions also need to be created in order to succeed. Hammer and Stanton (1994), the gurus of business process re-engineering suggest that leaders need to evoke or generate negative emotions in order to accomplish the difficult and unpopular task of reengineering an organization. They write: "To accomplish this [change] you must play on the two most basic human emotions: fear and greed. [...]. Fear can be used in many different ways as a catalyst for change". (p. 52) While we personally disagree that creating fear and greed is a sensible or, in the long term, efficient way to conduct change, this example shows that it is, of course, not only positive emotions that help to achieve goals. But positive emotions are certainly more socially acceptable. All the above are examples of how leaders attempt to impact their employees by managing or regulating emotions in order to achieve a personal or organizational goal.

When Leaders Cause Negative Emotions at Work

The above examples reflect the tendency within the leadership literature to focus on the positive effects of leaders on team members. However, from everyday experience we know that leaders can also have a very negative effect on team members and followers and some research does indeed suggest that leaders are often the cause of negative emotions at work. Frost (2003), for example, argues that there are two ways in which leaders can have a destructive impact and create painful, negative emotions. This can be done directly, by being the source or cause of negative emotions at work and, indirectly, through the way they handle negative emotions in followers.

According to Frost, leaders can be the source of especially intense negative emotions. Through his research he identifies a number of common causes of such emotions, including intention or malice, incompetence or weak and inadequate people skills, social insensitivity, betrayal or injustice, institutional forces (e.g. through implementing structural change or causing job insecurity).

The first author and a colleague asked 197 employees of a Government organization how frequently their supervisor was the cause of their negative emotions at work. The majority replied never or not very often, however about 25% said sometimes and 19% replied often or very often (Kiefer, Barclay, & Frost, 2005). The main ways in which supervisors caused their negative emotions was

Box 7: leaders reactions to negative emotions at work.

Ignoring and withdrawing

- He just does not care
- She walks away
- He pretends nothing happened

Not taking seriously and making it worse

- She tells me to not make a fuss and get on with it
- He makes it worse by his actions
- She ridicules me for getting upset

Taking action to remove the problem

- He tries to help
- She gets to the source of the problem
- He takes action and intervenes

Tending to emotion

- She shows me ways to cope with my anger
- He listens with care and respect
- She is really empathic

---

by treating them unfairly, being insensitive towards their situation and emotional issues and ignoring them. In addition, it was reported that leaders caused negative emotions institutionally by creating job insecurity and imposing heavy work-loads. Besides these direct ways in which leaders can cause negative emotions, there are also indirect ways. Kiefer and Barclay (2005) also asked employees how their supervisor reacted to their negative emotions at work. A range of different supervisor reactions, from not reacting at all to trying to deal with the problem was assessed. The behaviours can be grouped into three main categories, as shown in Box 7. Preliminary results show that the way leaders react to negative emotions matters: employees who feel their supervisors ignore their negative emotions or withdrawing from them, also report higher job strain, less trust in the company and more withdrawal from their organization. Taking action to remove the problem is however associated with better psychological well-being and more job engagement.

Implications for Management and Leadership

Given the especially social nature of leadership processes, we can make some plausible assumptions about the links between leadership and emotion and the way such links may work based on general research on emotions. However, it is important to note that that there is actually a very limited amount of research into emotions and leadership, particularly compared to the quantity of research into the other topics, such as emotional labour, discussed in this chapter. This is espe-cially true for the question how leadership is affected by emotion in an interna-tional business context. But of course emotions are highly contextual and culturally shaped and therefore understanding links between leadership and emo-tion becomes even more complex in an international context (Schyns & Meindl, 2006). The rules governing what emotions it is appropriate to display vary enor-mously across cultures and subcultures. While emotions and leadership will inevitably be connected in all cultures, it seems reasonable to assume that the nature of such connections is very different across different contexts and cultures. Both leadership *and* emotion are strongly dependent on culture and even organi-zational subcultures — thus individuals operating in an international business set-ting should be aware of the cultural differences in emotion display rules. Expressing or not expressing a certain emotion (e.g. anger or enthusiasm) will have different impacts in different cultures. These differences can be very subtle or very obvious, but either way they will strongly affect the way leaders express emotion, and how they are perceived.

Organizational Change and Emotion

While organizational changes have become a normal context in which organizations try to function, the success of fundamental changes such as mergers, layoffs or restructuring, is often being questioned. Low motivation for change and strong negative emotional reactions are viewed as common response to change and are often even held to be the cause of change project failures. So, is it the employees' fault, if organizational change programs do not deliver what shareholders and change architects' expect? The answer is not clear, but the quality of the change project itself or the change strategy is rarely questioned. More often there is talk about the "human factor" and "emotions" somehow interfering with the change project. A common concern among managers and practitioners is how people and their emotions can be effectively managed during change. In order to address this concern we need first to better understand what is going on in change and how and why organizational change is experienced emotionally.

In the remainder of this section, we first challenge the idea of the people and the problem during change projects and expose the stereotypical view of the role of emotions during change. Second, we discuss more comprehensively how and why change is experienced emotionally by drawing on our own and others' research. We conclude by summarizing some basic principles for dealing with emotions during organizational change.

How are Emotions Viewed in Change? The Human Factor: Nothing but Resistance, Fear and Stress?

The ideas held by managers and consultants about emotions during change are very similar to those found in some of the change literature. Such ideas are strongly related to some of the myths about emotions discussed at the start of this chapter. The assumptions typically made about change and emotion can be categorized into three main groups:

(a) *Organizational change elicits negative emotions, predominantly stress and fear*: The dominant assumption is that change elicits strong adverse emotional reactions. Such emotions are always negative and mainly about stress and fear. They are viewed as an obstacle to successful change, which therefore needs to be overcome or "managed away". This assumption and way of thinking leads to interventions that mainly target the individual such as stress management or self-management seminars. While this approach attempts to support the individual and provide more resources to cope with the changes, it also neglects the fact that there may be a whole range of different emotions in change, including positive ones. Interventions based on this assumption are therefore bound to be very narrow and limiting.

(b) *Negative emotions are part of resistance to change*: It is often assumed that resistance is the main reason why change projects do not work. It is clearly linked to the above notion that reactions to change are always strong and negative, but reveals an even stronger top-down bias. This perspective suggests that it is lower-status employees who are resisting change by not going along with or not being happy about proposed changes. From within this perspective, employees may be thought of as being afraid of change because of what they might lose, as being "change-lazy", or not able to understand the urgency or relevance of the change. Thus at the centre of this lies the assumption that the individual is unable or unwilling to make the change. Expressing negative emotions is here seen as an indicator of resistance. As a consequence of this view, management interventions target such emotions in order to overcome resistance, for example, by selecting "change-ready" individuals, and by communicating the reasons for change to help individuals understand and accept the need for change. This notion neglects the fact that emotions are a legitimate expression of human experiences and concerns. Viewing the expression and experience of emotion during change only in terms of resistance may mean not taking individual's emotional experiences seriously or viewing them as legitimate. At the same time, it also means that valuable information about the change process and how it is or is not working is not is not examined or explored as employees negative emotions and the reasons for their emotions simply viewed as resistance which needs to be overcome.

(c) *Emotions during change are an expression of loss, which go through distinct phases*: A further assumption is that emotions during change are about loss and therefore go through some sort of set of phases or stages. In general, phase models describe the course of a transition process or the course of adjustment to an event. In the change management literature, it has become common to draw, uncritically, on the work of Kübler-Ross (1970) who studied dying patents and described this process in terms of five distinct psychological phases: Denial and isolation ("not me, it can't be true"), anger ("why me?"), bargaining (trying to postpone the inevitable by "being good"), depression (sense of loss) and acceptance (contemplation, no anger or resentment). It has been suggested that the psychological response to radical change, especially mergers, can be understood within this framework describing personal bereavement (see Hunsaker & Coombs, 1988; Mirvis, 1985). According to this view, a productive and positive approach to change will not develop until the employee has reached the stage of acceptance (which is associated with positive emotions). The first three stages are associated with negative emotion and unproductive behaviour. These phases should, according to this perspective, therefore be kept as short as possible. Research on critical life events suggests that the adaptation takes around 12–18 months. This phase model approach has the advantage that it reminds us that adaptation to changes is a process that takes time. Nevertheless, the adequacy of such phase models drawing on the analogy of "loss" and "death", remain questionable though, due to the lack of empirical support. Furthermore, in the context of continuous and multiple changes, organizational change lacks a clear beginning and end, which makes questions the usefulness of such a heuristic.

Of course, these three basic assumptions are not completely wrong as many managers and employees observe and experience negative reactions on a day-to-day basis in changing organizations. The issue is, rather, whether these assumptions show the whole picture and if they are actually helpful in planning and conducting interventions. This seems unlikely as these assumptions are just that: Not based on sound evidence or the experiences of people going through change.

In the next section, we will discuss how a more comprehensive understanding of emotions at work can help improve our understanding of organizational change and thus its management.

How and Why is Change Emotional?

Research by the first author suggests that change is not merely about stress and fear, but about a wide range of issues leading to different feelings and that viewing negative emotions as resistance does not do justice to the ongoing processes (see Kiefer, 2002, for a more detailed discussion). Further, it shows that even in radical change, people also experience positive emotions, and not only on a senior management level.

The results presented here are based on several studies conducted in the context of organizational change (Kiefer, 2002; Kiefer & Müller, 2003). The emotional stories from the 397 individuals reported above (see p. 197) were analysed with respect to whether the story was related to organizational change. The results make clear that people experience change in relation to different aspects of their job and their life in the organization. We will use the four categories described earlier (see Table 7.3) to describe how organizational changes in particular affect everyday emotional experiences. In accordance with emotion psychology, we view emotions as a result of experienced events. Emotional experiences during change may, of course, differ depending on many aspects of the context, including the nature of the individual, the department, the organization, the kind of change and the phase of the change process. It is, however, important to see that both positive and negative emotions can be experienced at the same time, because they are connected to different aspects of the job in the context of change. Each of these aspects is influencing our attitudes and behaviours in different ways and therefore requires different management interventions. Here, we summarise some typical examples of events experienced during organizational change.

Typical change events in the category "Work tasks"   In this category, the events refer to the process ("We used to do this differently") and to the procedures of work ("This is organized very differently now, we first have to send it to department *x* before we can continue working"). Typical examples are the huge increases in workload during change because, for example, of the introduction of new products or new working procedures. Employees may also feel upset because they feel they cannot work effectively and do a good job because of continual changes. New processes are introduced and implemented successfully, and then a further change project is introduced and restructuring starts again. Thus, personal work standards of wanting to do a good job are often violated. Ongoing, continuous and multiple changes dominate the work task and the time for consolidation of changes or improvement is not perceived to be sufficient. Here, the negative emotions anger, frustration, impatience are common if the changes are felt to be hindering one's ability to do one's job effectively. On the other hand, joy and enthusiasm were experienced when the procedures and processes were improved ("This works much better now", "We finally got rid of this ridiculous procedure, "I enjoy doing this new task").

Typical change events in the category "Personal situation and future"   These are events that relate to their personal future (e.g. "Where in the new organization will I get a job?", "I'm moving to a new location which is closer to my home"), their status ("Personally, I am winner in this merger") and their competencies ("I worry I won't meet the requirements and demands set by the new management"). According to the situation, the person emotions vary from fear and insecurity to pride and satisfaction.

Typical change events in the category "Social relationships"   This is a category of change event hardly ever mentioned in the change literature. These are events and issues that are related to the way in which people work with or against each other as well as to team or group identity. Typical examples are the composition of a new team, for example, after a merger ("we've got to get used to each other") and the strengthening or weakening of teams/groups for example through restructurings ("This challenge binds us together"). In this category, there are also events, which are about leadership ("what is my new boss going to be like?") and the way in which supervisors treat their employees. Here, we find typical social emotions such as aggression, jealousy, envy but also thankfulness and liking.

Typical change events in the category "Relationship with the organization"
The majority of negative emotional events in change are about the employees' relationship with the organization and their management. Events in this category reflect peoples' attitudes towards the company and indicate the state of the psychological contract (see psychological contracts in this chapter). It is about identifying with the way in which the organization deals with stakeholders ("The early retirement scheme is great", "The way customers are treated is outrageous") and in which things are done. It is also about trusting the organization ("I don't believe a word they're saying"). There are many experienced emotions in this category, including hope and relief as well as disappointment, frustration, resignation and disbelief. Clearly, people experience a wide range of emotions connected to different aspects of their jobs in ongoing organizational change, which go far beyond stress. The data do not suggest that emotions should be seen as resistance. On the contrary, the data suggest that, for example, emotions express a feeling of being unable to perform the job according to one's personal job standards (category "work tasks"). Furthermore, the results indicate that emotions are not about organizational change itself, but about the way change is implemented as well as the attitude and behaviour of senior management in conducting changes. Also, although a few emotional experiences can be interpreted in terms of loss, most emotional stories are not about loss.

Using emotions as theoretical approach to understanding organizational change has framework helped understand how we can view emotions differently, namely as expression of valuable and different perspectives on the change process, and showing also that viewing emotions as only negative and in terms of loss or resistance or fear and stress is limiting.

What is the Role of Emotions in Change?

As discussed above, emotions, and in particular negative emotions, are often viewed as something commonly experienced during change and something that hinders the change process. In several studies, we explored first whether emotions were indeed reported more frequently during organizational changes than during periods when the organization was not going through change and, second, we explored possible roles of emotions in change.

The data show that the more change people experienced, the more they also reported negative emotions, in particular anger, mistrust, frustration, disappointment and aversion. However, further analysis showed that it was not change in itself that lead to more negative emotions, but the fact that individuals experience more work events linked to a deterioration in working conditions, an increasingly insecure personal situation and future and increasing lack of fairness, support and acknowledgement from senior management. The data further showed that these events were linked to a decrease in trust and an increase in withdrawal from the organization.

However, there was no link between ongoing changes and positive emotions. In other words, individuals experiencing more organizational change did not report more or fewer positive emotions than individuals who did not experience change. Nevertheless, positive emotions are not unimportant in organizational change and play a vital role in maintaining a functional work environment. Table 7.6 summarizes some roles of positive and negative emotions in change.

Table 7.6: Examples of roles of positive and negative emotions in organizational change.

Positive emotions	Negative emotions
• Provide a counterpart to negative emotions — balancing negative experiences	• Expression of violation of personal and professional standards, of values and beliefs, or a threat to personal well-being
• Building resources to deal with negative experiences	• Communicating one's beliefs to self and others
• Creating a space at work which is under personal control	• Motivating to improve the situation for the organization
• Positive emotions may be contagious in the team and increase not only individual well-being but also the team climate	• Fuel motivation to make a personal change for the better (e.g. leaving a dysfunctional workplace)
	• Sustaining and maintaining one's identity and remaining true to oneself in the midst of changes one does not believe in

Implications for Management

Earlier, we discussed that the general approaches to change and emotion are somewhat narrow and lead to a limited range of interventions. Using emotion as an approach to understanding organizational change has several practical implications for change management.

First, negative emotions are not themselves an obstacle to change and hence not need to be overcome or managed away. Successful change seems more likely where the emotions of all stakeholders are acknowledged. Emotions are always a legitimate expression of individual experience in change that can give us important clues about how and where the change process is going. Acknowledging emotions means taking people and their needs seriously.

Second, there cannot be a recipe for how to deal with emotions in organizational change. There cannot be a pre-fixed solution to an unknown problem. The framework makes clear that we need to understand the whole range of topics and feelings that are dominating the experience of a particular change. A question frequently asked by managers is "So what can we do to manage people effectively through change?" The answer is seemingly banal but unpopular: "it depends on what is going on". A thorough and sympathetic analysis of how people actually feel and what they are experiencing is the basis for understanding emotions in change. Leaders therefore need to investigate the kinds of issues and feelings that dominate during specific phases of the change process. Interventions and measures for dealing with negative emotional reactions after change should take account of all four categories of the emotional experience of change. Interventions may be direct or indirect and the focus can be on removing obstacles as well as on facilitating positive experiences. The interventions can and should be planned on different levels. It is important to decide when and where and on which level measures can or should be taken in order to manage people in change: Employees and managers need to be "targeted" as well as structures and procedures. Should one aim to reduce work load due to change or harmonize procedures in order to reduce the anger at work and/or do you wish to enhance (or make possible) enthusiasm or enjoyment at work? If you aim at reducing job insecurity, then again different measures are asked from trying to manage disappointment and lack of trust in the organization.

Third, it should never be the aim of management or consultants to practice first aid or short-term fixes during change. Our studies show that measures taken during change, not perceived to be sustained or serious, fuel cynicism and lead to questions about the credibility of the organization. Many stories about negative emotional experiences are about short-term and not-credible management actions. These sorts of interventions can easily backfire, and far from facilitating change may actually hold it back.

Summary and Conclusions

The aim of this chapter was to give a brief overview of the field of emotions at work. In practice, emotions are still often seen as somewhat out of place at work and as something that hinders efficiency. By going into emotion psychology in some detail, we intended to give the reader an alternative interpretation of the meaning and purpose of emotions in everyday working life. Throughout the chapter we have given various examples of how emotional processes work in organizations and why understanding these processes is both interesting and potentially important. Nevertheless, this research field is relatively young, and there are still many questions to answer.

At the present time, and to the best of our knowledge, there is hardly any research that investigates emotions at work in an international business context. However, there is some research into cultural differences in emotion. Parkinson, Fischer, and Manstead (2005) suggest five ways in which emotions may differ across cultures. First, different cultures have different rituals and occasions in which emotion may be experienced. So, for example, a culture that places great emphasis on achievement is also likely to place emphasis on rituals and occasions around rewarding and acknowledging achievement, which in turn will affect emotional experience. Second, cultures provide values that are then used to make sense of and appraise emotional events: The meaning of another person's sadness or what it tells us about that person, for example, varies across cultures. A third way in which culture affects emotion is through the way in which individuals within that culture are brought up to express and feel specific emotions. Fourth, people's presentation of their emotions is affected by cultural norms or standards through, for example, display rules. Last, culture seems to influence the way in which people respond emotionally to other people's emotion. Hence, the role of culture in emotion is complex and in turn is likely to play out in complex ways within organizations. Research into emotion at work still has a long way to go to develop even a basic understanding of the role of culture in emotion at work.

Leaders in international businesses need to be aware of how specific national or more local cultures may influence the experience, expression and meaning of emotion. For example, emotions that can be linguistically translated fairly easily and therefore may seem quite similar may still have very different meanings in different cultures. They should, however, also be aware that there is a risk of stereotyping other cultures' way of expressing and dealing with emotion. Developing such an awareness is no easy task yet, without it, our understanding of how emotion may play a role in work behaviour in the context of international business will remain limited.

References

Ashkanasy, N. M., Härtel, C. E. J., & Zerbe, W. J. (Eds). (2002). *Managing emotions in the workplace*. Armonk, NY: M.E. Sharpe.

Ashkanasy, N. M., Härtel, C. E. J., & Zerbe, W. J. (Eds). (2005). *Research on emotion in organizations: The effects of affect in organizational settings* (Vol. 1). Amsterdam: Elsevier.

Basch, J., & Fisher, C. D. (2000). Affective events–emotions matrix: A classification of work events and associated emotions. In: N. M. Ashkanasy, C. E. J. Härtel, & W. J. Zerbe (Eds), *Emotions in the workplace: Research, theory and practice* (pp. 36–48). Westport, CT: Quorum Books.

Brief, A. P., & Weiss, H. M. (2002). Organizational behavior: Affect in the workplace. *Annual Review of Psychology, 53*, 279–307.

Briner, R. B., & Kiefer, T. (2005). Psychological research into the experience of emotion at work: Definitely older, but are we any wiser? In: N. M. Ashkanasy, C. E. J. Härtel, & W. J. Zerbe (Eds), *Research on emotion in organizations: The effects of affect in organizational settings* (Vol. 1). Amsterdam: Elsevier.

Briner, R. B., & Totterdell, P. (2002). The experience, expression and management of emotion at work (5th ed.). In: P. Warr (Ed.), *Psychology at work* (pp. 229–252). Harmondsworth: Penguin Books.

Cacioppo, J. T., & Gardner, W. L. (1999). Emotion. *Annual Review of Psychology, 50*(1), 191–214.

Cherulnik, P. D., Donley, K. A., Wiewel, T. S. R., & Miller, S. R. (2001). Charisma is contagious: The effect of leaders' charisma on observers' affect. *Journal of Applied Social Psychology, 31*, 2149–2159.

Conway, N., & Briner, R. B. (2002). A daily diary study of affective responses to psychological contract violation and exceeded promises. *Journal of Organizational Behavior, 23*, 287–302.

Conway, N., & Briner, R. B. (2005). *Understanding psychological contracts at work: A critical evaluation of theory and research*. Oxford: Oxford University Press.

Dasborough, M. T., & Ashkanasy, N. M. (2002). Emotion and attribution of intentionality in leader–member relationships. *The Leadership Quarterly, 13*(5), 615–634.

Ekman, P. (1994). Strong evidence for universals in facial expressions: A reply to Russell's mistaken critique. *Psychological Bulletin, 115*(2), 268–287.

Ekman, P., & Friesen, W. V. (1971). Constants across cultures in the face and emotion. *Journal of Personality and Social Psychology, 17*(2), 124–129.

Fineman, S. (1993a). Introduction. In: S. Fineman (Ed.), *Emotions in Organizations* (Vol. 1, pp. 1–8). London: Sage.

Fineman, S. (Ed.). (1993b). *Emotions in organizations* (1st ed.). London: Sage.

Fineman, S. (Ed.). (2000). *Emotions in organizations* (2nd ed.). London: Sage.

Fredrickson, B. L. (2001). The role of positive emotions in positive psychology: The broaden-and-build theory of positive emotions. *American Psychologist, 56*(3), 218–226.

Frijda, N. H. (1986). *The emotions*. Cambridge: Cambridge University Press.

Frost, P. J. (2000). Narratives of compassion in organizations. In: S. Fineman (Ed.), *Emotions in organizations* (2nd ed., pp. 25–45). London: Sage.

Frost, P. J. (2003). *Toxic emotions at work*. Boston, MA: Harvard Business School Press.

George, J. (2000). Emotions and leadership: The role of emotional intelligence. *Human Relations*, *53*, 1027–1055.

Goleman, D. (1995). *Emotional intelligence. Why it can matter more than IQ*. London: Bloomsbury.

Hammer, M., & Stanton, S. A. (1994). *The reengineering revolution: A handbook*. New York: Harper Business.

Harré, R. (1986). *The social construction of emotions*. Oxford: Blackwell.

Hochschild, A. R. (1983). *The managed heart: The commercialization of human feeling*. Berkeley: University of California Press.

Humphrey, R. H. (2002). The many faces of emotional leadership. *The Leadership Quarterly*, *13*(5), 493–504.

Hunsaker, P. L., & Coombs, M. W. (1988). Mergers and acquisitions: Managing the emotional issues. *Personnel*, *65*(3), 56–63.

Kiefer, T. (2002). Understanding the emotional experience of organizational change: Evidence from a merger. *Advances in Developing Human Resources*, *4*(1), 39–61.

Kiefer, T., Barclay, L., & Frost, P. J. (2005). Understanding toxic emotions at work. Preceedings of the fifth European Academy of Mangement, Munich.

Kiefer, T., & Müller, W. R. (2003). Understanding emotions in organizational change: The role of identity in change. Paper presented at the Academy of Management Conference, Seattle.

Kübler-Ross, E. (1970). *On death and dying* (5th ed.). London: Macmillan.

Lazarus, R. S. (1991). *Emotion and adaptation*. Oxford: Oxford University Press.

Lazarus, R. S. (1999). *Stress and emotion. A new synthesis* (1st ed.). London: Free Association Books.

Lazarus, R. S., & Folkman, S. (1984). *Stress, appraisal and coping*. New York: Springer.

Lewis, K. (2000). When leaders display emotion: How followers respond to negative emotional expressions of male and female leaders. *Journal of Organizational Behavior*, *21*, 221–234.

Lord, R. G., Klimoski, R. J., & Kanfer, R. (Eds). (2002). *Emotions in the workplace. Understanding structure and role of emotions in organizational behavior*. San Francisco: Jossey-Bass.

McColl-Kennedy, J. R., & Anderson, R. D. (2002). Impact of leadership style and emotions on subordinate performance. *The Leadership Quarterly*, *13*(5), 545–559.

Mirvis, P. H. (1985). Negotiations after the sale: The roots and ramifications of conflict in an acquisition. *Journal of Occupational Behaviour*, *6*, 65–84.

Oatley, K., & Johnson-Laird, P. N. (1987). Towards a cognitive theory of emotions. *Cognition and Emotion*, *1*(1), 29–50.

Ortony, A., Clore, G. L., & Collins, A. (1988). *The cognitive structure of emotions*. Cambridge: Cambridge University Press.

Parkinson, B. (1995). *Ideas and realities of emotion.* London: Routledge.

Parkinson, B. (1996). Emotions are social. *British Journal of Psychology, 87,* 663–683.

Parkinson, B., Fischer, A. H., & Manstead, A. S. R. (2005). *Emotions in social relationships.* Hove, East Sussex: Psychology Press.

Payne, R. L., & Cooper, C. L. (Eds). (2001). *Emotions at work: Theory, research and applications in management.* Chichester: Wiley.

Pirola-Merlo, A., Hartel, C., Mann, L., & Hirst, G. (2002). How leaders influence the impact of affective events on team climate and performance in R&D teams. *The Leadership Quarterly, 13*(5), 561–581.

Rafaeli, A., & Sutton, R. I. (1989). The expression of emotion in organizational life. *Research in Organizational Behavior, 11,* 1–42.

Rousseau, D. M. (1989). Psychological and implied contracts in organizations. *Employee Responsibilities and Right Journals, 2,* 121–139.

Rousseau, D. M. (1995). *Psychological contracts in organizations: Understanding written and unwritten agreements.* Thousand Oaks, CA: Sage.

Russell, J. A. (1991). Culture and the categorization of emotions. *Psychological Bulletin, 110*(3), 426–450.

Salovey, P., Hsee, C. K., & Mayer, J. D. (1993). Emotional intelligence and the self-regulation of affect. In: D. Wegner, & J. W. Pennebaker (Eds), *Handbook of mental control* (pp. 258–277). Englewood-Cliffs: Prentice Hall.

Salovey, P., & Mayer, J. D. (1998). Emotional intelligence. *Imagination, Cognition, and Personality, 9,* 185–211.

Salovey, P., Mayer, J. D., Goldman, S. L. Turvey, C., & Palfai, T. P. (1995). Emotional attention, clarity, and repair: Exploring emotional intelligence using the trait meta-mood scale. In: J. W. Pennebaker (Ed.), *Emotion, disclosure, & health* (pp. 125–154). Washington, DC: American Psychological Association.

Scherer, K. R. (1984). Emotion as a multicomponent process. A model and some cross-cultural data. In: P. Shaver (Ed.), *Review of personality and social psychology* (pp. 37–63). Beverly Hills: Sage.

Scherer, K. R. (2000). Emotion. In: M. Hewstone, & W. Stroebe (Eds), *Introduction to social psychology: A European perspective* (3rd ed., pp. 151–191). Oxford: Blackwell.

Schyns, B., & Meindl, J. R. (2006). Emotionalizing leadership in a cross-cultural context. In: W. Mobley, & E. Weldon (Eds), *Advances in global leadership* (Vol. 4). Greenwich, CT: JAI Press.

Simon, H. A. (1982). Comments. In: M. S. Clark, & S. T. Fiske (Eds), *Affect and cognition* (Vol. 333–342). Hillsdale, NJ: Erlbaum.

Weiss, H. M. (2001). Introductory comments. *Organizational Behavior and Human Decision Processes, 86*(1), 1–2.

Weiss, H. M. (2002). Deconstructing job satisfaction. Separating evaluations, beliefs and affective experiences. *Human Resource Management Review, 12*(2), 173–194.

Weiss, H. M., & Brief, A. P. (2001). Affect at work: An historical perspective. In: R. L. Payne, & C. C.L. (Eds), *Emotions at work: Theory, research, and applications in management.* Chichester: Wiley.

Weiss, H. M., & Cropanzano, R. (1996). Affective events theory: A theoretical discussion of the structure, causes and consequences of affective experiences at work. *Research in Organizational Behavior, 18,* 1–74.

Weiss, H. M. & Beal, D. J. (2005). Reflections on affective events theory. In: N. Ashkanasy, W. J. Zerbe & C. E. Härtel (Eds), *Research on emotions in organizations: The effect of affect in organizational settings* (Vol. 1, pp. 1–21). Oxford: Elsevier.

Worline, M. C., Wrzesniewski, A., & Rafaeli, A. (2002). Courage at work: Breaking routines to improve performance. In: R. G. Lord, R. J. Klimoski, & R. Kanfer (Eds), *Emotions in the workplace* (pp. 295–330). San Francisco: Jossey-Bass.

Chapter 8

Approaches in Business Coaching: Exploring Context-Specific and Cultural Issues

Manfusa Shams

In this chapter, I would like to summarize major issues concerning the application of coaching approaches to diverse client groups and for cultural specific organizations.

I would like to propose that it is not enough to apply a particular approach for all client groups despite the apparent generalizability of an approach, rather coaching approaches should be devised to meet the needs of a group within a specific local context. For example, can we apply business-coaching approach to all businesses disregarding the context in which it is established? We cannot give any definitive answer, as there is little empirical research on the efficacy of business coaching (Horner, 2002). In addition, there is no groundwork to suggest that business coaching should be embedded within the contextual framework of a business for which coaching is sought. Although, the limitation of executive coaching has been identified, mainly for its failure to address the issues of individual differences (Harris, 1999), nonetheless, the failure of business coaching to incorporate context-specific coaching needs has not yet been discussed.

If a business is performed using an indigenous approach, then we must consider the possibility of developing an indigenous coaching approach tailored to the needs of context-specific client groups. In this case, it may be worth looking for a general coaching framework/approach addressing indigenous and individualized coaching needs, however, this can be a difficult task for researchers. Localized knowledge has a significant influence on the way a community functions (Shams, 2005), hence businesses originating from a local context must have such influences on the progress of businesses and for employee performance.

Developments in Work Organizational Psychology
Copyright © 2006 by Elsevier Ltd.
All rights of reproduction in any form reserved
ISBN: 0-08-044467-9

Since psychology practice is inherently context-specific and dependent on local languages (Ingrid, 2005), any issue with psychological practice in coaching must consider the context in which a coaching practice is developed, and from which a theoretical framework can be generated to satisfy clients' specific coaching needs. This has encouraged me to think if I am asking for a collection of context-specific coaching approach, rather than justifying the use of existing coaching approaches based on the theories, such as rational emotive therapy (Ellis, 1962), social learning theory (Bandura, 1977), humanist theories of motivation (Herzberg, 1966; Maslow, 1943), and positive psychology (Linley & Harrington, 2005), if so, how might we develop coaching approaches within a context since context-specific issues are generated from a broad environmental context?

For example, executive coaching approach calls for several significant steps to follow, such as an assessment phase; a feedback phase; a planning phase; an implementation phase; and a follow-up phase, these steps are general for any executive coaching practice, however, it is within each of these steps that a context-specific element should be included to enhance the performance of a local business and development for employees working for that business.

The literature of coaching is increasingly showing the diverse approaches and methods used to explicate coaching (Palmer & Whybrow, 2005), yet a clear lack of strong research base is also identified. The theoretical underpinning of coaching is argued in favour of developing a solid foundation for coaching psychology research. However, the developmental work is rather complex as it involves not only the definitional dilemma for coaching, but also requires a holistic approach (Leedham, 2005) to evaluate the benefits of coaching to get optimal satisfaction in performance, and desired improvement in skill acquisitions and related personal development. The high level of abstraction involved in defining coaching has been highlighted by Jackson (2005). This could be due to inadequate theorizing of coaching, however, some types of coaching are persistently showing the effectiveness of coaching to monitor, moderate and enhance human potentialities to excel in performance, for example, executive coaching, business coaching and life skills coaching (Zeus & Skiffington, 2000). The applicability of each of these popular approaches to a wide context, and for diverse population/client groups remains to be seen. The tendency to focus on the 'return on investment' in coaching fails to take into account the subjective experiences of the trainee/ coach (Leedham, 2005), and such as facilitation and expectations within a cultural context.

I would like to present the findings of an exploratory study where business functions are regulated by a cultural specific framework, hence demanding a context-specific coaching practice for business development.

Cultural Influences in Business Functions: An Exploratory Study

Discussions on cultural influences in business function, such as employee ratio from South Asian culture, implementation of South Asian cultural values and practices into organizational functions (business functions), and ensuing link with business partners from country of origin and elsewhere from the same cultural origin to ensure sustainable growth and development are ongoing. The information gathered from these sources will be beneficial to frame ideas for business coaching for this ethnic group and to address diversity in business coaching approaches.

Sixty-five to eighty percentages of all businesses in the world are accountables to family businesses (Nation, 2004). The size of the minority ethnic population was 4.6 million in 2001 (7.9 per cent of the total population of the United Kingdom, Census, April 2001, Office for National Statistics, 1999). With such a large number of ethnic minorities in the UK, family business research should detect cultural issues determining the functioning of family business, succession trends in business, overall business performance and success. It has academic and social policy implications. For example, contributions towards the development of coaching approaches tailored to meet the developmental needs of business organizations and employees within that culturally based businesses.

The psychological enquiry should also be directed towards the significant issues concerning large-scale involvement in family business by ethnic minorities in the UK. Although, there is an increasing literature to document family business among ethnic minority communities (Ram & Jones, 1998; Sanders & Nee, 1996; Janjuha-Jivraj & Woods, 2002), there is hardly any research examining cultural influence to execute and govern on, and determining of succession issues in South Asian origin family firms. The distinctive South Asian culture has paramount influence on the lifestyles of South Asian communities. The pervasive cultural influence can be traced in every spheres of the life course, as such any type of functions carried out within this culture must have significant cultural influence provided there is such opportunity to activate and practice cultural values and norms. This is evident in most of the self-employment categories for South Asians as this type of employment not only necessitates the growth and sustainability of cultural values and ideologies (Shams, 2002), but also demands the practice of cultural values to ensure economic sustainability.

The broad conceptualization of culture beyond the popular usage of nationality to encompass family business culture has been highlighted by Heck (2004). Cramton (1993) confirms that family beliefs and orientations are underlying economic foundation for business functions within a family setting. Heck (2004) furthermore asserts that family culture is distinct and effects family firm functioning independent of business functioning. Stafford (1999) show the importance of family culture determining family business. The diversity in family types suggests that it is important to examine family culture specific to families, such endeavour is evident only for a few studies so far (Zahra, Hayton, & Salvato, 2003). Recent research on transcultural businesses venture has provided significant insights on the challenging issues encompassing family businesses, which may pose as threat to the development of bilateral business alliance (Miller, Fitzgerald, Murrell, Preston, & Abelard, 2005). The discussion of family business must show appropriate concerns to local community in which family business operates; furthermore, local community context provides cultural impetus to sustain the pressure from non-family businesses. A theoretical groundwork was proposed by the author (Shams, 2005) for understanding the influence of local knowledge derived from local community functioning in conjunction with cultural practices.

The literature in Asian family business is dominated by the discussion on succession (Bachkaniwala, Wright, & Ram, 2001; Janjuha-Jivraj & Woods, 2002), entrepreneurship (Basu & Altinay, 2002), finance and business support (Smallbone, Ram, Deakins, & Baldock, 2003) and policy issues to support business enterprise (Ram & Smallbone, 2003). However, the process of transmitting 'culture' values to family business, which is both dictated by general South Asian business practice as well as typical South Asian family values (which is subjected to certain demographic variables, such as region from original country, religious background, marital status, parental employment status, migration pattern and length of immigration) remains to be documented through empirical research.

Research Methodology

A case study approach was used to gain an in-depth insight into cultural influences in business functioning. Case study approach is the most widely used method in family business research for its flexibility to access information on family business functioning, and to have the possibility of developing an effective partnership with the participating business through open discussions (Eisenhardt, 1989). The use of case study method, however, warrants careful interpretations of acquired information, specially, if cultural issues are overlooked in analyses, thereby affecting the quality of information gathered, leading to a misleading interpretation and discussion (Shams & Björnberg, 2006).

The cases comprised seven South Asian families from Indian origin, who migrated to the UK mainly via East Africa with the exception of one during the 1960s and 1970s. Rather than taking an opportunistic sample, a sample criterion was drawn. These include those Asian family business firms which are owned and managed by family members mainly and which have at least 25–30 employees from family and non-family members. All Asian family business firms either from a direct migration route or from an indirect route (via East Africa) can be included provided they meet the definitional criterion. Family business in the categories of restaurants, take-away, corner shops, grocery shops, clothing and small vendors were excluded from sample selection. This is because many of these businesses have short longevity and no generational contributions, and in some cases, they are mainly startup businesses from a single generation or a business enterprise from a local authority etc. Another important criterion was that interview must be carried out with the head of the family business or in the absence of head of the family, another family member who holds similar position and is knowledgeable about the ownership and management of family business.

Family business firms have strong reservations on taking part in research due to the fear of breaching confidentiality, making business strategies public and doubts about the benefits of taking part and giving valuable time which can be spent otherwise in business functions (Shams & Björnberg, Chapter 1). To overcome such deadlock in sample recruitment, several researchers have suggested establishing trust and mutual understanding about research process and exchange of information prior to the formal interview (Carson, Cromie, McGowan, & Hill, 1995; Pires & Stanton, 2003). Also use of extended social-networking within South Asian communities may facilitate sample recruitment and enabling access to sensitive information regarding family business. An interviewer from South Asian background (Indian origin) was appointed to carry out the task of formal negotiation and subsequent interviews with potential business firms. The interviewer utilized the extended social networking technique to approach prospective firms and use family contacts first and then secondary information about other firms from the family contacts. This technique has allowed yielding rich sources of information on a range of issues, such as leadership and family history, management structure, business size and change, family business culture and conflicts, succession issues and cultural influences in family business. The measures are standard questionnaire including all of the above issues and a genogram to trace the family history and involvement in family business. These two techniques have been used in a main study of family business with mainly white sample recently (Nicholson, 2003). Negotiation with

Asian family business firms began in October–December 2004 and data collection was completed during January–February 2005.

Cultural Representation in the Business Function: Business Size and Structure

The present sample belongs to medium to large size family businesses (minimum number of employee = 20 and maximum = 600). The percentage of employees from South Asian background in each of these firms is quite high indicating a high preference for employees making up the total workforce in family business from business founder and owner's cultural background. Thus, 71, 57, 86, 86, 57 and 86 per cent of board members, customers, owners of the business, advisors, suppliers and managers are from South Asian origin respectively. The representation of South Asian origin members at various levels of business structure is presented in Table 8.1.

A close examination of at least four firms shows the domination of cultural representation in business structure, which is summarized below.

Case A: Family business was set up around 20 years ago by two brothers who migrated from Africa (Kenya) to the UK with a present employee number of 200. The business growth is due to the success in pharmaceutical productions in England. The eldest brother has asserted the importance of maintaining cultural

Table 8.1: Employee structure in Asian family business: percentage of South Asian employees.

	0–20%	20–40%	40–60%	60–80%	80–100%	N/A
Managers	42	14	14	14	14	
Other employees	–	29	43	14	14	
Suppliers (including financial services)	29	–	29	43	–	
External business partners	57		14		14	
Advisors	43	29	14		14	
Board members	29		14	14	14	29
Customers		14	14	14	14	43
Business owners					100	

N/A = not applicable.

practice in business functioning as depicted below:

> being a small to medium sized firm, we work under an umbrella —
> the family. Because shares of owners are 50% each, the conflicts
> are to the minimum. We have an equal share to whatever.

This strength in family structure is also being confirmed in the reported employee structure of the firm. Around 80 per cent of all employees (board members, customers, owners of the business, advisors, suppliers and managers) with the exception of other employees (who have made 40–60 per cent from South Asian origin) is from South Asian origin. As the founder-link of the business confirms the strengths of family business culture as '*unity*'. No distinctive cultural weakness is reported.

Case B: The founder of the family business migrated from East Africa to the UK and set up the export/import and food distribution business almost 20 years ago with a business size (determined by the number of employees) of 28. The distinctive cultural strength has been reported as follows:

> working as a team, togetherness, hardwork/motivation, to expand,
> good network within family community.

The dominant cultural ethos in business function is furthermore confirmed by the employee structure. All employees (80 per cent approximately) belong to South Asian culture implying a strong preference for cultural representations in business functions.

Case C: A medium size family business of furniture retailer with an existing employee size of 80 set up by the founder about 25 years ago, the present owning generation is the second generation migrated from Africa to the UK. The employee structure for this business suggests a strong preference for cultural representation in the labour force with almost all employees belong to South Asian culture (60–80 per cent). Further confirmation of strong cultural influence came from the founder-link's verbatim about distinctive cultural strength:

> continual family support.

Case D: A medium size family business for steel manufacturing products run by the second generation with an employee size of approximately 200. The founder migrated from Kenya to the UK about 20 years ago. The business is the second holding being acquired originally from a business owned by a white family. The employee structure in terms of suppliers, employees, business partners and board members shows a strong preference for South Asian employees (40–80 per cent). This cultural preference is furthermore supported by distinctive cultural strengths as was written by the owner of the business below:

> at some point of time in the growth of business family agreed to work together pool both human and financial resources and promote unity and harmony.

The rest of the three cases also show dominance of employees from South Asian culture with at least 40 per cent of all employees from the same culture. The paramount influence of culture on family business is furthermore extracted from the part of the questionnaire, which asks for responses regarding language use, values and cultural practices in business function. The next section aims to discuss this aspect.

Cultural Representation in Business Function: Language Use, Values and Practices

The maintenance of cultural representation in business functions can only be ensured and enhanced through the implementation of certain functional elements, such as South Asian language use, family values in organizational culture and cultural ethos in business.

Language use   In contrast to cultural representation in employee structure, a rather non-dominance picture for language use has emerged for the four cases, with only 3 cases showing a strong preference to use South Asian language in advertising, product labelling, face-to-face communication with employees and customer service (one case only).

The use of South Asian language at various levels of business structure is presented in Table 8.2.

A detailed analysis for the three cases (where dominant cultural influence in terms of South Asian language use is demonstrated) is presented next. To show an overall integration of two dominant cultural factors (employee structure and language use) into Asian family business, the next section examines if an affirmative answer for language use corresponds to strong cultural influence in employee selection, and the responses are presented under each case study below.

Case A: It is interesting to note that despite highest number of South Asian employees occupying various positions in the labour force of this family business, the use of South Asian language is limited to only face-to-face communications

Table 8.2: Use of South Asian language in business functions.

	Yes (%)	No (%)
Advertising	29	71
Product labelling	29	71
Internal written communications with employees	86 (missing value = 14)	
Face-to-face communications with employees	57	43
Customer service	28	43 (missing values = 29)

although the business is identified quite strongly as a South Asian family business in its organizational culture in terms of implementing values and practices (family values embedded in cultural practices for business functions).

A close examination of the nature of business suggests the potential difficulties to implement the use of South Asian language in pharmaceutical industries without satisfying the drug regulatory committee's conditions for drug production and marketing. The use of South Asian language is thereby restricted to verbal communication with employees only. Cultural representation in business functions could have been accelerated if the business is linked with other businesses located in the South Asian region, for the present case no business link was reported with South Asian region.

Case B: The application of South Asian language in business function is more apparent in Case B. For example, South Asian language is being used in advertising, product labelling, face-to-face communications with employees and customer service. The only exception to the use of South Asian language in business function is internal written communication with employees. This family business has also indicated that they consider the business as South Asian in its organizational culture as they practice cultural values in business function. The nature of business for this case has facilitated the process of developing and maintaining a culturally based family business, for example, export/import and food distribution businesses may allow cultural practices such as the use of preferred languages in business.

Case C: Interesting result is obtained for this case when despite being consideration of the business as South Asian business in its organizational culture; no report of the use of South Asian language is made for business functions. This could be explicated in terms of the nature of business, which is furniture retailer in this case. As this business has got no formal link with South Asian or African region, there may not be enough impetus for the business to carry on cultural features in business function.

Case D: Similar to Case A, this business shows a preference for South Asian language only in face-to-face communications with employees and communications with local communities, although a high degree of recognition is given (score five on a five point rating scale for this item) for the business as being a South Asian in its organizational culture, particularly implementing values and practices. This finding is not surprising given that it is a steel product manufacturing company with long established family holdings in business functions. As the founder asserts the importance of cultural tradition below, in response to what has been the one or two major transitions in the business in the last five years, the answer was:

> in ... calculating family traditions philosophy and value.

This trend to enforce cultural representation into family business is setting an example for the next coming generation as most of the owners of the firms are from either first or second generation for the cases reported with the exception of Case D where third and fourth generations are involved in addition to second generation in order to groom younger generation into family business ensuring a sound transfer of responsibilities for, and integration into family business, as well as cultural features in business functions.

Diagram (8.1) highlights the major cultural features in practice for family business.

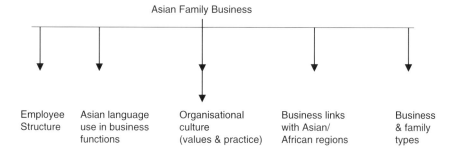

Diagram 8.1: Cultural practices in South Asian family business functions.

Cultural-Specific (Indigenous) Business Approach

The findings in this research are indicative of predominant cultural influences in business functions, especially a strong preference to uphold cultural practices in both employee structure and language use in business functions.

However, the application of cultural elements warrants a careful examination of business type and owner's perceptions of, and interests in the application of cultural practices in business functions. The literature so far has provided evidence of Asian family business as a provider for meeting the needs of local Asians as well as showing sustainable progress in maintaining an Asian cultural ethos in business functions (Aldrich, Zimmer, & McEvoy, 1989; Ram, 1994). Different explanations have been put forward to explicate cultural bias in employee selection other than a strong succession plan in practice. These explanations can be grouped together to suggest preferences for own ethnic groups in employee selection, thereby indicating a cultural-specific coaching practice is appropriate in this instance.

Culturalist Explanation

Family business is the outcome of maintaining family tradition in economic activities, with an aspiration to seek independence in the economic sector, and a family tradition to follow — cultural unity, integration, leadership and the contribution of family culture to business performance (Ainsworth & Cox, 2003). A contrasting view for culturalist explanation is to make culture accountable for normative control within family business (Cassey, 1999; Gabriel, 1999), thus developing a fundamentally gendered, hierarchical structure within a family business setting. It is therefore of significant importance to make further enquiry about the preference for cultural practice in business functions which may not be the genuine interests to promote Asian cultural elements rather it may be an issue of 'practical convenience' — to attract local community and to ensure a rapid growth in business for and by the Asians living in a particular region. Basu and Altinay (2002) asserted that culture is an essential determinant of entrepreneurial behaviour.

The research reported in this chapter has shown a strong preference for inclusion of cultural factors despite the size and nature of business supporting culturalist notion for business function, viz., to show sustainable growth in cultural unity, and an example for the execution of family tradition in business behaviour.

Economic Explanation

Contradicting the explanation of the 'availability of cheap labour' and family business as a patriarchal site' (Jones, Cater, De Silva, & McEvoy, 1989; Mitter,

1986), the recent explanation emphasizes on 'negotiated paternalism', a system of informal non-trade bargaining in which employees have more leverage that is commonly assumed (Ram, 1991), and Asian family business as a thriving economic unit on its own right, a desire for control over the individual work situation, thereby making a driving force to the sustainable progress of family business (Blackburn, 1994). This explanation overrides the derogatory image assigned to small businesses as being risky, hazardous and drudgery and poor economic return (Curran, 1986). The explanation for economic necessity as the driving force to the establishment of family business, especially for immigrant groups has also been highlighted in the literature (Barrett et al., 1986). For the present research, all family firms are established in Africa by the founder generation, which were later transferred to the UK, showing a strong favour towards the negotiated paternalism to the establishment of a secure economic base for the next generation.

Family Functions Explanation

The central tenet of this explanation thrusts on the very crucial existence issue of family business, which is strongly embedded into family structure. Therefore, any family dysfunctions will inevitably lead to a disruption in family business, and eventually family business may cease to exist within a short-time period. There is an inseparable bond between family and business (Heck, 2004). An extended explanation draws attention to the functional similarities between family and family business, for example, family climate is affecting the way the business is run, especially paternalism, gender and power relations (Ram & Jones, 1998). Family business is subjected to continuous negotiations between family members (Song, 1997) for its performance and growth, thus closure of a family business is quite often a decisional outcome from the founder or founder-link, as was expressed by the present sample. The strong link between household's dynamics and small business activity is coined as micro-business household by Wheelock and Baines (1998). The inextricable link between the family and small business activity, as well as the ways household may shape business behaviour has been critically discussed by Ram, Abbas, Sanghera, Barlow, and Jones (2001). They have provided authoritative arguments to show that the continuity of family business is not determined by the uncomplicated family collectivises, rather it is regulated by two powerful agents in family climate, viz., socialization and power relations. The importance of such family functions for the sustainable growth of family business has been highlighted by the four cases presented in the result section.

Family business can best be explicated in terms of cultural, economic, sectoral, spatial and political contexts. The overall strategy incorporating all these essential factors to unveil family business behaviour is called mixed embeddedness (Kloosterman, Leun, & Rath, 2000). The research reported here is supporting the notion of mixed embeddedness through the examination of two strong cultural factors in business functions, viz., employee structure and language use. Furthermore, the research is showing concerns about the future implications of extensive use of cultural elements in business functions, which may or may not be productive for the continuity of a family business. For example, any frequent and extensive use of South Asian language may limit business growth, especially for retail industry, manufacturing factory and pharmaceutical industry. On the contrary, it may also allow business growth as it allows multiculturalism to flourish through business functions. However, it is important to assess the motivation underlying the use of Asian employees and Asian languages — if it is to attract employees to declare solidarity in cultural integration rather than acquiring cheap labour (Barrett, Jones, Mcevoy, 1996) at the expense of divorcing quality of production.

It has been reported that family heritage and tradition can benefit the economic value of the family business (Narva, 2001), and the business environment and community in which they operate (Kleberg, 2001). Future research should aim to address to what extent cultural values and traditions projected onto business functions are restricted to business types and size of business, including family set up. It is also important to know if cultural practice in business functions is the result of institutional encouragement such as from the local government or is it the sole discretion from the founders to raise cultural tradition in the economic activities of a family. It is also equally important to assess to what extent business growth, quality of production and future development are strongly determined by cultural specific in-house coaching practices, and how such practices sustain the external pressures for integration into the wide business environment, including the ongoing coaching for employees to maintain cultural practice in business functions.

The findings drawn from this research are definitely raising the awareness of researchers, academics, practitioners and policymakers including family businesses about the significant influence of, and far-reaching effects for cultural practice in business functions with a positive implication for business growth and sustainability. It furthermore provokes interests to generate cultural-specific coaching practice for these organizations as they continue to maintain indigenous practices in business functions, and business growth is mainly a product of internalization of family values embedded within cultural practices in business.

Conclusion

In conclusion, I am leaving the tensions for developing indigenous coaching approach in this chapter, so that further debate on, and discussion about context-specific/indigenous coaching approaches can be made. I hope that the discussion may lead to the justification of a pragmatic and sustainable approach in coaching psychology, specifically to address diversity, and to affirm the need for an indigenous/contextualized coaching approach for business organizations. Approaches to business coaching are determined by the nature of business and pattern of business functions. The application of an indigenous cultural framework practiced by businesses can meet the demands of a context-specific coaching approach for the personal development of employees and business growth and for enhancing business growth.

References

Ainsworth, S., & Cox, W. J. (2003). Families divided: Culture and control in small family business. *Organization Studies, 24*(9), 1463–1485.

Aldrich, H., Zimmer, C., & McEvoy, D. (1989). Continuities in the study of ecological succession: Asian Businesses in three English cities. *Social Forces, 67*(4), 920–944.

Barrett, G. A., Jones T. P. & Mcevoy, D. (1996). Ethnic minority business: Theoretical discourse in Britain and North America. *Urban Studies, 33*(4), 783–810.

Bachkaniwala, D., Wright, M., & Ram, M. (2001). Succession in South Asian family businesses in the UK. *International Small Business Journal, 19*(4), 15–28.

Bandura, A. (1977). *Social learning theory.* Englewood Cliffs, NJ: Prentice-Hall.

Carson, D., Cromie, S., McGowan, P., & Hill, J. (1995). *Marketing and entrepreneurship in SME's: An innovation approach.* Hemel Hempstead: Prentice-Hill.

Basu, A., & Altinay, E. (2002). The interaction between culture and entrepreneurship in London's immigrant businesses. *International Small Business Journal, 20*(4), 371–393.

Blackburn, R. A. (1994). *Ethnic minority enterprise in Britain: Experience and trends.* Paper to conference on ethnic minority firms; developing good practice. University of Central England, 30 March.

Cassey, C. (1999). Come, join our family: Discipline and integration in corporate organizational; culture. *Human Relations, 52*(2), 155–178.

Cramton, C. D. (1993). Is rugged individualism the whole story? Public and private accounts of a firm are founding. *Family Business Review, 6*(3), 233–261.

Curran, J. (1986). The survival of the petit bourgeois: Production and reproduction. In: J. Curran, J. Stansworth, & D. Watkins (Eds), *The Survival of the Small Firm* (Vol. 2, 204–227). Gower: Aldershot.

Eisenhardt, K. M. (1989). Building theory from case study research. *Academy of Management Review, 14*(4), 532–550.

Ellis, A. (1962). *Reason and emotion in psychotherapy*. Secaucus, NJ: Lyle Stuart.

Gabriel, Y. (1999). Beyond happy families: A critical re-evaluations of the control-resistance-identity triangle. *Human Relations*, *52*(2), 179–203.

Heck, Z. K. R. (2004). A commentary on entrepreneurship in family vs. non-family firms: A resource-based analysis of the effect of organizational culture. *Entrepreneurship Theory and Practice*, 383–389.

Herzberg, F. (1966). *Work and the nature of man*. New York: Crowell.

Horner, C. (2002). *Executive coaching: The leadership development tool of the future?* MBA dissertation, Imperial College of Science, Technology and Medicine.

Janjuha-Jivraj, S., & Woods, A. (2002). Succession issues within Asian family firms. *International Small Business Journal*, *20*(1), 77–94.

Jones, T., Cater, J., De Silva, P., & McEvoy, D. (1989). *Ethnic business and community needs*. Report to the Commission for Racial Equality, Liverpool Polytechnic, Liverpool.

Ingrid, L. (2005). Reaching the parts that needs it? *The Psychologist*, *18*(2), 78–79.

Jackson, P. (2005). How do we describe coaching? An exploratory development of a typology of coaching based on the accounts of UK-based practitioners. *International Journal of Evidence-based Coaching and Mentoring*, *3*(2), 45–60.

Kleberg, S. S. (2001). Philanthropy: Adding value to family business. In: G. McCunn, & N. Upton (Eds), *Destroying myths and creating value in family business* (pp. 65–71). Deland, FL: Stetson University.

Kloosterman, R., Leun, J., & Rath, J. (2000). Mixed embeddedness: (In) formal economic activities and immigrant businesses in the Netherlands. *International Journal of Urban and Regional Research*, *23*(2), 253–267.

Leedham, M. (2005). The coaching scorecard: A holistic approach to evaluating the benefits of business coaching. *International Journal of Evidence-based Coaching and Mentoring*, *3*(2), 30–44.

Linley, A. P., & Harrington, S. (2005). Positive psychology and coaching psychology: Perspective on integration. *The Coaching Psychologist*, *1*, 13–14.

Maslow, A. (1943). A theory of human motivation. *Psychological Review*, *50*, 370–396.

Miller, M. G., Fitzgerald, S. P., Murrell, K. L., Preston, P., & Abelard, R. (2005). Appreciative inquiry in building a transcultural strategies alliance: The case of a biotech alliance between a U.S. multinational and an Indian family business. *Journal of Applied Behavioural Science*, *41*(1), 91–110.

Mitter, S. (1986). Industrial restructuring and manufacturing homework. *Capital and Class*, *27*, 37–80.

Narva, R. L. (2001). Heritage and tradition in family business: How family-controlled enterprises connect the experience of their past to the promise of their future. In: G. McCann, & N. Upton (Eds), *Destroying myths and creating value in family business* (pp. 65–71). Deland, FL: Stenston University.

Nation. (2004). *Baker & McKenzie: unique needs of family firms*. The Thailand (July 26).

Nicholson, N. (2003). *Leadership, Culture and Change in UK Family Firms*. Report of the First Stage Survey of Research. London Business School.

Office for National Statistics. (1999). *The ethnic minority populations of Great Britain: Latest estimates*. London: Office for National Statistics.

Palmer, S., & Whybrow, A. (2005). The proposal to establish a special group in Coaching psychology. London: *The Coaching Psychologist*, BPS.

Pires, G., & Stanton, J. (2003). Identifying and reaching an ethnic market: Methodological issues. *Qualitative market research: An international Journal*, 6(4), 224–235.

Ram, M. (1991). Control and autonomy in small firms: The case of the West Midlands clothing industry. *Work, Employment and Society*, 19, 43–60.

Ram, M. (1994). Unravelling social networks in ethnic minority firms. *International Small Business Journal*, 12(3), 42–53.

Ram, M., Abbas, T., Sanghera, B., Barlow, G., & Jones, T. (2001). Making the link: Households and small business activity in a multi-ethnic context. *Community, Work and Family*, 4(3), 327–347.

Ram, M., & Jones, T. (1998). *Ethnic minorities in business*. Milton Keynes: Small business Research Trust.

Ram, M., & Smallbone, D. (2003). Policies to support ethnic minorities enterprise: The English experience. *Entrepreneurship and Regional Development*, 15, 151–166.

Sanders, J., & Nee, V. (1996). The family's social capital and the value of human capital. *American Sociological Review*, 61, 231–249.

Shams, M. (2002). Issues in the study of indigenous psychologies: Historical perspectives, cultural interdependence and institutional regulations. *Asian Journal of Social Psychology*, 5(2), 79–91.

Stafford, K., Duncan, K. A., Danes, S. M., & Winter, M. (1999). A research model of sustainable family business. *Family Business Review*, 12(3), 197–208.

Shams, M. (2005). Developmental issues in indigenous psychologies: Sustainability and local knowledge. *Asian Journal of Social Psychology*, 8(1), 39–50.

Shams, M., & Björnberg, A. (2006). Issues in family business: An international perspective. In: P. R. Jackson, & Manfusa Shams (Eds), *Developments in work and organizational psychology*. London: Elsevier.

Smallbone, D., Ram, M., Deakins, D., & Baldock, R. (2003). Access to finance by ethnic minority businesses in the UK. *International Small Business Journal*, 21(3), 291–314.

Song, M. (1997). Children's labour in ethnic family business: The case of Chinese takeaway business in Britain. *Ethnic and Racial Studies*, 20(1), 690–716.

Wheelock, J., & Baines, S. (1998). Dependency or self-reliance? The contradictory case of work in UK small business families. *Journal of Family and Economic Issues*, 19(1), 53–74.

Zahra, S. A., Hayton, J. C. & Salvato, C. (2003). *Organizational Culture and Entrepreneurship in Family Firms: A Resource-Based Analysis.* Paper presented at the theories of the family enterprise conference. University of Pennsylvania, Philadelphia, December.

Zeus, P., & Skiffington, S. (2000). *The Complete Guide to Coaching at Work.* Roseville, NSW: McGraw-Hill.

Chapter 9

Working in Glass Houses: Managing the Complex Organisation

Paul R. Jackson

Introduction

The challenges that businesses face today are formidable. Accounting firms find that the confidence of their clients is dented not due to their own failings but because of a scandal involving a competitor, which has tainted the whole profession. Another company, a market leader in hearing aid technology, finds that its key product is made obsolete by advances in digital technology in an altogether different industry. A corporate re-branding exercise carried out with great care is rendered irrelevant by suddenly announced plans for a merger of their parent group with another. Many companies, and especially airlines, find that their carefully calculated investment plans have to be abandoned due to a terrorist attack thousands of miles away.

Markets are not just changing, they are often hyper-turbulent — volatile, complex and unpredictable — resembling nothing more than continual avalanches of uncontrollable chaos (Brown & Eisenhardt, 1997; Ilinitch, Lewin, & D'Aveni, 1998). Organisations are changing in fundamental ways, driven by these rapid changes in information and communications technology. One key result is the increasingly problematic nature of organisational boundaries, both internally and externally (Cross, Yan, & Louis, 2000). Boundaries are becoming increasingly permeable and transparent — the glass houses of the title of this paper — and structures are becoming more fluid (Volberda, 1998).

Developments in Work Organizational Psychology
Copyright © 2006 by Elsevier Ltd.
All rights of reproduction in any form reserved
ISBN: 0-08-044467-9

Organisations as Glass Houses: Transparent Organisational Boundaries

Externally, companies are seeking strategic alliances, often between competitors, and lean production systems (Womack, Jones, & Roos, 1990) depend heavily on long-term trusting relationships between members of supply chains. Companies are seeking to reduce the number of their suppliers, preferring close working relationships with fewer suppliers to competitive relationships among many. One consequence is that it is much less obvious where the organisational boundary is: a company such as Ford may have employees who work all of their time on the premises of a supplier, and the customer may have a much greater impact on working practices within a company (and therefore on employees) than the formal employer. Similarly, outsourcing of support functions leads either to core elements of a company's business being provided externally (perhaps on sites alongside similar functions for other companies) or to employees of another organisation working within a company's premises. As a final example, Cheney and Christensen (2001) report on remote provision of health care in Norway, where nurses in one location use video technology to work with doctors many hundreds of miles away on the treatment of a patient. Here, people are working as a 'team', yet they have never met or worked together in the same location. It is becoming less and less clear where organisational boundaries are. In similar vein (Hatch & Schultz, 2002), organisations are also increasingly exposed to the media as external stakeholders take greater interest in their internal workings.

Internally, boundaries are also becoming unclear as organisations change from a vertical, function-based form of structure to a horizontal, process-based structure (Daft, 2001). Process-based forms of work organisation have greatly weakened traditional definitions of jobs in terms of functional specialisms, and job descriptions are now much more fluid – workers are expected to do whatever it takes to get the job done (Parker, Wall, & Jackson, 1997). There is less-and-less buffering of internal organisational actors, and employees are much more likely to deal directly with external stakeholder groups:

- External suppliers as part of a just-in-time production system bring components directly to the point on the production line where they will be used rather than to a central stores department.
- Shopfloor workers can place an order for tools and equipment themselves rather than rely on supervisors dealing with suppliers on their behalf.
- Project teams working on the specification and manufacture of a new product consist of experts from both the customer and the supplier, and production staff work directly with technicians from the customer.

- Customers with a query on an order expect to talk directly with the person who can take action to resolve the difficulty.

In all these ways, there is less and less of a role for someone as buffer or intermediary between actors inside and outside the organisation (Pratt & Foreman, 2000). The increased permeability of organisational boundaries also implies a greater vulnerability to influences from the environment.

Organisational Options for Dealing with Environmental Complexity

Broadly, organisations can deal with complexity in two ways (Boisot, 1995; Boisot, & Child, 1999): either they can reduce it through specialisation or they can absorb it by adopting organisational forms that are flexible and by developing a repertoire of strategies for dealing with alternative risks. Boisot (1995) describes how the first response of *complexity reduction* uses codification (reducing data processing needs by categorisation and formalisation of procedures) and abstraction (discerning patterns and structures that underlie data) as a means of simplifying an organisation's transactions with its environment. The second approach is one of *complexity absorption*, which involves not specialisation to reduce complexity but the development of internal organisational forms and external alliances, which make it possible to respond to a wider range of environmental contingencies. Boisot and Child (1999) apply this distinction to an analysis of the ways of operating of western firms in China. Yeow and Jackson (submitted) studied two multinational companies in Singapore dealing with the Asian crash of 1997, and found that these strategies had starkly contrasting consequences for employee well-being.

This paper proposes a more detailed analysis of the second option for dealing with complexity, following Albert and Whetten (1985) who used the term holographic multiplicity to describe organisations where multiple identities are shared by all members. The key point of the argument proposed here is that such holographic organisations have characteristics which allow them to absorb environmental complexity.

The hologram was invented in 1948 by Dennis Gabor. It uses pure, coherent light from a laser. The light source is split into two beams. One beam, the reference beam, is directed at a light-sensitive plate, while the other is directed onto the object illuminating the object in the round, from all directions. The two beams are re-united to create what is called an interference pattern that is recorded on the light-sensitive plate.

The key difference between a holographic image and a normal photographic negative is that each part of the interference pattern in a holographic image can be used to re-create the whole picture. In a normal photographic image, however, there is a one-to-one correspondence between the original object and the negative, so that part of the object image is lost if part of the negative is removed. In a hologram, therefore, the whole image is enfolded in every component part just as every human cell contains all of the genetic code for the whole human body (Zohar & Marshall, 1994). The individual parts of the holographic image are not redundant: the picture re-created from one small part of a holographic image contains less detail than that from the whole image and from a different point of view. Nevertheless, what we get is a vase containing a bunch of flowers, and not just one daisy.

The metaphor of the hologram has been applied in a number of ways. For example, Keenoy (1999) analysed ways in which HRM can be understood from a holographic perspective. Pribram (1977) puzzled over the way in which memories do not appear to be physically located in a specific part of the brain, and concluded that the brain behaves as a hologram. This paper explores the extent to which the physical characteristics of the hologram can be used as a lens to understand organisational responses to complexity.

The Holographic Organisation

Four characteristics are proposed for the holographic organisation, which allow it to develop a repertoire of responses to environmental turbulence based on flexibility and adaptability. The most obvious is their holistic nature based on a shared vision and set of core values. Second, individuals within holographic organisations are active agents, empowered to manage local environmental demands effectively, partly because they are sanctioned to do so by management but also because they have the skills and resources necessary to be effective. Third, the structure of holographic organisations is that of a loosely coupled network, richly connected but not too much. Finally, holographic organisations are characterised by collective, distributed intelligence. Each key characteristic has an associated core task (see Table 9.1). The rest of this section examines each of the four characteristics and associated core tasks in turn.

The Whole Enfolded in Every Part

1. Symptoms of a problem   Every time you ring the organisation to find out what has happened to a delayed order, you are told something different. First, you are told that your order has been dispatched. Later, you find that the

Table 9.1: Key characteristics and associated core tasks in the holographic organisation.

Key characteristic	Core task
1. Holistic nature — the whole is enfolded in every part	Build a shared vision
2. Employees are empowered active agents	Build flexible work designs based on principled autonomy
3. Loosely coupled networks, richly connected but not too much	Manage relationships with stakeholders
4. Collective, distributed intelligence	Protect and promote the co-evolution of organisational intelligence

goods are out of stock at the warehouse (but this fact was not recorded on the order file), but are due in soon. You are promised that dispatch will happen soon, by someone who cannot know when that might be. In the end, you find that the delivery company has delivered the wrong product to the wrong address, and it is your responsibility to return it.

2. Customers who ring up with a problem are left to deal with multiple internal agencies themselves, simply because their initial contact was not with someone prepared (or sanctioned) to 'own' the problem. You are passed from one extension to another, and each person you talk to is friendly but can only deal with part of the problem and you have to explain it all again and again.

3. Contact staff cannot respond to all queries from a customer because they have only partial access to customer information. Imagine someone who can record a gas meter reading but cannot book a service call; or someone who can give information about the availability of grants for renewing obsolete equipment but cannot alter a bill payment method.

Building coherent identifications   What all the symptoms above share is the theme of disjointedness or incoherence: a compartmentalised response (Pratt & Foreman, 2000), where the experience of the organisation is quite different in different places and at different times. In stark contrast, the holistic character of the hologram implies an integrated response in which the same fundamental values are expressed throughout the organisation's culture (Hatch & Schultz, 2002).

Organisational culture has been examined at many levels. Most superficially, we make inferences about the culture of an organisation from the physical artefacts within its premises — paintings, pot plants, decorations, colours on walls and so on. Culture is also embodied in the policies and practices, which guide the day-to-day behaviour of employees, as well as in forms of work design. More deeply, culture includes the ways of thinking and taken-for-granted assumptions (often beyond the awareness of organisational members) that inform decision-making. At its deepest level, culture refers to fundamental values, and it is at this level that the first defining characteristic of the holographic organisation can be found. The degree of consensus in values within organisations has been used as one of the defining characteristics of strong cultures (Kotter & Heskett, 1992) in a study of 200 companies. Provided that the company value set included an emphasis on adaptation to environmental changes, strong cultures were found to be associated with excellent performance.

A number of authors have examined these distinctions in terms of different kinds of management control of employees. Both Weick (1995) and Perrow (1986) have pointed out that different forms of control are appropriate for more predictable and less predictable environments. Where the setting is relatively simple and predictable, standardisation of work procedures according to rules means that direct supervision ('first-order' control) is more pervasive. By contrast, what Perrow called 'third-order' control is more likely in complex environments. Third-order controls are also called 'premise controls' because "they influence the premises people use when they diagnose situations and make decisions" (Weick, 1995, p. 113). Premises are taken for granted assumptions and principles that limit the options considered in organisational acting and guide the choices made. They are pervasive throughout the organisation, and will not often be the subject of discussion because they are tacit. Organisational members will not challenge the premises on which their actions are based, and will regard such challenges by outsiders as incomprehensible. While a reduction in first-order control gives what Alvesson and Willmott (1996, 2002) call 'micro emancipation', greater scope for workers in defining timing and methods aspects of their work, they also point out that third-order control is a much deeper means of controlling worker identities and identifications.

Ethical work climate   One of the ways in which employee identifications have been related to the broader concerns of organisational stakeholders has been in terms of the ethical aspects of work climate. Barnett and Schubert (2002) examined the concept of what they call the *covenantal relationship* between the employees and the organisation, which they argue is based on two components: mutual concern for the welfare of the other and commitment to shared values. Such a mutual concern is a key component of a relational psychological contract, which is defined by broad principles (rather than detailed specific task specifications), is long-term (rather than short-terms), and open-ended (rather than fixed in duration) (see Rousseau, 1995). An ethical climate is defined as "the stable, psychologically meaningful perceptions members of organisations hold concerning ethical procedures and policies existing in their organisations" (Barnett & Schubert, 2002, p. 281).

Ruppel and Harrington (2000, 2001) broaden this argument by proposing that the existence of an ethical climate within an organisation is an important precursor to innovation, since successful innovation relies on the active commitment of employee stakeholders:

Policies and practices → ethical climate → trust → innovation → firm performance.

This linkage is also a critical part of the broader argument in favour of instrumental stakeholder theory (Jones, 1995). In so doing, they see trust in relational terms as "confidence that the self-interests of the company owners and managers will not necessarily take total precedence over the self-interests of the other stakeholders" (Ruppel & Harrington, 2001, p. 314).

Employees working within organisations with multiple identities are much more likely to be exposed to high levels of role conflict, as the demands of one role identity clash with those of another (Pratt & Foreman, 2000). Such role conflict sends powerful messages to employees about justice within the organisation and about whether senior managers can be trusted. Finally, Jackson (2004) showed how injustice and lack of trust are strong determinants of employee identification with the organisation (see also Smidts, Pruyn, & van Riel, 2001).

Multi-layered identifications   Shared employee identification with a common set of core values does not imply that employees are clones, or that everyone needs to behave in the same way. Rather, it means that common values are embodied perhaps in very different ways from one part of an organisation to another. For example, an organisation may have as a core value putting customers first. A design engineer could express that value by focusing primarily on what customers look for in a new product. Sales staff might express the value by ensuring that customer needs are explored thoroughly before advice is given on choice of product. Dispatchers may seek to identify the delivery mode that best suits the lifestyle of the customer. Thus the same fundamental values can be expressed in very different ways using diverse skill sets. Although these employees share the same values, they are not substitutable one for another and could not be considered as clones. Indeed, Scott and Lane (2000) show how organisational members' identifications are complicated and perhaps often contradictory.

An example of this can be seen in call centres. Call centres are an increasingly important way of using communication technology to provide flexibility of service to customers. In some organisations, such services are supplied by outsourcing the function to specialist suppliers, and advances in telephone and networking technology allow call centres to be located almost anywhere in the world. The role of employees in a call centre is particularly important, since they are often the only human contact between the customer and the organisation. From this point of view, they are the custodians of the corporate brand (and it is all the more surprising that working conditions in call centres are so poor (Sprigg, Smith, & Jackson, 2003), leading to them being described as 'the new sweat shops').

Call centre staff have a complicated position, since they have a commitment to the call centre provider as their employer as well as to the company to which they are providing a service. For example, Vertex Communications (part of United Utilities in the UK) run call centres for two mobile phone companies, Orange and T-Mobile, and they seek to promote Vertex corporate values in their employees. Yet those same employees are actively promoting different product brands in their work. Such staff are trained to provide a quality of service consistent with the standards of Vertex and also to provide a content of service (not just product knowledge, but also other aspects of the customer's brand) consistent with the customer's standards.

Employees as Empowered, Active Agents

Symptoms of a problem   Rigid demarcation lines between jobs create a normal response of '*that's not my job*' when workers are asked to do something which falls outside their job description. Thus, faults can be passed on through a system even when detected, simply because the person formally responsible for acting is a quality inspector at the end of the line. In this way, companies pay four times: they pay someone to make a mistake, someone to notice it but do nothing, someone whose job is to detect it and finally someone to rectify it. No wonder Crosby (1979) argued that quality is free, on the basis that it is always cheaper to do it right the first time. Related to the first symptom, a second classic symptom of a problem is the inertia shown by the symptom '*we've always done it this way*'. There is eminent sense in benefiting from prior experience (and this is often embodied in bureaucratic procedures and practices), but not when the world has changed. Related to this are symptoms three and four: *stick to the rules*, even when they do not apply, and *make sure you cannot be blamed* for something gone wrong. Both are defensive strategies used by employees who feel threatened within working environments low in trust.

Building flexible work designs based on principled autonomy   The term empowerment has many meanings and associations (see e.g., Parker & Wall, 1998). It is used here to refer to autonomy over aspects directly related to employees' work (Friedman, 1990). *Timing* and *method control* (Jackson, Wall, Martin, & Davids, 1993) concern the extent to which workers have discretion over when they perform work tasks (starting and stopping a particular piece of work, and the pacing of work once it is initiated) and over work methods (how work is done, the procedures followed or tools used). *Boundary control* or role breadth (see e.g., Wall, Corbett, Clegg, Jackson, & Martin, 1990a) refers to the extent of worker control over aspects of their work outside the core tasks themselves, such as scheduling of work, selection and training of new organisational members, monitoring quality standards and dealing directly with customers.

Principled autonomy is the term used for devolving control to workers over aspects of their work within the framework of a set of overall goals for their work, and consistent with organisational values (cf. Friedman's (1990) 'responsible autonomy and Perrow's (1986) 'third-order' control). There is now strong evidence of the benefits of such enhanced autonomy, and they include gains in performance, both quality and quantity (e.g., Jackson & Wall, 1991; Wall, Jackson, Corbett, Martin, & Clegg, 1990b; Wall, Jackson, & Davids, 1992), as well as benefits to workers in the form of job satisfaction and increased psychological health (Jackson & Parker, 2001). In a detailed analysis of performance data and fault reports, Jackson and Wall (1991) and Wall et al. (1990b) showed that the primary mechanism for improved performance was that workers were given authority to undertake tasks which previously were the responsibility of maintenance engineers. In other words, they were allowed to use knowledge they already had, whereas previously they had to wait for an 'expert' to arrive in order to undertake tasks which they were perfectly capable of performing themselves.

Empowerment also promotes new learning and therefore increases the adaptive competitive capability of the organisation. Leach, Jackson, and Wall (2001) reported findings of a feedback intervention in the Paper Finishing department of Photo-Co (not its real name), a manufacturer of photographic printing paper. Employees were given an active role in machine management, including new responsibilities for fault rectification, where previously they were only able to record faults and call out an engineer. The previous practice was seen as grossly inefficient, since engineers had identified that many faults were trivial (such as not connecting a machine to mains power), either caused by poor operator practice or easily rectifiable without their specialist expertise. Working with the engineers, the research team identified a set of 'operator-correctable faults', which workers were authorised to deal with themselves, together with the more serious faults, which required the specialist knowledge of the engineers. The intervention itself was very simple, achieved with almost no cost to the organisation.

Faults that could not be dealt with by operators themselves were recorded as they occurred on a board posted on the wall of the shopfloor as well as reported to engineers. If the engineers judged that operators themselves could take responsibility for a specific fault (perhaps with requisite training), then they worked with operators to achieve that. The results were dramatic and sustained. The number of operator-correctable faults reported went down by more than 50%, with an immediate impact sustained over 10 months. There was a decrease of 15% in downtime reflected in extra production value of £125k per annum in the department.

How was this benefit achieved? In part, it arose because workers were more careful and conscientious in applying what they already knew. As well as this though, the study showed enhanced fault management knowledge, especially for novices. Detailed interviews with employees showed that novices developed a greater understanding of production faults, they relied less on engineers to correct faults, and they had a greater understanding of the principles underlying faults. These changes were reflected in personal benefits to workers themselves: there was an increase in self-efficacy (personal confidence in capability to deal with problems) for novices in the department (though, not surprisingly, no change for experts who already had the capability to manage problems). Similar findings emerged from a study of workers in a steel mill (Leach, Wall, & Jackson, 2003).

This research adds to a growing body of empirical evidence (e.g., Jackson & Wall, 1991; Wall et al., 1990a, 1990b, 1992) which show how organisations and their members can benefit from employee autonomy over their local working environment. The findings can usefully be interpreted in terms of what Kauffman (1995) calls fitness landscapes — here fitness means *effectiveness.* The concept of a landscape represents the effectiveness payoff of alternative forms of action, and what the Leach et al. (2001) study demonstrates is an example of managerial action which had the effect of allowing employees locally to alter the pattern of ways in which they can be effective in their jobs, and thus their fitness landscape. The important implication from complexity theory is that this also changed the shape of the fitness landscape for others, illustrating co-evolutionary change. Engineers were now freed from dealing with many trivial tasks in order to work on more complex tasks for which they were uniquely equipped — their own fitness was enhanced, so that they could provide a better service, further enhancing effectiveness within their department. More broadly, management in the neighbouring department noted these findings and set out to implement the same intervention. In this way, increased evolutionary fitness in one part of the organisation served to change the shape of the fitness landscape elsewhere.

Holographic Organisations as Loosely Coupled Networks

Organisations as open systems   Katz and Kahn (1966) see it as self-evident not just that organisations are systems but that they are open rather than closed systems: "Social organisations are flagrantly open systems in that the input of energies and the conversion of output into further energic input consists of transactions between the organisation and its environment" (p. 15). In so doing they built upon earlier biological work of von Bertalanffy (1956, 1968) on general systems theory, and the concept of organisations as open systems is now a key element in much of management thinking.

Network density — the concept of coupling   Coupling refers to the number and quality of connections between individual elements in a system. Networks where every element is connected to every other one are very tightly coupled, while elements with no connections are scarcely networks at all. Between these two extremes are loosely coupled networks where elements are connected to others, but not too many. "A tightly coupled system has little slack and is one in which a process, or set of activities, once initiated, proceeds rapidly and irreversibly to a known or unknown conclusion" (Weick & Sutcliffe, 2001, p. 97).

A number of authors (Bak, 1997; Kauffman, 1995, 2000) have constructed computational models, so-called NK models, with varying numbers of linkages (K) among elements in systems of size N. They were interested in the consequences for the shape of the evolutionary 'fitness' of tuning the value of K. For low values of K, where interactions among elements are few, changes in one element have little effect on others, and the system will tend to converge at a 'frozen' stable state where no element can improve its fitness. The fitness landscape is very smooth, with a single peak of optimal fitness. On the other hand, systems with K at its maximum value (N-1) are those where every element is linked to every other one, and here a change in any element immediately has an impact on every other element. The result is a chaotic state where increases in fitness for one element cannot be sustained before changes elsewhere impact on it, and the system as a whole cannot reach a global maximum adaptive fitness. The fitness landscape is rugged, with multiple low peaks and no single optimal state.

Intermediate values of K reflect systems with some, but not many, linkages among elements such that changes in one element affect others, but the reverberations of changes are local rather than global. Here, elements can maintain adaptive changes and can also learn from the effects of changes elsewhere in the system. Systems with intermediate values of K are said to be in a poised state, sometimes called 'the edge of chaos' (Bak, 1997; Kauffman, 1995) and show characteristics of both of the previous types of system: the memory of previous experience characteristic of the frozen low-K system, and the openness to change of the chaotic high-K system. The edge of chaos state of intermediate levels of coupling is similar to the concept of loosely coupled systems discussed by Weick (1982).

Managing internal relationships   A high level of integration between successive parts of a production workflow is one of the defining characteristics of lean production systems (Jackson & Martin, 1996; Jackson & Mullarkey, 2000). Evidence from several empirical studies shows that such highly integrated systems are very vulnerable to external interruptions in supply, and also can have highly negative consequences for employee psychological well-being (e.g., Jackson, in preparation). Interactive complexity refers to the extent to which systems have many elaborate linkages and feedback loops (Perrow, 1986), and in such systems it is often impossible to anticipate the consequences of actions (Greening & Johnson, 1996; Weick & Sutcliffe, 2001).

Managing relationships across boundaries   The term 'stakeholder' is used to refer to any person or group who has an interest, or stake, in an organisation (Freeman, 1984), and is usually considered to have been developed by analogy with the more familiar term shareholder. Shareholders are the owners of an organization, and their stake is enshrined in law in most countries; but they are not the only ones whose stake has legal force. Employees and customers also have legal rights to be taken into account in the organisation's decision-making. Some stakeholders have direct interactions with the organization, while others (such as communities) are impacted upon by the organisation's actions without having any formal relationship with it. For example, the movie Erin Brokovich takes as its subject the efforts to achieve compensation of residents living around a plant owned by the Californian company Pacific Gas and Electric who suffered manifold severe medical problems as a result of chemical leakages from a cooling water pool. Similar issues arose among shanty town residents who had congregated around the Bhopal plant of Union Carbide in India when there was a disastrous release of chemicals following an explosion in 1983.

The boundary-spanning activities of organisational members are among the ones which are most critical for the survival and effectiveness of the organisation itself. One important reason for paying attention to what is happening beyond the organisation's boundaries is that things that matter to stakeholders can have profound impacts on the organisation. Monitoring stakeholder issues is one of the most important activities for a public relations or corporate communications function. Mitchell, Agle and Wood (1997) have presented a taxonomy of different kinds of stakeholder based on three dimensions of power, legitimacy and urgency. *Power* refers to the "the ability of those who possess it to bring about the outcomes they desire" (Salancik & Pfeffer, 1974, p. 3). *Legitimacy* is "a generalised perception or assumption that the actions of an entity are desirable, proper, or appropriate within some socially constructed system of norms, values, beliefs, and definitions" (Suchman, 1995). *Urgency* reflects "the degree to which stakeholder claims call for immediate action" (Mitchell et al., 1997, p. 867). Combining the three dimensions gives seven classes of stakeholder together with an eighth class of non-stakeholder.

Dominant stakeholders are the ones who matter most to managers because they possess both power and legitimacy, and this dominance will usually be reflected in a formal mechanism for managing the relationship. They include owners, investors, employees and government, and the company has good reason to pay continuing attention to their concerns and issues, which are salient to them. Large organisations will usually have specialist corporate communications or public affairs departments whose primary role is to manage relationships with such dominant stakeholders.

Other stakeholder groups may lack either the power or legitimacy of the dominant group, but ignoring their interests can turn out to be damaging to the company. *Dangerous* stakeholders are those who have power and pursue urgent claims, but they lack legitimacy. Despite the lack of legitimacy, organisations do well to take account of the actions and claims of dangerous stakeholders, since they can cause substantial damage. For example, some years ago, senior executives of transnational corporations were regularly kidnapped by South American terrorist groups and held to ransom. *Dormant* stakeholders possess power, which is not used, but could be. In other words, they may change from being dormant to being either dominant or dangerous. For example, laid-off employees may file for wrongful dismissal, may sabotage the plant or shoot people, or may speak out on radio programmes. Management may also pay attention to *discretionary* stakeholders (who possess legitimacy, but have no power or urgency to their claims) as recipients of corporate philanthropy. The motivation for building relationships with discretionary stakeholders may be normative, because it is seen as the ethical thing to do, or instrumental, because it brings commercial benefit to the company, perhaps as part of a marketing campaign to appeal to customers or investors (Donaldson & Preston, 1995). Finally, *dependent* stakeholders with legitimate, urgent claims but who lack power may become much more important to the company's activities when they become aligned with powerful others in pursuit of their claims.

Many organisations adopt a traditional approach to dealing with stakeholders, following a 'telling' model (Grunig, 1992) and allocating responsibility for a specific stakeholder to a specialist internal function. Thus, the human resources function deals with employee stakeholders, the sales or marketing function deals with customers, the purchasing function deals with suppliers, investor relations deals with shareholders and investment analysts and public affairs deals with media. The folly of this compartmentalisation is easy to see. For example, van Riel (1995) gives the graphic example of two pieces from the Dutch newspaper *Het Financieele Dagblad* for 28th November 1989, both concerning the tobacco company BAT Industries. The company placed an advertisement announcing a 22% increase in profits under the by-line 'More value for your shares'. On the same day, there was also an announcement of the closure of the Amsterdam cigarette factory employing 123 workers. The message would appear to be that the closure of the factory (with harm to the employee stakeholders and their local communities) was the means whereby the company was able to achieve the benefits offered to shareholder stakeholders. Such fragmented, indeed contradictory, communications are at the least embarrassing and quite possibly harmful to the company's reputation.

However, the need for consistency in communicating with stakeholders runs much deeper than this. The conventional stakeholder map is far from accurate, since stakeholder groups are overlapping in complex ways, and the same individual may belong to several stakeholder groups simultaneously. Employees also are increasingly shareholders, and thus have a stake as owners of the organisation that employs them. Many employees are also customers, and through being such may also belong to consumer groups which might be lobbying against the organisation for its practices or pricing policies. Employees may also belong to political parties, and thereby have a stake in influencing government actions, which might have profound impacts on the organisation. Such multiple stakeholder role sets are common, and they make the hope of tailoring communications to specific stakeholders (and perhaps hiding bad news from others) an increasingly forlorn one.

The rapid advance of the Internet has also had an impact on how companies relate to their stakeholders. Instantaneous global communication has compressed both time and space, so that the actions of a company in one part of the world cannot easily be hidden. Dramatic examples of the consequences of this include the ways in which activist non-governmental organisations have brought to public attention the working conditions in factories, which supply products to companies like Nike. The company has had to devote considerable effort, first to denying responsibility for the actions of its suppliers (on the grounds that they do not belong to Nike) and later to working with its suppliers to define and enforce better working conditions for employees.

Boundary scanning activity is fundamentally important to protect the evolutionary survival of an organisation. At the very least, organisations need to listen to what stakeholders say, need to understand what issues they care about and the values that underlie them, in order to see danger coming. While this advice sounds obvious, even large organisations, such as Shell can find themselves caught out (Fombrun & Rindova, 2000; Wheeler, Rechtman, Fabig, & Boele, 2001) when they pay meticulous attention to one group of stakeholders (governments and the science community) but neglect others (community groups, the 'green' lobby and activists). Such boundary scanning activity also needs to be pro active. A reactive policy of merely responding to urgent claims from stakeholders is common, but is fraught with hazard. Not only is the organisation denying itself opportunity to plan ahead, but it is choosing to allow small problems to grow into big ones before it does anything. Furthermore, a purely reactive strategy affords no opportunity for true dialogue, working with stakeholders to shape the development of issues and how they might be expressed in claims upon the company (Murphy, 2000).

Protect and Promote Organisational Intelligence

Organisational learning We earlier saw how principled autonomy allows workers to use the knowledge they have and also to develop new expertise. While this is clearly important, Rycroft and Kash (1999) argue that individual learning also needs to be propagated throughout an organisation. They cite the Adler and Cole (1993) comparison between Volvo's Uddevalla plant (run on the basis of highly autonomous work teams) and the Toyota-General Motors NUMMI joint venture (run on lean production lines). They conclude "differences in the ability to integrate individual learning into system-wide learning were an important factor in the failure of the former and the success of the latter" (p. 63). The effective protection and promotion of organisational knowledge is a critical element in the holographic organisation, a characteristic shared by the ideas of Peter Senge in his work on the learning organisation (Senge, 1990).

Receiver — referenced communication Much of the communication within organisations is driven by senders, who decide what information is needed and the most effective way of transmitting it. This has formed the basis of one of the most influential models of communication, based on the work of Shannon and Weaver (1949). An alternative view is offered by receiver-referenced communication, where all the agents in a system who seek to coordinate their efforts let others know what is happening to them. Thus there is a rich flow of information, but choices are not determined by decisions on what should be sent but rather by receivers selecting what is relevant to their situation.

Relevance is thus context-sensitive, and that decision is made by the receiver and not by the sender. The value of information to task performance is made locally by the receiver and not remotely by the sender. This implies that receivers will selectively ignore sources of information, and indeed Kauffman (1995, pp. 267–269) argues that ignoring information is a critically important element in effective communication.

An example is taken from Rochlin (1989) in a study of life aboard the US Naval carrier *Carl Vinson*:

> "Almost everyone involved in bringing aircraft on board is part of one of several constant loops of conversation and verification, taking place over several different channels at once. At first, little of this chatter seems coherent, let alone substantive, to the outside observer. With experience, one discovers that seasoned personnel do not 'listen' so much as they monitor for deviation, reacting almost instantaneously to anything that does not fit their expectations of the correct routine. This constant flow of information about each safety-critical activity is designed specifically to assure that any critical element that is out of place will be discovered by someone before it causes problems" (p. 167).

Uncoupling of Identities and Practice — The Case of BNFL at Sellafield

In 1997, British Nuclear Fuels Limited (BNFL) had developed methods for re-processing spent nuclear fuels. They opened a Demonstration Plant at Sellafield in Cumbria, and planned to open a mixed oxide fuel (MOX) production plant for processing MOX pellets for export to lucrative markets in Eur ope, Japan and the US.

Two years later, the Chief Executive of BNFL, John Taylor, resigned and the contracts of the non-executive directors were not renewed. The partial privatisation of BNFL planned to net the Treasury £1.5 billion was postponed until at least after the next election. Customers in Germany, Sweden and Switzerland announced that they no longer wished to buy from BNFL, and potential US re-processing contracts worth £4.5 billion were also lost. The company's accounts moved from a profit of £218 million to a loss of £337 million the next year. Furthermore, several European governments renewed calls for the whole Sellafield site to be closed, and newspapers even reported damage to the company's ability to recruit graduates. How could such a dramatic deterioration of fortune come about? The answer is simple and an immensely sobering example of the power of the link between the internal practices of an organisation and its relationships with its external stakeholders.

The immediate cause of BNFL's problems was that figures related to measurements of the size of MOX pellets sent to a Japanese customer were suspected of having been faked. At first, the company denied this, but later admitted the truth. They then agreed on the return of the fuel to the UK at BNFL's expense together with paying compensation of £40 million to Japanese customer. Two investigations were instigated by the Health and Safety Executive's Nuclear Installations Inspectorate (NII), one of the faking of quality data, and the other of supervision at Sellafield.

The report in February 2000 found that five employees charged with manual measurement of pellets had measured a batch of pellets, then cut and pasted blocks of figures to avoid measuring everything. They changed a few figures to make them look more realistic. The work was trivial and repetitive, and in addition was technically unnecessary (although a term of the contract with the customer) since all the pellets had already been measured automatically by computer-controlled instruments. It also transpired that workers had been following the same practices for four years, involving materials for a number of European customers. These long-lasting practices had escaped management attention for so long because changes within the company had led to downsizing too far — middle management had been reduced in number so much that they were unable to monitor workers effectively and were largely invisible on the site.

Furthermore, there were more deep-rooted problems of which the data faking was but a symptom. The formal policy of BNFL, of course, placed safety at the heart of its practices, and there was a strong 'vision for safety' at Board level. The reality at Sellafield however was rather different. The NII report (HSE, 2000) found that there were 58 different safety policies across the site so that contractors moving from one area to another could not be sure what practices were in force in a particular area. Safety had been demoted from a Board-level responsibility, and a review of safety policy was still awaiting Board approval after a delay of two years.

Conclusions

The concept of the holographic organisation captures much of modern management thinking on the most effective ways of dealing with complexity and rapid-paced unpredictable change. In developing this metaphor, the purpose of the paper has been to embed the internal and external communications of organisations with their stakeholders within the very fabric of organisational identity and practices. There is no room in this view for corporate communication as simply image management; rather corporate communication is about the continuing production of organisational identities within day-to-day practices. Communication is an integral part of what it means to be an organisational member.

References

Adler, P. S., & Cole, R. E. (1993). Design for learning: A tale of two auto plants. *Sloan Management Review*, *34*, 85–94.

Albert, S., & Whetten, D. A. (1985). Organizational identity. In: B. M. Staw, & L. L. Cummings (Eds), *Research in organizational behavior* (Vol. 14, pp. 179–224). Greenwich, CT: JAI Press.

Alvesson, M., & Willmott, H. (1996). *Making sense of management: A critical analysis.* London: Sage.

Alvesson, M., & Willmott, H. (2002). Identity regulation as organisational control: Producing the appropriate individual. *Journal of Management Studies*, *39*(5), 619–644.

Bak, P. (1997). *How nature works: The science of self-organised criticality.* Oxford: Oxford University Press.

Barnett, T., & Schubert, E. (2002). Perceptions of the ethical work climate and covenantal relationships. *Journal of Business Ethics*, *36*(3), 279–290.

Boisot, M. (1995). *Information space: A framework for learning in organisations, institutions and culture.* London: Routledge.

Boisot, M., & Child, J. (1999). Organisations as adaptive systems in complex environments: The case of China. *Organization Science*, *10*(3), 237–252.

Brown, S. L., & Eisenhardt, K. M. (1997). The art of continuous change: Linking complexity theory and time-paced evolution in relentlessly shifting organizations. *Administrative Science Quarterly*, *42*(1), 1–34.

Cheney, G., & Christensen, L. T. (2001). Organisational identity: Linkages between internal and external communication. In: F. M. Jablin, & L. L. Putnam (Eds), *The new handbook of organisational communication: Advances in theory, research, and practice* (pp. 231–269). Thousand Oaks: Sage.

Crosby, P. (1979). *Quality is free.* McGraw Hill: New York.

Cross, R. L., Yan, A. M., & Louis, M. R. (2000). Boundary activities in 'boundaryless' organizations: A case study of a transformation to a team-based structure. *Human Relations*, *53*(6), 841–868.

Daft, R. L. (2001). *Organization Theory and Design (7th ed.): South-Western College Publishing.* Cincinnati, Ohio.

Donaldson, T., & Preston, L. (1995). The stakeholder theory of the corporation: Concepts, evidence and implications. *Academy of Management Journal*, *20*, 65–91.

Fombrun, C. J., & Rindova, V. P. (2000). The road to transparency: Reputation management at Royal Dutch/Shell. In: M. Schultz, M. J. Hatch, & M. Holten Larsen (Eds), *The expressive organisation: Linking identity, reputation, and the corporate brand* (pp. 77–96). Oxford: Oxford University Press.

Freeman, R. E. (1984). *Strategic management: A stakeholder approach.* London: Pitman.

Friedman, A. (1990). Management strategies, techniques and technology: Towards a complex theory of the labour process. In: D. Knights, & H. Willmott (Eds), *Labour process theory*. London: Macmillan.

Greening, D. W., & Johnson, R. A. (1996). Do managers and strategies matter? A study in crisis. *Journal of Management Studies*, *33*(1), 25–51.

Grunig, J. E. (Ed.) (1992). *Excellence in public relations and communication management.* Hillsdale, NJ: Lawrence Erlbaum Associates.

Hatch, M. J., & Schultz, M. (2002). The dynamics of organisational identity. *Human Relations, 55*(8), 989–1018.

HSE. (2000). *HSE Team Inspection of the Control and Supervision of Operations at BNFL's Sellafield Site. Retrieved, from the world wide web: http://www.hse. gov.uk/nsd/team.htm*

Ilinitch, A. Y., Lewin, A. Y., & D'Aveni, R. (Eds). (1998). *Managing in times of disorder: Hypercompetitive organizational responses.* Thousand Oaks: Sage.

Jackson, P. R. (2004). Ethical work practices and organisational commitment: Ethics as the ordinary embodiment of organisational identity. *Ethical Space: The International Journal of Communication Ethics, 1*(2), 23–29.

Jackson, P. R., (in preparation). *Workflow integration, work design and employee well-being.* Unpublished manuscript, Manchester Business School.

Jackson, P. R., & Martin, R. (1996). The impact of just-in-time on job content, employee attitudes and well-being: A longitudinal study. *Ergonomics, 39*(1), 1–16.

Jackson, P. R., & Mullarkey, S. (2000). Quick-response manufacturing: Lean production teams in garment manufacture. *Journal of Occupational Health Psychology, 5*, 231–245.

Jackson, P. R., & Parker, S. K. (2001). *Change in manufacturing: Managing stress in manufacturing.* London: HSE Publications.

Jackson, P. R., & Wall, T. D. (1991). How does operator control enhance performance of advanced manufacturing technology? *Ergonomics, 34*, 1301–1311.

Jackson, P. R., Wall, T. D., Martin, R., & Davids, K. (1993). New measures of job control, cognitive demand and production responsibility. *Journal of Applied Psychology, 78*, 753–762.

Jones, T. M. (1995). Instrumental stakeholder theory: A synthesis of ethics and economics. *Academy of Management Review, 20*(2), 404–437.

Katz, D., & Kahn, R. L. (1966). *The social psychology of organisations.* New York: Wiley.

Kauffman, S. (1995). *At home in the universe.* Oxford: Oxford University Press.

Kauffman, S. (2000). *Investigations.* Oxford: Oxford University Press.

Keenoy, T. (1999). HRM as hologram: A polemic. *Journal of Management Studies, 36*(1), 1–23.

Kotter, J. P., & Heskett, J. L. (1992). *Corporate culture and performance.* New York: Free Press.

Leach, D. J., Jackson, P. R., & Wall, T. D. (2001). Realising the potential of empowerment: The impact of a feedback intervention on the performance of complex technology. *Ergonomics, 44*, 870–886.

Leach, D. J., Wall, T. D., & Jackson, P. R. (2003). The effect of empowerment on job knowledge: An empirical test involving operators of complex technology. *Journal of Occupational and Organizational Psychology, 76*, 27–52.

Mitchell, R. K., Agle, B. R., & Wood, D. J. (1997). Towards a theory of stakeholder identification and salience: Defining the principle of who and what really counts. *Academy of Management Journal, 22*, 853–886.

Murphy, P. (2000). Symmetry, contingency, complexity: Accommodating uncertainty in public relations theory. *Public Relations Review*, *26*(4), 447–462.

Parker, S. K., & Wall, T. D. (1998). *Job and work design: Designing jobs for well being and effectiveness.* London: Sage.

Parker, S. K., Wall, T. D., & Jackson, P. R. (1997). That's not my job: Developing flexible employee work orientations. *Academy of Management Journal*, *40*, 899–929.

Perrow, C. (1986). *Complex organisations* (3rd ed.). New York: Random House.

Pratt, M. G., & Foreman, P. O. (2000). Classifying managerial responses to multiple organizational identities. *Academy of Management Review*, *25*(1), 18–42.

Pribram, K. (1977). *Languages of the brain.* Monterey, CA: Wadsworth Publishing.

Rousseau, D. M. (1995). *Psychological contracts in organisations: Understanding written and unwritten agreements.* Thousand Oaks, CA: Sage.

Ruppel, C. P., & Harrington, S. J. (2000). The relationship of communication, ethical work climate, and trust to commitment and innovation. *Journal of Business Ethics*, *25*(4), 313–328.

Ruppel, C. P., & Harrington, S. J. (2001). Sharing knowledge through intranets: A study of organizational culture and intranet implementation. *IEEE Transactions on Professional Communication*, *44*(1), 37–52.

Rycroft, R. W., & Kash, D. E. (1999). *The complexity challenge: Technological innovation for the 21st century.* London: Pinter.

Salancik, G., & Pfeffer, J. (1974). The bases and uses of power in organisational decision making: The case of a university. *Administrative Science Quarterly*, *19*, 453–473.

Scott, S. G., & Lane, V. R. (2000). A stakeholder approach to organizational identity. *Academy of Management Review*, *25*(1), 43–62.

Senge, P. (1990). *The fifth discipline: The art and practice of the learning organisation.* London: Century.

Shannon, C. E., & Weaver, W. (1949). *The mathematical theory of communication.* Urbana, IL: University of Illinois Press.

Smidts, A., Pruyn, A. T. H., & van Riel, C. B. M. (2001). The impact of employee communication and perceived external prestige on organizational identification. *Academy of Management Journal*, *44*(5), 1051–1062.

Sprigg, C. A., Smith, P., & Jackson, P. R. (2003). *Call centres.* London: Health and Safety Executive.

Suchman, M. C. (1995). Managing legitimacy: Strategic and institutional approaches. *Academy of Management Review*, *20*, 571–610.

van Riel, C. B. M. (1995). *Principles of corporate communication.* London: Prentice-Hall.

Volberda, H. W. (1998). Toward the flexible form: How to remain vital in hypercompetitive environments. In: A. Y. Ilinitch, A. Y. Lewin, & R. D'Aveni (Eds), *Managing in times of disorder: Hypercompetitive organizational responses* (pp. 267–296). Thousand Oaks: Sage.

von Bertalanffy, L. (1956). General systems theory. *General Systems*, *1*, 1–10.

von Bertalanffy, L. (1968). *General systems theory: Foundations, development, applications.* New York: Braziller.

Wall, T. D., Corbett, J. M., Clegg, C. W., Jackson, P. R., & Martin, R. (1990a). Advanced manufacturing technology and work design: Towards a theoretical framework. *Journal of Organisational Behavior*, *11*, 201–220.

Wall, T. D., Jackson, P. R., Corbett, J. M., Martin, R., & Clegg, C. W. (1990b). Advanced manufacturing technology, work design and performance: A change study. *Journal of Applied Psychology*, *75*, 691–697.

Wall, T. D., Jackson, P. R., & Davids, K. (1992). Operator work design and robotics system performance: A serendipitous field experiment. *Journal of Applied Psychology*, *77*, 353–362.

Weick, K. E. (1982). Management of organisational change among loosely coupled elements. In: P. S. Goodman, & Associates (Eds), *Change in organisations: New perspectives in theory, research and practice* (pp. 375–408). San Francisco: Jossey-Bass.

Weick, K. E. (1995). *Sensemaking in organisations*. Thousand Oaks, CA: Sage.

Weick, K. E., & Sutcliffe, K. M. (2001). *Managing the unexpected: Assuring high performance in an age of complexity*. San Francisco: Jossey-Bass.

Wheeler, D., Rechtman, R., Fabig, H., & Boele, R. (2001). Shell, Nigeria and the Ogoni. A study in unsustainable development: III. Analysis and implications of Royal Dutch/Shell group strategy. *Sustainable Development*, *9*(4), 177–196.

Womack, J. P., Jones, D. T., & Roos, D. (1990). *The machine that changed the world*. New York: Macmillan.

Yeow, P., & Jackson, P. R. (unpublished). The impact of economic hyper-turbulence on employees in Singapore: The moderating role of HR practices. Unpublished manuscript, Centerburg Business School.

Zohar, D., & Marshall, I. (1994). *The quantum society: Mind, physics and a new social vision*. London: Flamingo.

Chapter 10

Future of Work and Organisational Psychology: Implications for International Business

Manfusa Shams and Paul Jackson

The internationalisation of business has brought many challenges to the academic community, and the growth of International Business as a distinctive discipline within Management Research is based in large measure on contributions from other disciplines. This book focuses on some of the things that Work Psychology can offer. Drawing on the critical discussions made in each chapter, this chapter attempts to give an overview of major issues for the future of International Business and Management. First, we will consider the landscape of IB research, building on current debates within the discipline. Second, we explore the 'balance of trade' between Work Psychology and IB, and consider what contribution Work Psychology can make to IB. In the final section, we examine the potential for collaboration between the two disciplines.

The Landscape of International Business Research

As a sub-discipline of Management, IB is intrinsically multidisciplinary, drawing upon such areas as marketing, finance, economics, business history and organisational behaviour. Its distinctiveness lies in two respects: the focus on *international* management, doing business across national boundaries; and also in the need to integrate the perspectives of these management specialisms. In the language of complexity theory (Yeow & Jackson, this book), the landscape of IB research is thus rugged in its topography. No single disciplinary perspective dominates IB (though economics provides a strong foundational base for many IB scholars) and this leads to controversy as scholars from different backgrounds compete in the paradigms they use to interpret and evaluate potential new knowledge. Related to its multidisciplinary character, there is now a recent debate over the issue of whether IB needs a single big question. Buckley (2002) posed the question, and in so doing suggested that there was no single question that unified IB scholars. Peng (2004) responded by arguing that IB does need such a question and that the IB's big question has always been: "what determines the international success or failure of firm." (p. 100).

There is a good and a bad side to this debate. On the positive side, diversity in perspectives can bring constructive controversy and energise research efforts towards creative advancement. On the negative side, controversy and diversity can weaken the identity of the IB community (see further discussion of this point in the context of mergers in Jackson & Dackert, this book). This is the basis of the Peng argument, where he suggests that it serves to energise and unite scholars (by focusing research effort) and will enhance the prestige of the discipline. Identifying a number of big questions is, in our opinion, important. They reflect the judgements of the major scholars in a discipline about which are the regions of the knowledge landscape that are most promising and which define what is distinctive about IB as a discipline — i.e. what IB is, in contrast with neighbouring areas such as Strategy or Economics. While we do not set out directly to address the issue of the identity of IB as a scholarly community, the ideas developed throughout this book can be applied to that debate (by way of example, the recent European International Business Association conference held in Oslo contained a panel consisting of one of the current authors, Jackson, and a number of eminent IB scholars, where the standing and the future of the discipline of IB were debated).

Developing the Discipline of International Business: The Contribution of Work Psychology

A strong theme throughout this book is the impact of changes in work organization, which have been brought about by the rapid development of information and communications technologies. Turner, Parker and Williams identify a number of challenges which could arise in particular for the safety at work as a result of the increased ethnic diversity of organisations and of the much greater prevalence of virtual teams working across geographical boundaries. The same theme is picked up by Sparrow in his consideration of how globally distributed teams can develop effective knowledge sharing. More fundamentally, individuals working in organisations which cut across national and cultural boundaries face much tougher challenges in understanding who they are and whom they work for. McLean Parks and Smith describe very eloquently how difficult it can be to work out where boundaries lie in modern organisations, and the consequences of these difficulties for both personal and social identity. The chapter by Jackson and Dackert focuses on the important issue of planned change in organisation boundaries through mergers and joint ventures. Here, it is clear that threats to identity are powerful determinants of the success of such planned changes. To some extent, IB scholars are aware of the importance of identity processes and trusting relationships in relation to joint ventures (see, for example (Child & Faulkner, 1998)), but this book offers insights from Work Psychologists that will serve to enrich their understanding. Buckley (2002) described three themes in IB research, and we now consider briefly how Work Psychology can contribute to each theme.

Explaining the flows of foreign direct investment (FDI)   How do firms get better performance in international markets through FDI compared with non-FDI firms such as licensing or exporting? A separate and important question is the extent to which FDIs involve not just capital flows (the domain of the finance specialist) but also knowledge flows (from head offices to subsidiaries, and also from subsidiaries to head offices). Here is one area of contribution for the Work Psychologist in understanding what we mean by knowledge, how to promote knowledge accumulation and dissemination (through learning), what factors promote or inhibit knowledge development, and how to build knowledge communities (see Jackson, 2005).

Explaining the existence, strategy and organisation of MNEs   How to overcome the liability of foreignness in competition with local firms? Potential contributions from Work Psychology are in the realms of identity, especially in relation to belongingness and otherness. Identity and identification processes are examined in several chapters of this book. Jackson and Dackert explore the power of mergers to bring group identity into salience, and for those identities to either facilitate or undermine the success of an inter-organisational merger. Turner, Parker and Williams examine identity issues at the level of the work team, and show how identification of individuals with their team influence and how safely the team works together. The chapters by Sparrow and McLean Parks and Smith both describe the role of organisational identification from the point of view of the challenges that organisations face when they seek to work across national boundaries. Sparrow points to the effect that this has for the role of the Human Resource professional, while McLean Parks and Smith describe in detail the investments that individuals make in organisations and the corresponding investments made by organisations in individuals.

Globalisation and the internationalisation of firms How to develop the resources and competences in order to perform abroad? Social psychology has much to say about the factors, which lead to success or failure in cross-national mergers and international joint ventures (see Jackson & Dackert, this book). Sparrow (this book) also discusses the personal and interpersonal competences that firms require who wish to operate internationally with a specific focus on the impact of globalisation on one function within firms — human resource management. He emphasises the importance of distinguishing between *global* (the management of activities through 'global mindsets') and *international* (the management of a workforce from around the world); and highlights how HRM professionals are seeking to deal with the implications of both sets of issues. The chapter brings out once again (see also Shams & Bjornberg) the significance of cultural values in international management. In this respect, he looks at two aspects, both of which are critically important:

- *Employee engagement* — how to bind employees to the organisation when those employees hold very different values both within and between countries.
- *Globally distributed teams* — how to develop effective knowledge sharing within teams which are formed across countries.

One important conclusion of this chapter is that the success of businesses internationally depends on the development of what Sparrow calls an international mindset, but the chapter also brings out the difficulties involved in its development because of the 'stickiness' of nationality in defining managers' prescriptions for how things should be done. This issue has been highlighted in the chapter by Shams, especially in relation to the business coaching approaches.

Shams and Bjornberg present a critical overview of recent developments in research on family businesses, an area neglected both within IB and within management research as a whole. The chapter begins by emphasising just how widespread family businesses are: it is estimated that between 65 and 80% of all businesses worldwide are family businesses. Family businesses tend to be small, they are often set up by members of ethnic minority groups within a community, and they are often international in structure where the family provides a link between migrants and their country of origin. The chapter draws our attention to a number of characteristics of family businesses that make them particularly valuable as a focus for research in IB.

Management research (including IB) tends to be rather restricted in focus, and examination of the family business forces us to take into account the interplay between business and family functions. Families are obviously defined by biological linkages between their members, but the structure of these relationships is also defined by powerful social factors that are well described in the chapter by Shams and Bjornberg. One strong implication of these social factors is that IB research needs to reconceptualise the significance of culture, especially with respect to the ways in which culture is embedded within families. The concept of culture is becoming less salient in IB research, and this chapter is one of the number in this book (see for instance, Jackson and Dackert on mergers; Sparrow on global teams; Turner, Parker and Williams on safety cultures), which reminds IB scholars of how important culture is to the effective functioning of global organisations. The focus on family businesses reminds us that culture is much broader and deeper than the values and the ways of thinking: countries also express their cultural values through their institutions and the structure of labour markets. Many family businesses (and especially among immigrant ethnic minority communities) develop as they do because of patterns of discrimination within national labour markets. Work psychologists are recognising the need for perspectives beyond the individual level of analysis, and IB scholars need to do the same.

Methodology and design issues Psychologists are socialised into recognising the importance of strong research design as a basis for sound inference (they are not alone, of course, in this). It is no surprise therefore that Turner, Parker and Williams pay particular attention in their chapter on the design of the studies that they review. They are quite rightly critical, for example, of claims of safety benefits arising from simple comparisons between samples of teams organised in different ways. Instead they draw our attention to the importance of two features:

- The identification of confounding factors that could explain an observed result.
- Examination of mechanisms that could explain how effects come about.

Many studies in Work Psychology utilise weak forms of design, and the same is true of much of management research. One important lesson that IB scholars can learn from Work Psychology is to adopt more rigorous forms of research design.

Where is the Potential for Collaboration between Work Psychology and International Business?

IB and social science The balance of trade between IB and social science disciplines — argument between Peng and Buckley here. Mostly, the feeling is that IB has imported concepts from elsewhere in support of its research endeavours, rather than exported its concepts and paradigms — IB as a discipline without a theory. The focus of this book is on the exchange between IB and Work Psychology. We have deliberately not sought to give a representative picture of Work Psychology here; rather we have sampled from a variety of leading scholars in the discipline. We asked them to consider how current thinking within Work Psychology informs and is informed by changes in the global work environment.

As a result, the chapters show diversity in approach, focus and style — these are both a strength and a weakness of an edited collection, which we encouraged in our authors. We did not force on them a strict requirement to write in a particular way, or to a set agenda. Some chapters (e.g. Turner, Parker & Williams) summarise a programme of research by the authors, which is driven by key concepts and paradigms within Work Psychology. Others emphasise issues and then illustrate the thinking of leading Work Psychologists when applied to those issues. This diversity gives freshness to the collection of chapters, but it inevitably will lead some reviewers to become frustrated. We do not offer a systematic body of research from Work Psychology, which will enable the reader to appreciate all that the discipline can offer to IB. Instead we hope to attract readers to find new ways of thinking for their own research across the diversity of chapters here. As an aid to that process, the first chapter both sets the scene and points forward to the central contribution of each chapter. Finally, we will sum up how we see IB and Work Psychology working synergistically together.

Multilevel perspectives   In common with much of management research (Klein, Tosi, & Cannella, 1999) IB is intrinsically multilevel in character (Buckley, 2002):

- the international competitive advantage of nations;
- how firms compete internationally; and
- micro-level of individuals and groups within firms operating internationally.

While IB research has addressed all three levels of analysis, its natural focus is on the firm level (Peng, 2004). For the most part, scholars in Work Psychology concern themselves primarily with the micro-level analysis; and firms and nations are taken as the context within which individual experience and behaviour can be understood. Management scholars have recognised the importance of building multilevel theories, and of exploring cross-level impacts. The chapter by Yeow and Jackson accepts that explanations need to recognise the multilevel nature of our experience as humans, but then argues that we can more productively engage in theorising when we consider how firms, industries and societies are emergent phenomena. So, macro-level phenomena are not simply the context for understanding micro-level phenomena; rather higher-order structure emerges from the individual actions of agents at a lower level in a hierarchy of social systems (Simon, 1996).

The chapter by Turner, Parker and Williams demonstrates powerfully how important it is to recognise the hierarchical nature of organisations when investigating factors influencing effectiveness. While their review focuses on workplace safety, its implications are much broader, since a wide variety of factors have been identified to impact upon safety at work and many of them operate across levels. Thus, the climate of a work team has been shown to be fundamental to how safely individuals within it operate (an example of a team-level variable impacting on individual-level performance).

Verbeke (2003) comments that IB research draws upon a variety of functional areas within management such as finance, marketing and organisational behaviour. Consequently, there will always be a variety of lenses through which IB-phenomena can be viewed. Therefore, any approach that focuses on a specific issue runs the risk of degenerating into fragmentation into these functional specialisms unless there is a strongly coherent conceptual underpinning. He makes this point in reviewing an edited book by Kotabe and Aulakh (2002), *Emerging Issues in International Business Research*, and our own collection runs the risk of being characterised in just the same way. Is there a coherent conceptual underpinning to the Work Psychology perspectives presented by our authors?

Two-way street   IB research has been dominated by a globalisation agenda (Buckley & Ghauri, 2004) — the movement of firms out of predominantly western economies into developing economies (including FDI). However, this movement has been challenged in new ways: through the anti-globalisation movement and through the rapid emergence of nations (particularly China and India) into the global economy. While, we have a large literature now on doing business in China, written primarily from the perspective of western companies; what we will soon see is studies of Chinese outward investment. One example of this is the takeover of IBM's PC operation by Lenovo, and the UK is seeing increasing signs of Chinese businesses seeking to build global brands of their own rather than to continue being the invisible factory of the world providing products sold under western brand names.

Ralston (2001) introduces a symposium where he says that much of recent work has "emphasised the impact that developed — primarily Western — countries have had on the less developed regions of the world" (p. 1). The purpose of that symposium was to provide some balance: "our ongoing adjustment to a single, global economy is a two-way street, and that it is relevant to direct some thought towards the impact flowing *from* the developing economies, as well as *to* these economies in order to appreciate more fully the synergistic effect of this two-way influence." (p. 1)

A deeper perspective   Very soon scholars in IB will face the same tensions and debates as those in indigenous psychology (Jackson, 2005; Shams, 2005); see also (Boisot & Child, 1999). Why should we be arrogant enough to assume that the theories we use to understand western business practices and organisational forms are easily and appropriately trans-located to understanding how the

Chinese do business? Instead, we should expect and encourage greater diversity in theoretical frameworks and methodologies as Chinese scholars seek to understand what is happening around them.

In part, what we argue is consistent with the view presented by Ricart et al. (2004) in their analysis of the changing world, which faces MNCs. They describe the challenges of a move from serving what they call the "top of the pyramid in underdeveloped countries" (p. 178) to the untouched markets at the bottom of the pyramid. We agree with them that this requires new ways of thinking, but propose that what is needed is a more fundamental step for scholars which is more akin to a paradigm shift. Instead of starting from the perspective of how we can understand, for example, Chinese outward investment using our familiar western mindsets, we suggest instead an indigenous mode of theorising, which is grounded in the culture, history, and thinking of China. Such scholarship will almost certainly prove difficult to understand for those of us raised in a western tradition, and probably a real challenge to journal editors. However, such challenges are the only way for there to be step change in theorising in a world whose economic centre of gravity is rapidly shifting to the East.

As well as psychology, IB draws upon a broad spectrum of fields of social science such as economics, finance, sociology and business study, and as such encounters the problems of coherence and integration (Caves, 1998). Therefore, discussion drawing on from only one discipline such as work and organisational psychology can be risky because of its prescriptive nature (Shi & Wright, 2001).

International and cross-national businesses always ask for theory and research addressing the dynamics of organisational behaviour (Scandura & Serapio, 1998). There still lacks in-depth theoretical discussion supported by empirical study to convene a debate on the future progression of international business and management from a multidisciplinary perspective.

In addition, developments in cross-cultural business ventures (e.g., Lloyd-Reason, Damyanov, Ovidiu, & Will, 2005) pose a significant challenge for scholars in work and organisational psychology, which they have been slow to meet. We started this project as a result of identifying significant time lags in the cross-fertilisation of new research from one discipline to another. While our initial aim in preparing this edited collection was to expose IB students and scholars to some of the latest thinking in our own discipline of Work Psychology, we end with a much richer perspective by finding that IB in turn poses significant challenges to other disciplines. As a result, the balance of trade of ideas (to use the metaphor of Peng, 2004) is rather more equal than we had supposed.

The discussion made in this book has clearly highlighted the following developmental issues in work and organisational psychology in relation to the future of international business and management as depicted in Figure 10.1.

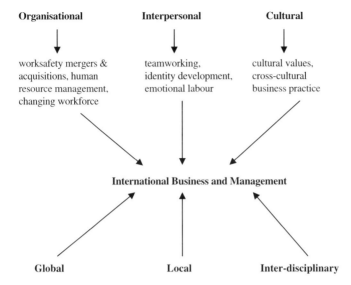

Figure 10.1: Selected developments in Work and Organisational Psychology influencing International Business and Management.

   The top three factors have been the focal points of discussion in this book within the bottom three areas. Thus, global, local and interdisciplinary issues are the grounded contexts within which discussions on selected areas in work and organisational psychology are made to show its influence on international business and management.

   We have been enriched by the exposure to the thinking of world-class scholars in IB, and we hope that readers of this volume will in turn be enriched by seeing what leading Work Psychologists have to say.

References

Boisot, M., & Child, J. (1999). Organisations as adaptive systems in complex environments: The case of China. *Organization Science*, *10*(3), 237–252.

Buckley, P. J. (2002). Is the international business research agenda running out of steam? *Journal of International Business Studies*, *33*, 365–373.

Buckley, P. J., & Ghauri, P. N. (2004). Globalisation, economic geography, and the strategy of multinational enterprises. *Journal of International Business Studies*, *35*, 81–98.

Caves, R. E. (1998). Research in international business: problems and prospects. *Journal of International Business Studies*, *29*(1), 15–45.

Child, J., & Faulkner, D. (1998). *Strategies of cooperation: Managing alliances, networks, and joint ventures.* Oxford: Oxford University Press.

Jackson, P. R. (2005). Indigenous theorising in a complex world. *Asian Journal of Social Psychology, 8,* 51–64.

Klein, K. J., Tosi, H., & Cannella, A. A. J. (1999). Multilevel theory building: benefits, barriers, and new developments (special topic forum on multilevel theory building). *Academy of Management Review, 24*(2), 243–248.

Kotabe, M., & Aulakh, P. (2002). *Emerging issues in International Business research,* Cheltenham, UK: Edward Elgar Publishing.

Lloyd-Reason, L., Damyanov, A., Ovidiu, N., & Will, S. (2005). Internationalization process, SMEs and transitional economics: A four-country perspective. *International Journal of Entrepreneurship & Innovation Management, 5*(2), pp. 206–226.

Peng, M. W. (2004). Identifying the big question in international business research. *Journal of International Business Studies, 35,* 99–108.

Ralston, D. A. (2001). Introduction to the symposium. *Journal of International Business Studies, 32,* 1–3.

Ricart, J. E., Enright, M. J., Ghemawat, P., Hart, S. L., & Khanna, T. (2004). New frontiers in international strategy. *Journal of International Business Studies, 35,* 175–200.

Scandura, T.A., & Serapio, M.G. (Eds). (1998). *Research in international business and international relations: leadership and innovation in emerging markets.*USA: Elsevier.

Shams, M. (2002). Issues in the study of indigenous psychologies: Historical perspectives, cultural interdependence and institutional regulations. *Asian Journal of Social Psychology, 5*(2), 79–91.

Shams, M. (2005). Developmental issues in Indigenous psychologies: Sustainability and local knowledge. *Asian Journal of Social Psychology, 8*(1), 39–50.

Shi, X., & Wright, C. P. (2001). Developing and validating an international business negotiator's profile. *Journal of Managerial Psychology, 16*(5), 364–389.

Simon, H. A. (1996). *The architecture of complexity* (3rd ed.). Cambridge, MA: MIT Press.

Verbeke, R. B. A. (2003). Review of 'Emerging issues in International Business research'. *Journal of International Business Studies, 34,* 312–313.

Author Index

Subject Index